RECONCILIATION
AND REVIVAL

James R. Mann in 1909. Reproduced from the Collections of the Library of Congress, 515503, LC negative number LC–USZ62–55627.

RECONCILIATION AND REVIVAL

James R. Mann and the House Republicans in the Wilson Era

HERBERT F. MARGULIES

Contributions in American History, Number 166

GREENWOOD PRESS
Westport, Connecticut • London

Library of Congress Cataloging-in-Publication Data

Margulies, Herbert F.
    Reconciliation and revival : James R. Mann and the House
Republicans in the Wilson era / Herbert F. Margulies.
        p.   cm.—(Contributions in American history, ISSN 0084–9219
; no. 166)
    Includes bibliographical references (p.   ) and index.
    ISBN 0–313–29817–3 (alk. paper)
        1. United States—Politics and government—1909–1913.   2. United
States—Politics and government—1913–1921.   3. Mann, James R.
(James Robert), 1856–1922.   4. Republican Party (U.S. : 1854–)—
History—20th century.   I. Title.   II. Series: Contributions in
American history ; no. 166.
    E766M33   1996
    320.973′09′041—dc20   95–36434

British Library Cataloguing in Publication Data is available.

Library of Congress Catalog Card Number: 95–36434
ISBN: 0–313–29817–3
ISSN: 0084–9219

First published in 1996

Greenwood Press, 88 Post Road West, Westport, CT 06881
An imprint of Greenwood Publishing Group, Inc.

Printed in the United States of America

The paper used in this book complies with the
Permanent Paper Standard issued by the National
Information Standards Organization (Z39.48–1984).

10 9 8 7 6 5 4 3 2 1

to
Elena, Joshua, Zachary, and Isaac

Contents

Preface

It was the misfortune of the Democratic party to be in control of the presidency and the Congress when a major economic depression struck the United States in 1893. President Grover Cleveland's policies divided his party and failed to reverse the course of the economic cycle. Republicans capitalized on the situation in the off-year election of 1894 and the presidential election of 1896. The new president, William McKinley, and his successor, Theodore Roosevelt, working closely with Republican Congresses, proved successful. A majority of the electorate became confirmed in its Republicanism. Fundamental voter attitudes did not again change until the Great Depression of the 1930s.[1]

The "fourth-party period" was not all serene for the Republicans. With the emergence of the Progressive movement the party experienced sectional and ideological tensions. The process, evident during the final Roosevelt years, became more severe and destructive during William Howard Taft's presidency. In 1910 the Democrats regained control of the House of Representatives. In 1912 Roosevelt and dissident Republicans challenged Taft's renomination. Defeated in that effort, Roosevelt formed the Progressive party and ran as its presidential candidate. As a result of the schism, culminating Republican misfortunes dating to 1907, Woodrow Wilson, a Democrat, won the presidency, and his party gained control of Congress. Roose-

---

[1]Jerome Clubb, William Flanigan, and Nancy Zingale, *Partisan Realignment: Voters, Parties and Government in American History* (Beverly Hills, Calif.: Sage Publications, 1980), 260–262; Lewis L. Gould "The Republican Search for a National Majority," in *The Gilded Age*, ed. H. Wayne Morgan (Syracuse: Syracuse University Press, 1970), 184.

velt came in a strong second to Wilson, while Taft ran a poor third. The very
survival of the Republican party was for a time in doubt.

One casualty of Republican discord and defeat was Joseph Cannon, who
came under increasing attack for being reactionary and dictatorial as Speaker
of the House. Following the Democratic victory in 1910, Cannon declined
to further lead what had become a minority. In 1911 House Republicans
chose James R. Mann as minority leader, and he continued in that role into
1919.

Even before his election as minority leader, Mann had chaired the important Committee on Interstate and Foreign Commerce in the Sixty-first Congress, 1909–1911. As Taft, from the very start of his administration, disappointed progressive Republicans in Congress and large segments of the public, Mann took on the complementary tasks of helping to establish for his
party a creditable legislative record and keeping to a minimum division
among House Republicans.

When Wilson took office, and Democrats assumed control of the Senate
as well as the House, Mann's task became more important and more complicated. There was no Republican in the White House, former President Taft
was discredited, and leadership of Senate Republicans fell to the lackluster
Jacob Gallinger of New Hampshire. Mann and the House Republicans represented the party before the electorate to a very considerable degree. It was
Mann's job to show the flag for the Republican party—to criticize cogently
many of the proposals and actions of both Democrats and Roosevelt's "Bull
Moose" Progressives and to put forth attractive Republican alternatives
where possible. Conservatives predominated among House Republicans, and
clearly the party's future lay on the conservative side. Mann had to accommodate to that reality, which in any case accorded with his inclinations. At
the same time, Mann needed to keep content the substantial number of progressive Republican congressmen and voters who had remained in the party
in 1912.

The Republicans recovered substantially in the election of 1914, while the
challenge of the Progressives waned. Meanwhile, however, war broke out in
Europe. Voters and congressmen became divided within each major party
about the conflicting goals of neutrality and neutral rights, and eventually
about declaring war. As on domestic matters, it behooved Mann to put forth
creditable Republican criticisms and alternatives while not, in so doing, worsening the divisions within his party. Similar challenges faced Mann after the
nation entered the war, though illness cut short his wartime service.

In November 1918, days before the Armistice, the Republicans won both
the Senate and the House. In 1920 they won Congress more decisively, and
their presidential candidate, Senator Warren G. Harding, took the presidency
in a landslide. The party faced many problems through the 1920s, yet it retained control. The political storms of the Taft years, the Bull Moose challenge, and the Wilson interlude had been weathered. By this time Mann's

leadership of the GOP was over because of ill health and antagonisms he had aroused.

Mann was hardly alone in effecting the outcome. The Republicans benefited from their full and seasoned national organization, the attractiveness of their issues and candidates, voter habits, the mistakes and inherent weaknesses of Democrats and Moosers, the impact of external events such as a business slump in 1913 and 1914, and more. Mann's contribution can not be quantified. A detailed study of what he did to accomplish Republican reconciliation and revival in the period 1909–1919 does, however, show that Mann made a greater contribution than any other individual. It shows, also, that he contributed to the GOP's gradual tilt towards the right, a factor related to the party's rejuvenation. This book is that study, the first of its kind.

Mann's lawmaking accomplishments, which were very considerable, are dealt with only as they relate to his party role, and similarly with his life story. Thus, though Mann served in Congress from 1897 until his death in 1922 and before that had an interesting career in Chicago law and politics, this book deals only in summary fashion with the early and final years, as well as the period of his rise in the House, focusing instead on the years of his greatest influence, which were also the period of Republican crisis and revival.

James Robert Mann (1856–1922) lived in the Hyde Park district of Chicago, which included many of the "better people." His early career in law and politics culminated in four years as a crusader for honesty on a highly corrupt city council. An active and increasingly prominent Republican spokesman, in 1896 he won election to the House of Representatives.

Mann rose slowly but steadily in the House by dint of extraordinary legislative talents, favorable associations, and acceptable viewpoints. The most important of his associations was with Speaker Cannon, who drew Mann into his "kitchen cabinet" and named him chairman of the Committee on Interstate and Foreign Commerce in 1909. Mann's ideas were those of a moderate American conservative, optimistic and probusiness.

Though more conservative than reformer, during the years of Roosevelt's presidency Mann led the House in adoption of the Pure Food and Drug Act and the bill that created the Department of Commerce and Labor and the Bureau of Corporations. In 1910 he pushed through the bill for which he is best remembered today, the Mann Act, directed against organized prostitution. More important, in the same year, and with great effort and skill, he steered through the House and the joint conference committee the Mann-Elkins Act, strengthening railroad regulation.

After the Democrats won control of the House in 1911, Mann managed no more bills. But since most legislation came to the floor free of binding commitments in the Democratic caucus, Mann was able to author many successful amendments, and he persisted in an earlier role, that of "Great Objector" to wasteful minor bills that required unanimous consent for consideration.

As a legislator, Mann tried to be constructive, and he was. Dovetailing with this activity, he had a strong institutional sense, which manifested itself in varied and sometimes strange ways. He had little tolerance for the careless or slipshod in the wording of a bill or disposition of a parliamentary question. His sharp jibes at offending members accorded oddly with his collegial purposes. Mann was also a strong partisan. Sometimes his remarks clearly reflected that. On other occasions, though, they blended with his legislative and institutional concerns in a complex mix that even he may not have fully understood. Thus, for example, he might wax caustic against Democrats for disgracing the House by pushing through a bad bill.

After he became minority leader, Mann assumed no committee assignments, but instead made himself familiar with, even expert about, all pending legislation. He tended to "hog the show," often at the expense of ranking Republicans on the committees reporting bills, as well as younger members. On balance his party benefited, for through him it spoke with a single and highly competent voice. Resentments developed, however, fueled also by Mann's sharp tongue, and these contributed to his defeat for Speaker in the Republican caucus in 1919. The price Mann paid was personal. The party had gained from what he had done. Mann continued as something of an elder statesman of considerable but not fully exerted power in the years 1919–1922.

House colleagues recognized Mann as something special and praised him in their memoirs and elsewhere. They noted especially his industry and parliamentary skills, but commented also on his courage, honesty, and ability as a strategist. John Nance Garner, reflecting on a House career of thirty years, called Mann "The most useful legislator I ever met." Another prominent Democrat, Finis J. Garrett of Tennessee, said of Mann, "Probably more legislative acts stand to his credit than to that of any other representative in our national history." "Mr. Mann's industry and intelligent criticism is the marvel of his colleagues," the Reading Clerk of the House wrote a friend in 1910. [2]

---

[2] Bascom N. Timmons, *Garner of Texas; A Personal History* (New York: Harper and Brothers, 1948), 111; *Congressional Record*, 67th Cong., 4th sess., 1714 (14 January 1923) (hereafter cited as *CR* 67:4); E. L. Lampson to David Hurlburt, 11 August 1910, vol. 14, James R. Mann Papers, Library of Congress. Lampson called Mann "the most useful member of the House." There is an abundance of similar comments. See especially Champ Clark, *My Quarter Century of American Politics* (New York: Harper and Brothers, 1920), vol. 2: 342–43; James F. Byrnes, *Speaking Frankly* (New York: Harper and Brothers, 1947), 30; James A. Frear, *Forty Years of Progressive Public Service* (Washington, D.C.: Associated Writers), 1937, 144; Fiorello H. La Guardia, *The Making of an Insurgent: An Autobiography, 1882–1919* (Philadelphia: J.B. Lippincott, 1948), 135; James E. Watson, *As I Knew Them: Memoirs of James E. Watson* (Indianapolis: Bobbs-Merrill, 1936), 62; Elizabeth T. Kent, *William Kent,*

Despite his importance, Mann was not among the truly famous of his time. He never served as Speaker, as Cannon and Champ Clark did, nor did he ever run for president or seriously contend for his party's nomination. The explanation for that lies partly with the politics of his home state, and partly in Mann's own qualities. He lacked "gravitas" and so was never taken as seriously as he deserved. He was too blunt, too quick with a biting remark, too impulsive, too involved with small matters, too much a man of the House. Not himself a person of wealth or family, he did not move in lofty business and social circles, nor did he speak much outside of the House.

Mann has fared even less well in history. His name lingers on in connection with the Mann Act and the Mann-Elkins Act, but his other legislative accomplishments and his role as a party leader receive little note. The decline of political history is surely a factor, and what political history is written about these years focuses on presidential elections, progressives of all parties, and Wilson. Senators, moreover, customarily get more attention than representatives. Study of Mann has also been inhibited by the fact that only a smattering of correspondence remains in his papers at the Library of Congress, although some useful letters do survive. The collection consists mainly of newspaper clippings about Mann provided by a clipping service.

Aspects of Mann's career have been chronicled by Virginia Phillips and Rena Mitchell in master's theses and by the very able historian L. Ethan Ellis. Ellis dealt with Mann as one of the more important congressmen from Chicago studied in his dissertation, most of which was published in 1930, and in an article on Mann as a legislator. These writings, though all to the good, do not describe Mann's leadership role in the House in any detail.[3]

A similar generalization might be made about the literature on Republican reunion and revival generally and the place of the House of Representatives in particular. Two of the best accounts, by Gerald McKnight and Howard Greenlee, are unpublished dissertations. McKnight dealt most fully with the House Republicans, but only for the years 1913–1916. The most useful published work deals with the multi-faceted topic briefly and/or tangentially. Especially valuable among the brief overall accounts are essays on the Re-

---

Independent: A Biography (n.p.: Privately published, 1951), 247 n. 14; and for the comments of Nicholas Longworth and Joseph Cannon, *CR* 67:4, 1716, 1724 (14 January 1923).

[3]Virginia Phillips, "The Early Congressional Career of James R. Mann: A Conservative in the Progressive Era, 1897–1913" (M.A. thesis, American University, 1959); Rena Mitchell, "The Congressional Career of James R. Mann" (M.A. thesis, University of Chicago, 1938); L. Ethan Ellis, *A History of the Chicago Delegation in Congress, 1843–1925,* (Springfield: Illinois State Historical Society, 1930); Ellis, "James R. Mann, Legislator Extraordinary," *Journal of the Illinois State Historical Society*, 46:1 (Spring, 1953): 28–43.

publican party by Lewis Gould and William Harbaugh. Aspects of the subject, limited either in terms of the years covered or topically, include a book by Horace Merrill and Marion Merrill that carries the story of congressional Republicans to 1913, James Holt's admirable study of Republican insurgents, James Oliver Robertson's book on Republican progressives after 1916, and Norman Wilensky's monograph on the Taft Republicans of 1912. Several Republicans who served in the House in the period 1909–1919 have received biographical treatment.[4] There is, then, some literature on Mann and some of the House Republicans and the larger subject of Republican reunion and revival. But much more remains to be done.

With respect to Mann and his relationship to Republican renewal, more can be done, despite the paucity of correspondence in the Mann Papers. Useful correspondence exists in collateral collections. The newspaper clippings in the Mann Papers, augmented by other newspaper and magazine stories, offer additional information and insight if they are used with care. These sources would not themselves be nearly enough if they are not combined with another source that is uniquely valuable for the study of the career of James R. Mann. When the House was in session, Mann was there and active, briefed on everything that came before the House and not shy to comment and, as best he could, to lead for his party. Neither committee work nor even lunch, chocolate that he ate at his seat, would divert him. He spent more

---

[4]Gerald D. McKnight, "A Party Against Itself—The Grand Old Party in the New Freedom Era, 1913–1916" (Ph.D. diss., University of Maryland, 1972); Howard Scott Greenlee, "The Republican Party in Division and Reunion, 1913–1920" (Ph.D. diss., University of Chicago, 1950); Gould, "Republican Search for a National Majority"; and Lewis L. Gould, "The Republicans under Roosevelt and Taft," in *The Progressive Era*, ed. Lewis L. Gould (Syracuse: Syracuse University Press, 1974), 55–82; William H. Harbaugh, "The Republican Party, 1893–1932," in *History of U.S. Political Parties*, vol. 3, *1910–1945: From Square Deal to New Deal* ed. Arthur M. Schlesinger, Jr., (New York: Chelsea House Publishers in association with R.R. Bowker Co., 1973), 2069–2128; Horace S. Merrill and Marion G. Merrill, *The Republican Command, 1897–1913* (Lexington: University Press of Kentucky, 1971); James Holt, *Congressional Insurgents and the Party System, 1909–1916* (Cambridge, Mass.: Harvard University Press, 1967); James Oliver Robertson, *No Third Choice: Progressives in Republican Politics, 1916–1921* (New York: Garland, 1983); Norman M. Wilensky, *Conservatives in the Progressive Era: The Taft Republicans of 1912* (Gainesville: University of Florida Press, 1965). Studies of House Republicans include Herbert F. Margulies, *Senator Lenroot of Wisconsin: A Political Biography, 1900–1929* (Columbia: University of Missouri Press, 1977); Thomas Robert Bullard, "From Businessman to Congressman: The Careers of Martin B. Madden" (Ph.D. diss., University of Illinois at Chicago Circle, 1973); and Robert Edward Drayer, "J. Hampton Moore: An Old Fashioned Republican" (Ph.D. diss., University of Pennsylvania. 1961).

time on the House floor than any man in history, some said.[5] Furthermore, his strong institutional feeling as well as pride caused him never to revise his remarks for *the Congressional Record*.[6] For the career of James R. Mann, the principal source, and an immensely valuable one, is the Congressional Record. The Record is clearest as to what Mann did. Often, in addition, taken alone or in combination with other evidence, it suggests some of the consequences of his actions for the Republican party, the main concern of this book.

I have been helped in this enterprise by more people than I can practicably name. My colleague Cedric B. Cowing, however, deserves special thanks for his close reading of several chapters. More than any other, Professor Lewis L. Gould of the University of Texas at Austin assisted me. He generously shared research notes from several manuscript collections and carefully and judiciously reviewed all my chapters. Finally, I am obliged to my wife Fran for unfailing encouragement and good-natured tolerance of my musings on Mann.

---

[5]*Washington Herald*, 30 July 1911, vol. 16, Mann Papers; *Washington National Tribune*, 16 December 1913, vol. 20, Mann Papers.

[6]*CR* 63:1, 1884 (3 June 1913), 13027 (30 July 1914); *Chicago Record-Herald*, 9 November 1913, vol. 18, Mann Papers.

RECONCILIATION
AND REVIVAL

Introduction

When James Robert Mann won the first of fourteen successive elections to the U.S. House of Representatives in 1896, he was forty years old. He had already done enough and said enough to indicate the kind of congressman he would be.

Unmistakably, he was his father's son. William Henry Mann pioneered as a horticulturist and nurseryman in central Illinois. He served as a private in the Mexican War and a captain in the Civil War, and with others of the northern army he became a staunch Republican. He was civic minded and helped establish what became the University of Illinois. [1] "Jim" absorbed his father's love of farming, faith in science and in progress, patriotism, Republicanism, and a strong desire to be useful. From both parents he learned to be industrious, and from some mysterious genetic combination he derived acute intelligence.

The late nineteenth century was a time of strong political parties and "bosses." While Mann was a passionate enemy to the corruption that accompanied party politics, he understood the need for party leadership in both the political and legislative settings. Thus, as he rose in politics in Chicago, he cooperated with the principal Republican leader in his area, Thomas "Doc" Jamieson, and even, in 1896, with the powerful Cook County leader, William Lorimer, who was strongly opposed by reformers. While serving on the city council Mann worked with the aggressive businessman-politician Martin

---

[1] Rena Mitchell, "The Congressional Career of James R. Mann" (M.A. thesis, University of Chicago, 1938), 4; J. H. Burnham, *History of Bloomington and Normal in McLean County, Illinois* (Bloomington, Ill.: Burnham Publishing Co., 1879), 143, 147; *Chicago Record-Herald*, 9 November 1913, vol. 18, James R. Mann Papers, Library of Congress.

Madden, though he freely differed with Madden in opposing liberal utility franchises. When a young reformer friend, William Kent, aspired to a council seat, Mann advised him to first see Jamieson.[2]

Mann's behavior was inconsistent with his resolve. Intense, on the council he spoke in a "radical manner on the simplest subject," and occasionally he intemperately lashed out at errant colleagues. But always he quickly made amends.[3]

The political bosses were uncertain allies, but they needed Mann in his various candidacies and as a campaign speaker. On a smaller scale, Mann was like a New York contemporary, Theodore Roosevelt, or Wisconsin senator John C. Spooner, a constitutional authority and strong party spokesman. These men were luminaries who lent respectability, luster, and ability as orators to tickets made up in the main of lesser candidates. Luminaries of this sort came to the bosses with bargaining power and exacted a large measure of independence on public policy questions in exchange for their cooperation.

Mann developed a loyal constituency in the area of his residence, the northern suburbs of the sprawling village of Hyde Park. Annexed to Chicago in 1889, this commodious area bordering on Lake Michigan hosted University of Chicago people after 1891. It was well stocked with businessmen-reformers, Republican and Protestant in the main, who wanted "good government." They found like-minded allies elsewhere in Chicago and drew powerful support from a reform-minded press headed by the *Tribune* and the *Daily News*.[4]

Mann was a luminary by virtue of private and public attainments. Though his family was hard hit by the depression of the 1870s, he matriculated at the University of Illinois and at the Union College of Law in Chicago, serving as valedictorian at both schools.[5] He soon became a leading real estate attorney and from his earnings acquired property.[6]

---

[2]Elizabeth T. Kent, *William Kent, Independent: A Biography* (n.p.: Privately published, n.d.), 109.

[3]*Chicago Times-Herald*, 8 June 1895, vol. 5, Mann Papers; *Chicago Herald*, 24 October 1893, 7 November 1893, vol. 1, Mann Papers.

[4]Michael Patrick McCarthy, "Businessmen and Professionals in Municipal Reform: The Chicago Experience, 1887–1920" (Ph.D. diss., Northwestern University, 1970), 3–5; Jean F. Block, *Hyde Park Houses: An Informal History, 1856–1910* (Chicago: University of Chicago Press, 1978), 45, 70; David Paul Nord, *Newspapers and New Politics: Midwestern Municipal Reform, 1890–1900* (Ann Arbor: UMI Research Press, 1981), 35, 53, 60.

[5]*Chicago Journal*, 23 April 1894, vol. 1, Mann Papers.

[6]L. Ethan Ellis, "James R. Mann, Legislator Extraordinary," *Journal of the Illinois State Historical Society* 46 (Spring 1953):29; *Congressional Record*, 64th Congress, 1st session), p. 7929 (13 May 1916) (hereafter cited as *CR* 64:1).

Mann's career as an officeholder began in 1887 with election to his community's school board. Other local offices followed, ones that required ability, such as village attorney. In 1892 he won election to the city council, where, surrounded by boodlers, he championed graft-free government. He continued on the council into 1896.

Mann served his party as an effective campaign speaker. In 1894 he emerged as a major statewide figure when he addressed the party convention as temporary chairman. Mann laid out his main ideas and attitudes in that speech. In a gravelly but tireless voice,[7] he linked his party to past and future economic growth. In the period 1860–1890, he said, under Republican guidance the United States "became the wonder and admiration of the world for a marvelous growth and rate of progress never equaled by any other nation. The spirit of man was lifted to lofty tops. American energy, American capital, genius, and industry were fostered, encouraged and protected." Democrats had interrupted the march of progress, and the country wallowed in a major economic depression, but restoral of Republican rule could reverse that, he said, for underlying opportunity remained. " We shall find the same natural conditions existing here, the same bright sun, the same fertile soil, the same rich ores, the same fair fields, the same bright minds, the same willing hands and hearts."

Chiefly needed, Mann told the convention, was tariff protection, as against President Grover Cleveland's proposal to drastically cut rates. Mann stood on orthodox Republican ground in urging on the federal government a strong promotional role, as through the protective tariff. Regulation at the federal level was in its infancy, and business-minded Republicans were not yet talking of the dangers of intrusive government.

But Mann was practical and knew that the McKinley tariff of 1890 had contributed to the party's defeat that year and in 1892. Characteristically, he cautioned temperateness in protectionism. In a similar moderate vein, without being specific, he also urged legislation that would mollify laboring men in the face of disturbed industrial relations.[8]

Mann's election to Congress in 1896 was fortuitously timed. It came as part of a Republican national sweep that put William McKinley in the presidency and gave Republicans firm control of House and Senate. Success in competitive midwestern states and northern industrial cities augured well for the future. Taken in combination with the party's victory in 1894, the 1896 election seemed to open the way for a long period of Republican control. But to accomplish that, the party would have to fulfill the people's hopes by its legislative and administrative actions. Ahead, then, for Mann, lay both challenge and opportunity.

---

[7] Ellis, "James R. Mann: Legislator Extraordinary" 32.
[8] *Chicago Tribune*, 26 July 1894, vol. 1, Mann Papers.

The new congressman was stockily built and seemed shorter than his five feet nine inches. A black beard bordered his features and turned increasingly gray and then white with the years, as did his full mustache. Mann's eyes, supplemented by pince-nez and overhung by shaggy brows, were clear blue and penetrating; they were his outstanding feature. His nose was sharp and pointed.[9] He was married and had one child, a son. Mann's robustness related to his love of farming. Throughout his years in Congress, he maintained farm land in his district and worked it when he could, while relying on a hired hand when he was away.

The key years of Mann's long service in the House were 1909–1919, when first informally, then formally, he led his party. The years 1897–1909 constituted an apprenticeship, when Mann gathered experience and increasingly demonstrated a gift for accomplishment, based on extraordinary acuity and industry.

In these apprenticeship years he had trouble over reelection only once. His district, from the South Chicago lakeshore suburbs in the north to the Indiana border in the southeast, was safely Republican. Redistricting in 1902 scarcely changed it. Renomination was more of a problem than reelection, but the good-government element of the northern suburbs remained reliable, in the main, and Mann won even stronger support in the industrial and heavily ethnic areas of the Calumet River in the south, where he repeatedly secured federal appropriations. In a young attorney, Edwin W. Sims, Mann found a capable guardian of his political interests. The only major test came in 1906, when Mann was challenged in the Republican primary as being too conservative. His successful championship of the Pure Food and Drug Act that spring and a congratulatory letter from President Theodore Roosevelt helped Mann meet the challenge.[10]

National political developments in the period 1897–1909 conduced to some of Mann's accomplishments and to his rise; they also eventuated in major problems for the Republicans that Mann, as his party's future leader, would have to face. The GOP fortified its national standing in the McKinley years and for a time under Theodore Roosevelt, who succeeded to the presidency in September 1901 when McKinley was assassinated. Operating in an

[9]Ellis, "James R. Mann: Legislator Extraordinary" 32; *Chicago Tribune*, 26 July 1894, vol. 1, Mann Papers; Mitchell, "Congressional Career of James R. Mann," 8.

[10]Kenneth C. Martis, and Ruth A. Rowles, *The Historical Atlas of United States Congressional Districts, 1789–1983* (New York: Free Press, 1982), 227; *Daily Calumet*, 1 April 1899, vol. 9, *Mann Papers; Chicago Herald*, 18 July 1915, vol. 22, Mann Papers; L. Ethan Ellis, *A History of the Chicago Delegation in Congress, 1843–1925* (Springfield: Illinois State Historical Society, 1950), 78; *Chicago Tribune*, 22 July 1906, and other reports, vol. 29, Mann Papers; Mann to "My Dear Sir," 17 July 1906, box 3, William Kent Papers, Sterling Library, Yale University; *Chicago Chronicle*, 9 October 1906, vol. 13, Mann Papers.

atmosphere of renewed prosperity and national confidence, the party focused on popular promotional policies. In addition to the Dingley tariff of 1897, the Gold Standard Act of 1900, and establishment of the Department of Commerce and Labor in 1903, the Republicans expanded trade opportunities through the acquisition of Hawaii, the Philippines, and the right to build a canal in Panama.

Ultimately the Progressive movement caused the Republicans great trouble, but not at first. The public became more fearful of the trusts and great corporations that sprang up in the nineteenth and early twentieth centuries and worried about their influence in politics. Muckraking journalists increasingly spread alarm after 1902. At the federal level, demand arose for more regulation. Theodore Roosevelt boldly championed the cause, and Republicans in Congress found it prudent to follow his lead. Three 1906 measures, the Hepburn Act, increasing the power over railroads of the Interstate Commerce Commission, the Pure Food and Drug Act, and the Meat Inspection Act, reflected the party's accommodation to progressivism.

Surprisingly in light of later events, in the House Speaker Joseph Cannon of Illinois enjoyed bipartisan popularity and full Republican support. Cannon became Speaker in 1903 at the age of sixty-seven, and by fostering party discipline he restored the place of the House relative to the Senate, to the delight of members. Even then he was an uncouth reactionary, but colleagues liked him for his blunt frankness, common sense, and humor. Because he himself influenced Roosevelt, he did not block the president's measures until 1907.[11]

In that year Roosevelt advanced proposals, as for limiting labor injunctions, that probusiness Republican congressmen would not accept. He also acted in ways that congressmen considered high-handed, as by creating new forest reserves before Congress could assert its authority. When it became clear that Roosevelt would adhere to an earlier promise and not seek reelec-

[11]George Rothwell Brown, *The Leadership of Congress* (1922; reprint, New York: Arno Press, 1974), 135; Blair Bolles, *Tyrant from Illinois: Uncle Joe Cannon's Experiment with Personal Power* (New York: W. W. Norton and Company, 1951) 4–10; William R. Gwinn, *Uncle Joe Cannon: Archfoe of Insurgency* (New York: Bookman Associates, 1957), 4, 78–79; George W. Norris, *Fighting Liberal: The Autobiography of George W. Norris* (New York: Macmillan Company, 1945), 108; James E. Watson, *As I Knew Them: Memoirs of James E. Watson* (Indianapolis: Bobbs-Merrill, 1936), 56–57; L. White Busbey, *Uncle Joe Cannon: The Story of a Pioneer American* (New York: Henry Holt and Company, 1927), 217–19; Henry Cabot Lodge to Nicholas Murray Butler, 11 May 1904, Lodge folder, Nicholas Murray Butler Papers, Butler Library, Columbia University; Lewis L. Gould, *The Presidency of Theodore Roosevelt* (Laurence: University Press of Kansas, 1991), 147–48.

tion, congressional Republicans felt free to blame him for a 1907 financial panic and to resist his proposals. [12]

In the House Cannon used the Rules Committee, over which he presided, to block Roosevelt's measures. Inevitably, he and the tight House rules came under attack from outside Congress and inside. Publishers, who privately blamed him for blocking efforts to lower the cost of print paper, attacked "Uncle Joe" as reactionary and autocratic. The American Federation of Labor fought him too, as did temperance groups. [13]

House Democrats became more unified and progressive under the able leadership first of John Sharp Williams of Mississippi and then, in December 1908, of Champ Clark of Missouri. They set out to capitalize on the new issues of Cannon and the rules, and in that connection they encouraged dissident Republicans to organize for rules reform. In December 1908 over thirty Republicans, called "insurgents," began to hold weekly meetings on the rules and perhaps displacement of the Speaker in the next Congress. [14]

Mann's response to these events was to enthusiastically support promotional policies, to accommodate early regulatory reform, and to fully back Cannon. In the course of acting on these policies, he steadily rose in the House Republican hierarchy, partly due to Cannon but mainly through legislative accomplishment.

Mann took full advantage of his assignment in 1897 to the Committee on Interstate and Foreign Commerce. The committee steadily gained in importance by dint of Supreme Court rulings, the growing complexity of the economy, and the movement for regulation. The chairman, William P. Hepburn of Iowa, a Civil War veteran and policy moderate, said of Mann: "I have thought that if the theory of transmigration of souls is true and he hereafter appeared in a later incarnation, he would have the semblance of a mule with four hind legs all in active operation." But what mattered was that Hepburn

---

[12]William H. Harbaugh, *The Life and Times of Theodore Roosevelt* (New York: Oxford University Press, 1975), 326; John Milton Cooper, Jr., *The Warrior and the Priest: Woodrow Wilson and Theodore Roosevelt* (Cambridge, Mass.: Belknap Press of Harvard University Press, 1983), 109–10; Gould, *Presidency of Theodore Roosevelt* 275–81, 244–45.

[13]George Roger Mayhill, "Speaker Cannon under the Roosevelt Administration, 1903–1907" (Ph.D. diss., University of Illinois, 1942), 10; Scott William Rager, "The Fall of the House of Cannon: Uncle Joe and His Enemies, 1903–1910" (Ph.D. diss., University of Illinois at Urbana-Champaign, 1991), 88–91, 96–97, 113–16; Bolles, *Tyrant from Illinois*, 112, 115–18; Samuel Gompers, *Seventy Years of Life and Labor* (New York: E. P. Dutton and Company, 1925), 2:113–14, 224–45, 255–58.

[14]James Holt, *Congressional Insurgents and the Party System 1909–1916* (Cambridge, Mass.: Harvard University Press, 1967), 17; David J. Foster to Frank Greene, 16 April 1909, box 2, Frank L. Greene Papers, Library of Congress; Kenneth W. Hechler, *Insurgency: Personalities and Politics of the Taft Era* (New York: Russell and Russell, 1964), 44–49.

found in Mann an able and industrious helper of similar outlook, and increasingly he delegated responsibility to him. Thus Mann took conspicuous leadership on several major issues. [15]

An early flirtation with jingoism before the Spanish-American War quickly gave way to an abiding antimilitarism in Mann's thinking. But with regard to pursuit of markets, especially in Asia, Mann was boundlessly optimistic and enthusiastic.[16] Panama Canal Zone legislation especially engaged his interest and activity, and by 1905 he had charge of all canal bills.[17]

Though wedded more to promotionalism than regulation, Mann regarded regulation as more constructive than antitrust measures. Also, through 1906 he wanted to advance Roosevelt's programs, while seeking personal achievement as well. Nor was regulation wholly antibusiness; often it protected some businesses against others. Thus Mann willingly took a large role in advancing regulatory laws. In 1903 he took charge in committee and the House of the noncontroversial Elkins antirebate bill. He also managed the bill creating the Department of Commerce and Labor and himself drafted a mild but innovative regulatory feature for a Bureau of Corporations, subsequently strengthened in the Senate.[18]

After the 1904 election Roosevelt gave sustained attention and top priority to railroad regulation. Over a two -year period Mann lent much assistance to Hepburn, who wanted to sponsor the committee's bill, and the legislation that eventuated in 1906 reflected Mann's work.[19]

---

[15]DeAlva S. Alexander, *History and Procedure of the House of Representatives* (Boston: Houghton Mifflin, 1916), 307; John E. Briggs, *William Peters Hepburn* (Iowa City: State Historical Society of Iowa, 1919), 288–92, 309, 320–23, 420 (the quote is from page 420); Martin J. Sklar, *The Corporate Reconstruction of American Capitalism, 1890–1916: The Market, the Law, and Politics* (Cambridge, Eng.: Cambridge University Press, 1988), 238–39.

[16]*CR* 55:2, p. 5846 (13 June 1898); *CR* 55:3, pp. 1812–27 (13 February 1899); *Chicago Record*, 20 September 1898 and *Chicago Inter-Ocean*, 6 October 1898, vol. 9, Mann Papers.

[17]*CR* 55:3, p. 1827 (13 February 1899); *CR* 57:1, p. 7440 (26 June 1902); *Chicago Post*, 19 December 1901, vol. 9, Mann Papers; *Chicago Daily News*, 11 November 1904, vol. 28, Mann Papers; *Chicago Tribune*, 10 March 1907, vol. 13, Mann Papers; Mitchell, "Congressional Career of James R. Mann," 31.

[18]Gould, *Presidency of Theodore Roosevelt* , 105–7; Mann in *CR* 63:2, p. 14939 (10 September 1914); Sklar, *Corporate Reconstruction*, 185; Arthur M. Johnson, "Theodore Roosevelt and the Bureau of Corporations," *Mississippi Valley Historical Review* 45 (March 1959): 574–75; Mitchell, "Congressional Career of James R. Mann," 32.

[19]Ellis, *History of the Chicago Delegation in Congress*, 50–52; Cannon in CR 67:4 p. 1724 (14 January 1923); John M. Blum, *The Republican Roosevelt* (Cambridge, Mass.: Harvard University Press, 1954) 88–105; Thomas K. McCraw, *Prophets of*

On the pure food and drug issue, Hepburn permitted Mann to lead, with the result that the Chicagoan awakened the House to his abilities. Characteristically slow to embrace thoroughgoing reform, by 1904 Mann was won to the approach of Dr. Harvey W. Wiley of the Agriculture Department, the pioneer of the reform, and the two closely collaborated. The matter culminated spectacularly in 1906, when Mann converted the House chamber into a chemical laboratory and expertly demonstrated processes of food and whiskey adulteration and fraud in weights and measures. "It was a triumph of preparedness," a member later observed.[20]

Mann performed lesser legislative services as well, in which he came to be seen as acting for Cannon. Indeed, the two Illinois men did share mutual regard, while sometimes disagreeing. Cannon came to rely on Mann for advice as to committee assignments.[21] On the floor Mann, with Cannon's help and approval, earned for himself the titles "Watchdog of the Treasury" on appropriation bills and "the Great Objector" on bills requiring unanimous consent for consideration. On the latter, he would pepper a bill's sponsor with questions and only if satisfied would he withhold objection. While his interventions were unwelcome at first, eventually Mann earned grudging admiration for blocking bad legislation.[22] He often served as presiding officer in Committee of the Whole and displayed parliamentary mastery.[23] He also headed the fairest of three election committees.[24]

In 1908 Cannon gave Mann a special assignment that would have important though unforeseeable consequences. Rather than open the door to tariff legislation before the elections, Cannon met publisher agitation over the cost of print paper by putting Mann in charge of a special investigating committee. Mann then superintended an exhaustive inquiry that took the committee to Canada and various American states, yielded six volumes of testimony,

Regulation: Charles Francis Adams, Louis D. Brandeis, James M. Landis, Alfred E. Kahn (Cambridge, Mass.: Belknap Press of Harvard University Press, 1984), 62.

[20]James Harvey Young, *Pure Food: Securing the Federal Food and Drug Act of 1906* (Princeton, N.J.: Princeton University Press, 1989), 158–59, 139–40, 205–06, 216–19, 255–57; Oscar E. Anderson, *The Health of a Nation: Harvey W. Wiley and the Fight for Pure Food*, 143–44, 159, 181–86; Wiley to Mann, 23 January 1904, vol. 11, Mann Papers; Harvey W. Wiley, *An Autobiography* (Indianapolis: Bobbs-Merrill, 1930), 228; Alexander, *History and Procedure*, 299.

[21]Mitchell, "Congressional Career of James R. Mann," 19; Brown, *Leadership of Congress*, 206; Joseph W. Graff to James R. Mann, 25 July 1905, and Mann to Joseph Cannon, 1 August 1905, Office of the Historian, U.S. House of Representatives.

[22]Samuel W. McCall, *The Business of Congress*, 70; Mitchell, "Congressional Career of James R. Mann," 52; Alexander, *History and Procedure*, 133.

[23]McCall, *Business of Congress*, 28, 33; Brown, *Leadership of Congress*, 192; "Men We Are Watching," *Independent* 111 (4 February 1909): 259.

[24]Mitchell, "Congressional Career of James R. Mann," 28; Randall B. Ripley, *Congress: Process and Policy* (New York: W.W. Norton and Company, 1979), 39.

and resulted in a report that was surprising for its unanimity and recommendations. It called for tariff cuts on print paper and pulp if Canada removed restrictions and subsidies. Sereno Payne of New York, chairman of the Ways and Means Committee, accepted Mann's proposals for inclusion in the tariff bill that he was preparing for the next Congress, soon to meet in special session.[25] Mann would later closely follow the fate of these provisions.

Hepburn failed of reelection, and observers correctly speculated that Cannon would pass over the more senior William Wanger of Pennsylvania and make Mann head of the Interstate and Foreign Commerce committee.[26] Mann's apprenticeship was over. It ended just as his party's political troubles were about to intensify. Incoming Republican President William Howard Taft wanted tariff reduction, but Old Guard Republicans disagreed. "Cannonism" had become an issue within the party and between the parties. On other issues, too, such as the labor injunction, Republicans were divided, while Democrats were ready to capitalize on burgeoning progressive sentiment in the country. As a leader in his party, Mann would have to wrestle with these problems and more, while also seeking to advance from his committee creditable legislation. The tasks were formidable, but Mann was confident, dedicated to his party's program and interests, and zealous for the thrust and parry of the legislative game.

---

[25]L. Ethan Ellis, *Print Paper Pendulum: Group Pressures and the Price of Newsprint* (New Brunswick, N.J.: Rutgers University Press, 1948), 43–48; *CR* 62:1, p. 4733 (31 July 1909); L. Ethan Ellis, *Newsprint: Producers, Publishers and Political Pressures* (New Brunswick, N.J.: Rutgers University Press, 1960), 39.

[26]*Chicago Record-Herald*, 6 November 1908, vol. 29, Mann Papers.

1

Rules Battles and Legislative Successes: November 1908–March 1911

William Howard Taft faced an impossible situation. His party was divided, and some among the regulars and insurgents spoiled for a fight. The regulars held the leadership positions in both houses and were numerically dominant, but the insurgents were encouraged by the rising tide of progressivism as expressed in newspapers, magazines, and the 1908 elections, and by the belief that Taft, the chosen heir of Roosevelt, was an ally. The hapless Taft, however, felt that to accomplish anything he had to work through the established leadership, as Roosevelt had. But Roosevelt's successes had occurred before most progressive Republicans came to Washington. Now they were there and were not prepared to be understanding. As events unfolded, Taft came under attack from them and their journalist allies, and he recoiled away from them and towards the regulars. In so doing, he confirmed the growing suspicions among insurgents and lost much of his national popularity. As division in the party grew, matters steadily worsened for both Taft and his party, which headed for defeat in 1910 and schism in 1912.

If the challenge that faced Taft in 1909 was far greater than anything Roosevelt had faced in 1901, the political skills that he brought to the task were much inferior to Roosevelt's. Some of his ideas and attributes were not suited to the times. Above all, he was clumsy at public relations and was not even much concerned about that presidential function until too late. A tendency to procrastinate, to play too much golf, and to travel too much to no purpose compounded his difficulties, which were magnified by the weakness of his staff.[1]

---

[1]Lewis L. Gould, *Reform and Regulation: American Politics from Roosevelt to Wilson*, 2nd ed. (New York: Alfred Knopf, 1986), 124; Donald F. Anderson, *William*

James R. Mann was concerned with more than just the direction and success of the Republican party, but his party role was a significant one. Even
activities that sprang mainly from other motives, such as legislative accomplishment, impacted on his party. In the Sixty-first Congress, from March
1909 to March 1911, Mann took moderately progressive positions on legislation consistent with continuing promotionalism. His accomplishments were
considerable, most notably in further advancing railroad regulation in the
Mann-Elkins Act. Although these accomplishments were not sufficient to
salvage Taft's reputation nor to save the party from defeat in 1910, they kept
the Republican party as a safe haven for most progressive Republicans when
in 1912 Roosevelt tried to win them to his party. Moreover, Mann's moderate legislative posture, together with occasional instances of independent action, worked to his advantage when in the next Congress he assumed party
leadership after Cannon stepped down. With regard to "Uncle Joe" and the
rules, Mann remained loyal in the face of several Democratic-insurgent attacks in 1909 and 1910, while also seeking compromises. The difficulties
were overwhelming though, and the only saving grace for the party was that
the damage, though severe, was reduced when the Democratic victory in
1910 largely removed Cannon and the rules as sources of major discord and
embarrassment.

The call for a special session to convene 15 March 1909 meant that in the
House the first order of business would be choice of a Speaker and adoption
of rules. The insurgents began to prepare soon after the 1908 elections and,
indeed, initiated their battle during the last session of the Sixtieth Congress.
The regulars offered a concession--creation of "Calendar Wednesday" when
committees would be called in succession and could bring to the floor reported bills of a public character—but most insurgents wanted much more
and prepared for battle in the new Congress. As noted, the urgency of the
cause lessened after that Congress, but some issues persisted and new ones
arose, so insurgency and its close relative, progressive Republicanism, remained important in Republican politics. The House insurgents of 1909 were
rebels against their party's leadership and against what they saw as undemocratic House and party rules. All progressive Republicans were insurgents,
but not all insurgents were progressives. A leader among the non-progressive
insurgents, and typical of them in being an easterner, relatively conservative,
and consistently loyal to Taft, was Augustus P. Gardner of Massachusetts.
Though humorous and amiable, Gardner was also given to righteous anger
and rebellion. Like his father-in-law, Senator Henry Cabot Lodge of Massachusetts, Gardner wanted to limit immigration through a literacy test, but in
1906 he was foiled by Cannon. He was a skilled parliamentarian and a dan-

Howard Taft: A Conservative's Conception of the Presidency (Ithaca, N.Y.: Cornell
University Press, 1973), 214-19, 224-28.

gerous enemy, but one who commanded Cannon's respect.[2] Others of the nonprogressive insurgents, such as Charles N. Fowler of New Jersey, came to insurgency out of pique over committee assignments.[3] Indeed, some of the progressives shared that grievance. There were also those who joined the insurgents because of pressure from various quarters, such as constituents displeased at Cannon on general principles and for blocking local projects. In the case of many Wisconsin members, the urgings of Senator Robert M. La Follette, the dominant politician in their state, led them to oppose Cannon.[4]

Insurgency was rooted in the progressive movement of Republican and agrarian states such as Minnesota, Iowa, Wisconsin, Kansas, Nebraska, and North and South Dakota, and states on the Pacific Coast. The representatives from these states wanted to replace Cannon and democratize the rules to open the way for such reforms as Roosevelt had advocated in 1907 and 1908.[5] Insurgency came naturally to them. They rose to power in their states in opposition to party "bosses"; their main battles had been intraparty; and their goals and weapons were anti-party devices such as the primary election.

The progressives were numerically dominant among the insurgents and led in organizing efforts. Victor Murdock of Kansas, a fiery red-haired editor, solicited support on rules reform from newly elected men, and was himself talked of as a candidate for Speaker.[6] Edmund H. Madison of Kansas and John M. Nelson of Wisconsin joined Gardner in convening insurgents. Madison, a respected lawyer not known for radicalism, lent weight to the

---

[2]L. White Busbey, *Uncle Joe Cannon: The Story of a Pioneer American* (New York: Henry Holt and Company, 1927), 258; Blair Bolles, *Tyrant from Illinois: Uncle Joe Cannon's Experiment with Personal Power* (New York: W.W. Norton and Company, 1951), 72.

[3]John D. Baker, "The Character of the Congressional Revolution of 1910," *Journal of American History* 60 (December *1973):*679; Claude Ercell Barfield, "The Democratic Party in Congress, 1909-1913" (Ph.D. diss., Northwestern University, 1965), 15-16.

[4]Howard W. Allen, *Poindexter of Washington: A Study in Progressive Politics* (Carbondale: Southern Illinois University Press, 1981), 35; Kenneth W. Hechler, *Insurgency: Personalities and Politics of the Taft Era* (New York: Russell and Russell, 1964), 42-43.

[5]James Holt, *Congressional Insurgents and the Party System, 1909-1916* (Cambridge, Mass.: Harvard University Press, 1967), 16-17; Richard Lowitt, *George W. Norris: The Making of a Progressive, 1861–1912* (Syracuse: Syracuse University Press, 1963), 27; Robert Sherman La Forte, *Leaders of Reform: Progressive Republicans in Kansas, 1900-1916* (Laurence: University Press of Kansas, 1974), 261.

[6]La Forte, *Leaders of Reform*, 140; Irvine Lenroot to Murdock, 16 February 1909 and Arthur Kopp to Murdock, 17 February 1909, box 22, Victor Murdock Papers, Library of Congress.

cause.[7] The man who later emerged as principal insurgent leader was George Norris of Nebraska, initially conservative but by 1908 a progressive. Norris had a fine mind and "a streak of patience that was part of his combative equipment."[8]

James R. Mann took the lead in defense of Cannon and the rules. On 6 November 1908, Charles Fowler announced himself a candidate for speaker. Cannon was undisturbed, but even so Mann promptly wrote all Republicans elected to the new House. He said that Illinois would present Cannon's name, invited their support, and asked for replies. Soon he announced that over half had pledged themselves to Cannon. At the same time, Mann criticized rules proposals designed to weaken the Speaker. The rules had been in effect since the Fifty-fourth Congress and had proved their worth. "And all the talk about the tyranny of the Speaker is rot." Unless the Speaker could block "endless debate and interminable filibustering," the tariff bill, with a thousand schedules, could not pass, he said. [9]

The reform movement became dangerous as insurgents and Democrats worked towards a common rules program. In its final form the old rules would continue for a time, but ad interim the Speaker might appoint only members of Ways and Means, which would work on the tariff bill in the special session, and four very minor committees. An enlarged Rules Committee consisting of six Democrats, five regulars, and four insurgents, and excluding Cannon, would be elected, and it would recommend a full set of rules in December. Presumably, the majority would propose to strip the Speaker of the power to name committees, making them elective. The party division in the new Congress would be 219–172. Just 24 insurgents, voting with a solid Democratic bloc, would be enough to adopt the reform proposal, and it was clear that there would be more than that. The only hope, from Mann's standpoint, was to detach some Democrats from the coalition.[10]

The key Democrat was John Fitzgerald of Brooklyn, the leader of the Brooklyn and Tammany delegation. Like Mann, he was a master parliamen-

---

[7]A. Gardner, E. H. Madison, and John M. Nelson to "Dear Sir," 19 January 1909, box 10, Herbert Parsons Papers, Butler Library, Columbia University; George W. Norris, *Fighting Liberal: The Autobiography of George W. Norris* (New York: Macmillan Company, 1945), 148; La Forte, *Leaders of Reform*, 40.

[8]Norris, *Fighting Liberal*, 89; Mark Sullivan, *Our Times: The United States, 1900-1925* (1930, reprint: New York: Charles Scribner's Sons, 1971), 4:381.

[9]James R. Mann to James S. Sherman, 18 November 1908, James S. Sherman Papers, New York Public Library; William R. Gwinn, *Uncle Joe Cannon, Archfoe of Insurgency* (New York: Bookman Associates, 1957), 158-59; *Chicago Inter-Ocean*, 2 December 1908, vol. 13, James R. Mann Papers, Library of Congress.

[10]Hechler, Insurgency, 57, 50; Paul DeWitt Hasbrouck, *Party Government in the House of Representatives*, 4; David J. Foster to Frank Greene, 16 April 1909, Box 2, Greene Papers; John Fitzgerald in *CR* 61:1, p.26 (15 March 1909).

tarian, a scrupulous watchdog of the Treasury, hard headed and conservative, and very able. As of 1912, Washingtonians said that he and Mann sometimes worked together, and in that year Fitzgerald invited "Jim" to join his Appropriations Committee on a trip to Panama.[11] It is not clear when their collaboration started, but at some point well in advance of the Sixty-first Congress the two discussed moderate rules reforms that would not substantially reduce the Speaker's powers. Mann later claimed parentage for one of three proposals that Fitzgerald prepared to sponsor. The proposal that Mann drew would create a Unanimous Consent Calendar that would be in order on two Mondays each month and in the last six days of a session. Members might call up from that calendar public bills that had been favorably reported without going first to the Speaker. Mann thought that its greatest virtue was in letting members know when a bill would come up. A second proposal was to guarantee the right to put a motion to recommit a bill before a final vote, thus allowing the minority party to spell out its alternative to the bill. The final reform was to require a two-thirds vote to set aside Calendar Wednesday, instead of a simple majority. These were useful reforms, but Mann saw them as not appreciably changing things and therefore tolerable.[12] Their main virtue was that they were acceptable to regular Republicans and some Democrats.

By 10 March, when Taft met with several insurgents, it was clear that Cannon would be reelected, since Taft had drawn back from earlier opposition, and no single strong opponent had emerged.[13] The movement for rules reform remained vibrant, however. Reassured by Cannon the day before of cooperation on the tariff if the president would back him, Taft now told the insurgents that he would not help them on the rules. Even so, more than the requisite 24 stood firm, ready to vote with the Democrats. When Champ

---

[11]Hechler, *Insurgency*, 54; Champ Clark, *My Quarter Century of American Politics* (New York: Harper and Brothers, 1920), 2:342; Medill McCormick to Sir Horace Plunkitt, 13 September 1917, box 2, Joseph Medill McCormick Papers, Hanna-McCormick Family Papers, Library of Congress; Irving Fisher to William Howard Taft, 11 September 1912, series 6 reel 423, William Howard Taft Papers, Library of Congress: Fitzgerald to Mann, 12 October 1912, vol. 16, Mann Papers.

[12]*Chicago Record-Herald*, 20 November 1909, vol. 13, Mann Papers; *CR* 63:2, p. 4885 (14 March 1914); *CR* 61:2, p. 1549 (7 February 1910); Chang-Wei Chiu, *The Speaker of the House of Representatives since 1896* (1928; reprint, New York: AMS Press, 1968), 186-87; Hasbrouck, *Party Government*, 5; *Chicago Tribune*, 16 March 1909, vol. 13, Mann Papers.

[13]*Chicago Record-Herald*, 20 November 1909, vol. 13, Mann Papers; *CR* 63:2, p. 4885 (14 March 1914); *CR* 61:2, p. 1549 (7 February 1910); Chang-Wei Chiu, *The Speaker of the House of Representatives since 1896*, 1928; reprint, New York: AMS Press, 1968, 186-87; Hasbrouck, *Party Government*, 5; *Chicago Tribune*, 16 March 1909, vol. 13, Mann Papers.

Clark won caucus approval for his proposal to elect an enlarged Rules Committee controlled by a Democratic-insurgent coalition to recommend sweeping rules reform, observers thought that Cannon's powers were seriously in jeopardy.

In the first order of business when the House convened on 15 March, Cannon was elected Speaker, though 12 die-hard insurgents voted for other Republicans. Then came the rules showdown. John Dalzell of Pennsylvania, Cannon's close ally on past Rules Committees, moved adoption of the old rules. His motion lost, 189-193, as 29 insurgents voted with the Democrats in opposition. Then came Champ Clark's proposal and a shocking reversal of fortunes. Sixteen Democrats now joined the regular Republicans to defeat Clark's motion, 180–203. Cannon quickly recognized Fitzgerald to offer his proposals, which included adoption of the old rules amended by his three reforms. Prodded by Mann, the House agreed to debate the motion for an hour rather than vote immediately. Mann and Dalzell consumed half of the thirty minutes controlled by Fitzgerald in defense of the Democrat's motion, further evidencing the prior collaboration that had occurred. It proved a success, as 188 regular Republicans joined 23 Democrats to adopt the motion, 211–173.[14]

Historians have explained the Democratic defections, mainly by New York and Georgia members, as caused by promises from Cannon of tariff and other favors.[15] The explanation is true but incomplete. Fitzgerald's motion was consistent with long-held views, and there is no reason to doubt his sincerity, even if he had other motives besides. Furthermore, whatever their ulterior purposes, the defecting Democrats needed a plausible facade, and Fitzgerald's moderate reforms provided it. In helping to develop a program on which regular Republicans and Fitzgerald Democrats could agree, Mann contributed to the outcome.

One effect of the deal was to allow for efficient attention to legislation during the regular session, rather than very prolonged debate on a new set of rules. This was a point Mann made in arguing for Fitzgerald's motion.[16] On the negative side, Fitzgerald's reforms, which would have been well received under other circumstances, failed to mollify the insurgents. They emerged from the contest embittered against Cannon and, in most cases, disillusioned with Taft. In that connection, the president's cabinet choices, including five

---

[14]*CR* 61:1, pp. 20–24, 15 March 1909; Jerome Martin Clubb, "Congressional Opponents of Reform, 1901–1913" (Ph.D. diss., University of Washington, 1963), 131; Gwinn, *Uncle Joe Cannon*, 174.

[15]Hechler, *Insurgency*, 49–63; Claude E. Barfield, "'Our Share of the Booty' The Democratic Party, Cannonism, and the Payne-Aldrich Tariff," *Journal of American History* 57 September 1970: 10-11.

[16]*CR* 61:1, pp. 29–30 (15 March 1909).

corporation lawyers, augmented suspicions. Furthermore, insurgents were encouraged to persevere by favorable publicity, which also drew fence-sitters to them.[17] For his part, Cannon became embittered towards the insurgents, contemptuous of them, and determined to punish them.[18] The Democrats took no retribution against their defectors, but adopted a rule binding all to any party agreement approved by two-thirds in caucus.[19] As their 1910 prospects increasingly improved, gradually they became more cohesive, and effective, and progressive under the leadership of Champ Clark.[20]

The day after the House organized, President Taft sent a message to Congress on the tariff. The clerk read for two minutes and then stopped. Everyone expected him to resume, but there was no more.[21] While some congressmen applauded Taft's brevity in contrast to Roosevelt's long-windedness, many reformers were shocked at Taft's seeming passivity. Although members clashed over several schedules, on balance the bill that emerged from the House on 9 April under the guidance of Ways and Means Chairman Sereno Payne contained many tariff reductions and significant administrative reforms that would encourage trade. It was widely approved in the country. Though Mann commented on various schedules, by far his greatest concern was for the rates on wood-pulp and print paper. The Payne bill embodied the suggestions of the committee he had headed, for a reduction of the tariff on print paper from six to two dollars per ton, and free admission of wood-pulp if Canada abandoned export restrictions. In an hour-and-a-half speech in which he displayed and discussed woods, pulps and papers, Mann argued for these rates. He predicted that if protection on wood-pulp continued, the nation would soon exhaust its supply of spruce trees.[22]

---

[17]Paolo E. Coletta, *The Presidency of William Howard Taft*, (Laurence: University Press of Kansas, 1973), 59-60, 50; Scott William Rager, "The Fall of the House of Cannon: Uncle Joe and His Enemies, 1903–1910" (Ph.D. diss., University of Illinois at Urbana-Champaign, 1991), 137-38; John P. Phillips to Victor Murdock, 15 March 1909, box 22, Murdock Papers; George Rothwell Brown, *The Leadership of Congress*, (1922; reprint, New York: Arno Press, 1974), 144.

[18]Busbey, *Uncle Joe Cannon*, xviii, 246–47; Brown, *Leadership of Congress*, 147.

[19]John B. Wiseman, *The Dilemmas of a Party Out of Power: The Democracy, 1904–1912* (New York, Garland, 1988), 127

[20]John Milton Cooper, Jr., *Pivotal Decades: The United States, 1900-1920* (New York: W.W. Norton and Company, 1990), 147.

[21]Robert M. La Follette, *La Follette's Autobiography: A Personal Narrative of Political Experiences* (1913; reprint Madison: The University of Wisconsin Press, 1960), 187; Claude G. Bowers, *Beveridge and the Progressive Era* (New York: The Literary Guild, 1932), 334.

[22]Paul Wolman, *Most Favored Nation: The Republican Revisionists and U.S. Tariff Policy, 1897–1912* (Chapel Hill: University of North Carolina Press, 1992), 143–47; L. Ethan Ellis, *Print Paper Pendulum: Group Pressures and the Price of Newsprint* (New Brunswick, N.J.: Rutgers University Press, 1948), 57–58, 62; *CR* 61:1, pp.

Despite opposition from some manufacturers, these provisions survived, and Mann voted for the bill.

In the Senate Nelson Aldrich of Rhode Island, responding not only to his own inclinations but to strong pressure from Republicans whose votes he needed, including "hides" senators, wrote a highly protectionist bill in the Finance Committee. The bill outraged Republican Senators La Follette, Albert Beveridge of Indiana, and Jonathan Dolliver of Iowa, and they led a spectacular and prolonged fight in opposition. In the end, though 10 Republicans voted against the bill, the Senate approved it, 45–34.[23] Among the rates increased over the Payne bill's was that on print paper, set at four dollars a ton. On wood-pulp the bill would threaten Canada with high countervailing duties unless all restrictions were removed. Mann warned that if those provisions survived the joint conference, he would vote against the bill. [24]

Cannon disappointed Taft by appointing high-tariff men as conferees and excluding the moderate Ebenezer J. Hill of Connecticut.[25] Unhappy with the Aldrich bill, Taft strongly intervened in the conference and won concessions on hides, lumber, coal, and other schedules, to the extent that he could accept the conference report. It displeased western progressive Republicans, however, who saw it as serving eastern manufacturing interests and hurting their constituents both as consumers and producers. Mann was also displeased, for the conferees set the print-paper rate at $3.75 per ton and only slightly modified the Senate's wood-pulp provisions.[26]

In a detailed speech Mann spelled out his objections. Then he voted for recommittal, which lost 191–186, and against the bill, which carried, 195–183. Fifteen progressive Republicans opposed the bill. In the Senate 7 progressive Republicans voted "nay" when it passed there.[27] The progressives opened themselves to retaliation. For Mann, a leader among regulars, the result was different: His votes strongly fortified his reputation for occasional headstrong independence, and that reputation would be to his and his party's advantage after he became minority leader.

Congress adjourned after finishing with the tariff, not to reassemble until December. In the intervening months the Republicans further divided, and Taft saw his reputation as a Rooseveltian progressive continue to decline.

645–53 (31 March 1909). See also CR 61:1, 331–32 (26 March 1909) and p. 1269 (9 April 1909).

[23]Gould, *Reform and Regulation*, 126–27; Merrill and Merrill, *Republican Command*, 283–84, 294.

[24]Ellis, *Print Paper Pendulum*, 62–63; CR 61:1, pp. 4366–67 (9 July 1909).

[25]Gwinn, *Uncle Joe Cannon*, 184; John M. Nelson, speech mss., n.d. (1909), box 16, John M. Nelson Papers, Library of Congress; CR 61:1, p. 5092 (5 August 1909).

[26]Allen, *Poindexter of Washington*, 73; Ellis, *Print Paper Pendulum*, 64.

[27]CR 61:1, pp. 4730–32, 4755 (31 July 1909); Baker, "Character of the Congressional Revolution of 1910," 681–82; Hechler, *Insurgency*, 145.

The new tariff law was unpopular in the nation, and newspaper publishers, unhappy over pulp and paper schedules, severely criticized it. Public reaction was calm, however, until Taft, in a 17 September speech at Winona, Minnesota, called Payne-Aldrich "the best tariff bill that the Republican party ever passed." Equally damaging, animosity towards progressive critics, especially Senator La Follette, was eroding Taft's judgment and sense of fairness.[28]

While Taft was widely misunderstood, Cannon was understood quite well. When the tariff bill passed, he announced committee assignments. The Speaker deposed three insurgents from chairmanships, though in the case of "Gussie" Gardner there were extenuating circumstances. He also punished other enemies, for example, by naming two able but radical new Members to the worst committee, on Ventilation and Acoustics.[29]

After Taft's Winona address, in speeches of his own Cannon called for a purge of antitariff progressives in 1910 primaries. He enlisted the head of the Republican Congressional Campaign Committee, William B. McKinley of Illinois, in the cause. Cannon saw himself as counterattacking, for the followers of Senators La Follette and Albert Cummins of Iowa in particular were preparing to attack regulars in 1910. The long-developing intraparty battle for control in Wisconsin, Iowa, and some other states had indeed assumed a national dimension. Now La Follette and Cummins, backed by the reform press, effectively capitalized on Cannon's unpopularity and his call for their political extinction. When Congress convened in regular session, insurgents met together and prepared to resume the rules fight whenever opportunity arose. [30]

Privately, Taft hoped that Cannon would announce himself as not a candidate for Speaker in the next Congress and sympathized with the movement to reduce his powers.[31] But in the interests of his legislative proposals, he put aside resentment over Cannon's handling of the tariff, posed amiably with him in October, and in December conferred with him about the new session.[32] The President's program, as put to Congress on 7 December, was ambitious and progressive. Some of the good it might have done for his reputation was obviated, however, when he again offended publishers in de-

[28]Sullivan, *Our Times*, 4:363; L. Ethan Ellis, *Reciprocity, 1911: A Study in Canadian-American Relations* (New Haven, Conn.: Yale University Press, 1939), 12–13; Gould, *Reform and Regulation*, 128; Pringle, *Life and Times of William Howard Taft*, 1:430.

[29]Gwinn, *Uncle Joe Cannon*, 184; John M. Nelson, speech mss., n.d. (1909), box 16, Nelson Papers; *CR* 61:1, p. 5092 (5 August 1909).

[30]Bolles, *Tyrant from Illinois*, 197–99; Barfield, "Democratic Party in Congress," 47–48

[31]Taft to Otto Bannard, 20 December 1909, series 8, reel 499, and to Guy Mellon, 17 January 1910, series 8, reel 500, Taft Papers.

[32]Rager, "Fall of the House of Cannon," 158; Gwinn, *Uncle Joe Cannon*, 195.

crying the low postal rates on newspapers and magazines as "an enormous subsidy."[33]

Matters worsened early in January with the news that Taft had withheld patronage from four congressmen and proposed to expand the blacklist. The president was uncomfortable with the patronage weapon, but in an exchange of letters with George Norris he said that he would not give patronage to those opposing the party program or his administration.[34] At just this time the long simmering dispute over Secretary of Interior Richard Ballinger boiled over. Chief Forester Gifford Pinchot, closely associated in the public mind with his friend Theodore Roosevelt and with conservation, wrote a public letter denouncing Ballinger, even though Taft had already cleared the secretary of charges relating to the disposition of coal lands in Alaska. Taft had to fire Pinchot, regardless of political consequences. La Follette had taken up the conservation battle in his magazine in August and on 18 December made his first direct public attack on Taft. The prospect loomed that other progressives would follow behind the shield of Roosevelt's policies, and the president would be positioned on the standpat side in an all-out bipolar battle.[35]

Eventually that happened, but not yet. In mid-January most progressives in the House drew back from conflict with Taft. Fearing a Democratic win in the 1910 elections, they wanted to cooperate with the president in support of his program.[36] Taft, in turn, made it clear that he would not interfere in the fight on Cannon and the rules.[37] The fires of conflict were hardly out, especially since the issue of Cannon and the rules remained, as did intense fac-

---

[33]Donald Anderson, *William Howard Taft*, 209–10.

[34]Harlan Hahn, "President Taft and the Discipline of Patronage," *Journal of Politics* (28 May 1966):371–372, 377; Stanley Solvick, "William Howard Taft and the Insurgents," *Papers of the Michigan Academy of Science, Arts, and Letters* 45 (1963):292–93; Norris, *Fighting Liberal*, 135–137.

[35]*La Follette's Weekly Magazine*, 1:33 (21 August 1909), 14–15, 1:50 (18 December 1909), 3–4.

[36]Frank Vanderlip to James Stillman, 3 February 1910, 11 February 1910, part B, series 1, box 3, Frank A. Vanderlip Papers, Butler Library, Columbia University; Henry Adams to Elizabeth Cameron, 24 January 1919, Worthington Chauncey Ford, ed. *Letters of Henry Adams* 1892–1918 (Boston: Houghton Mifflin, 1938), 531; John J. Esch to W. B. Tscharner, 14 January 1910, vol. 21, John J. Esch Letterbooks, State Historical Society of Wisconsin, Madison; David Sarasohn, "The Insurgent Republicans: Insurgent Image and Republican Reality," *Social Science History* 3 (1979): 242.

[37]David J. Foster to Frank Greene, 14 January 1910, box 2, Greene Papers; Miles Poindexter to W. D. Smith, 24 January 1910, series 1, file 23, Miles Poindexter Papers, University of Virginia, Charlottesville.

tional strife in several states.[38] They were enough abated, though, to open the prospect of a productive session.

As forecast, in August Cannon appointed Mann Chairman of the Committee on Interstate and Foreign Commerce. Mann quickly advanced important promotional and regulatory bills. On the first, a Panama Canal governance bill, he succeeded in the House but was balked in the Senate, as had happened before. He did better with a bill to curb the "white slave" trade, the famous Mann Act. The law is noteworthy in two respects. It opened the way to federal involvement in addressing an evil that defied the will or capacity of state and local governments; and it further pioneered in establishing a federal police power over things bearing little relationship to commerce under the constitutional authority to regulate interstate and foreign commerce.

Congress had passed a "white slave" law in 1907 under the power to control immigration, and prosecutions proceeded while an Immigration Commission mined for information. Chicago was a site of investigation, prosecutions, and publicity. Edwin W. Sims, Mann's political lieutenant, was a zealous prosecutor who also worked with the Immigration Commission. When in 1909 the Supreme Court found the federal law unconstitutional, Sims, convinced that "white slavery" existed on a large scale, urged Mann to sponsor new legislation and prepared a draft bill. Mann saw the need, thought the power to regulate commerce applicable, and felt that with that power as the basis for his committee's jurisdiction, he could use other constitutional powers as well to make the bill comprehensive.[39]

By 1910 sober investigation and reporting were giving way to exaggeration and sensationalism. But if among the public there was excessive credulity about massive importation of women and girls lured unwittingly, over the "missing girl," over imprisonment in brothels, and over a prostitution trust, it is nevertheless true that the prostitution business had become highly organized and elaborate, and that prostitutes were less free than earlier to quit and often suffered violence.[40]

---

[38]Hahn, "President Taft," 283–84; Norman M. Wilensky, *Conservatives in the Progressive Era: The Taft Republicans of 1912*, (Gainesville: University of Florida Press, 1965), 5.

[39]Ruth Rosen, *The Lost Sisterhood: Prostitution in America, 1900–1918* (Baltimore: Johns Hopkins University Press, 1982), 117–19; *CR* 61:2, p. 804 (19 January 1910); *Chicago Tribune*, 25 November 1909, vol. 29, Mann Papers.

[40]Rosen, *Lost Sisterhood*, 119; Walter C. Reckless, *Vice in Chicago* (1933; reprint, Montclair, N.J.: Patterson Smith, 1969), 32–34; Barbara Meil Hobson, *Uneasy Virtue: The Politics of Prostitution and the American Reform Tradition* (New York: Basic Books, 1987), 141–45.

Mann and Sims saw Taft on 24 November and persuaded him to include the subject in his program.[41] In committee Mann encountered strong constitutional objections from three Deep South Democrats, but two southerners gave the bill significant support—Thetus Sims of Tennessee and James Russell of Texas. More dangerous to Mann's bill was a rival one developed in the Committee on Immigration and Naturalization that also enjoyed bipartisan support. Both bills were comprehensive and included topics and constitutional supports more natural to the rival committee. Mann rejected compromise overtures and on 21 December reported his bill. Heated feelings between the committees and their friends endangered the legislation more than anything else. Superficially, the battle was for glory, but from Mann's standpoint there was more to it. Congress would tread on dangerous constitutional ground, so for the measure to survive in the courts it had to be surehandedly drawn. Mann felt that his bill was but that the rival Bennet-Sabath bill was not.[42]

In his committee report Mann presented the need for the bill, the provisions, and the constitutional justification. The most important section of the bill, the second, made it a felony to abet transportation in interstate or foreign commerce of a girl or woman for prostitution, debauchery, "or any other immoral purpose." Section six required those who harbored an alien woman for purposes of prostitution within three years of her arrival to file information with the commissioner-general of immigration. Since there was no federal antiprostitution law, this requirement, it was argued, would not involve self-incrimination. Mann further defended the constitutionality of the section on the basis of an international agreement to which the United States had adhered in 1908. The rest of the bill he defended as falling within the federal commerce power and beyond the police powers of the states. [43]

The Immigration Committee bill came up first, on 11 January. At Mann's suggestion the House agreed to debate for three hours, half of the time controlled by New York Republican William Bennet for the committee, the opposition time controlled by Mann. The Chicagoan then yielded most of his time to southern Democrats, who belabored the bill as unconstitutional. Mann did not share their reasoning, but in ending debate for his side, he agreed with their conclusions because of flaws of draftsmanship, which he pointed out. He was frank to charge carelessness, including failure to study the Supreme Court decision that overturned the 1907 law, "in this mad race

---

[41]*Providence Journal*, 25 November 1909, vol. 29, Mann Papers; Barfield, "Democratic Party in Congress," 262.

[42]*CR* 64:1, p. 4958 (27 March 1916); *Chicago Tribune*, 20 December 1909, vol. 29, Mann Papers.

[43]U.S. Congress, House, "White Slave Traffic," 21 December 1909, 61st Cong., 2nd Sess., H. Rep. 47, pp. 1–14; *CR* 61:2, pp. 804–5 (19 January 1910).

to obtain priority." Everis Hayes, Republican of California, soon took the floor to say, "Mr. Speaker, the spectacle of the gentleman from Illinois making a vicious and wholly unwarranted attack upon a committee of the House is nothing unusual. It is an exhibition that we often have." Adolph Sabath, a second-term Democrat from Chicago, later explained that he had been charged with incorporating the interstate commerce aspects into the committee's bill and virtually admitted flaws, while arguing for speedy adoption in the knowledge that the Senate could correct the defects. If Mann was vindicated by these remarks, prospects for a good bill had not been improved by his attack. He lost on a motion to recommit, 36–174, and the bill was adopted without a record vote. [44]

By the following Calendar Wednesday, Mann had mended most of his fences and was in a position to call up his own bill. Hayes objected to consideration, but lost a vote on that. In the debate that followed, Bennet supported Mann's bill as complementary to his own, which would at least bear on the District of Columbia and the territories. Bennet also praised Mann for originating the idea of using the commerce power. For his part, Mann said that his bill was not in contradiction to the Bennet-Sabath bill. Then he said that "the other day I possibly may have said something which was said more strongly than should have been said." He went on to give main credit to the Immigration Committee for "the agitation of this subject."[45] The outcome now was assured, and the following week the House passed the bill. [46]

The Senate stripped the Immigration Committee bill of everything that overlapped with Mann's, and in that form it became a minor law.[47] The Mann bill it accepted without amendment. In 1913 the Supreme Court unanimously upheld the constitutionality of the Mann White Slave Traffic Act. Though far from Mann's greatest achievement, the law would perpetuate his name in history.

Mann had other committee bills in process, the most important of them a railroad bill. First, however, he found himself defending the rules against an all-out and unexpected attack. Insurgents began to smell blood on 7 January. Members of a joint committee to investigate the Ballinger-Pinchot dispute were to be selected. Encouraged by Democrats, George Norris moved that the committee members be elected rather than appointed by the Speaker. Twenty-six insurgents joined the Democrats to adopt the motion, 149–146. The alliance persisted and the insurgents were able to secure the election to the committee of Edmund Madison and the exclusion of Payne and Dalzell.

---

[44]*CR* 61:2. pp. 517–29 (11 January 1910), pp. 545–51 (12 January 1910).
[45]*CR* 64:1, p. 4958 (27 March 1916); *CR* 61:2, pp. 808, 805 (19 January 1910).
[46]*CR* 62:1, p. 1141 (26 January 1910).
[47]*Ibid.*, p. 3291 (17 March 1910).

Heartened by this first victory over Cannon, insurgents waited for a chance to reopen the whole question of the rules.[48]

On 15 March the insurgents and Democrats successfully combined to eliminate an appropriation for cars for the speaker and the vice president, and also won a lesser appropriation battle. The following day Edgar Crumpacker, a regular Republican from Indiana, intruded on Calendar Wednesday in trying to get consideration for an amendment to the Census Act on the grounds that his motion was constitutionally privileged, since the Constitution provided for taking a census. Cannon, perhaps to retaliate against his tormentors by striking at the recently created Calendar Wednesday, ruled the motion in order. His ruling was appealed, and after hot debate 42 Republicans joined the Democrats to overturn the Speaker's ruling, 112–163, the first time in ten years the House had overruled a Speaker on a point of order. "Near insurgents" had heard from constituents about Cannon and also about the tariff. They hoped to deflect voter anger about the latter through action against the former and to appear as reformers. "Today's affair may not be the climax by any means," a journalist wrote.[49]

On 17 March, with Calendar Wednesday no longer at issue, the House reversed itself and permitted Crumpacker to get action on his bill. George Norris saw his opportunity, and hours later he moved adoption of new House rules to exclude the Speaker from the Rules Committee and change its size, composition, and method of selection. He claimed that his motion too was constitutionally privileged, since the Constitution gave the House power to make its rules. Dalzell made a point of order against the resolution, but Cannon declined to rule immediately, instead requesting debate on the point of order. Prospects were dim on the basis of the voting in recent days, and time was needed to send out for regulars who were away for St. Patrick's Day festivities.[50]

Four times Cannon sought adjournment, and each time the insurgent-Democratic coalition voted him down. The House stayed in continuous session through the night and into the next afternoon in an atmosphere of high excitement and rancor. Frustrated at their inability to get a vote, a number of insurgents told of past mistreatment by Cannon. On the other side, Mann's speech was later best remembered, though he did not deliver it until after

---

[48]Hechler, *Insurgency*, 64; Evans C. Johnson, *Oscar W. Underwood: A Political Biography* (Baton Rouge: Louisiana State University Press, 1980), 128; Minutes, insurgent meetings, 8 January 1910, box 16, Nelson Papers.

[49]Geoffrey Morrison, "Champ Clark and the Rules Revolution of 1910," *Capitol Studies* 2 (1974): 52; *Chicago Tribune*, 17 March 1910, vol. 29, Mann Papers; Baker, "Character of the Congressional Revolution of 1910," 685–88; *Chicago Record-Herald*, 17 March 1910, vol. 29, Mann Papers.

[50]Hasbrouck, *Party Government*, 6–7; CR 61:2, p. 3292 (17 March 1910).

midnight.[51] The impact of his words cannot be determined, but perhaps his spirited and creditable arguments on the point of order, for the rules, in defense of Cannon, and in opposition to the Democrats helped regulars get through a difficult time with the sense of being right, while adding to the discomfort of "near insurgents" and insurgents over their alliance with the Democrats and over some of their positions. Certainly, Mann's performance enhanced his own stature as a future leader for his party. Though he overstated his case, it was a strong one, especially on the point of order against Norris's motion. For the moment, at least, his opponents were concerned with ends, substantive and symbolic, more than with means and thus were vulnerable to his attack.

Prior to his speech, Mann made the point that while the Constitution provided for both census and House rules, "we have not yet taken the census, but we have made the rules." Later, as matters dragged on, Democrats cried "Filibuster." "Mr. Speaker," Mann commented, "it is a remarkable thing that the moment that side of the House sits in partial control of the House the effort is to stifle debate." Finally, he delivered his speech, and he began with the point of order. Mann argued that to allow anyone at any time to raise a rules question would mightily fortify filibusterers, especially if a group of members took turns putting rules motions. Democrat Henry Clayton of Alabama said that Cannon, by his refusal to rule, was conducting a filibuster, "and acting like a czar." Mann won fresh applause from Republicans when he replied that "when the Speaker permits debate he is accused of being a czar, and when the Rules Committee by a rule adopted by the House cuts off debate, he is accused of being a czar for stopping debate. It will never be possible to satisfy my distinguished friend from Alabama so long as there is a Republican Speaker in the chair." He said that Democratic leader John Sharp Williams had filibustered in the Sixtieth Congress and suggested that he, Mann, might do the same if the Democrats came to power, given this parliamentary weapon. He reminded members of the frequent inability of the House to act prior to rules changes begun by Speaker Thomas Reed in 1890. Filibustering then was based on faulty rules, which could be changed, Mann said. The new filibustering would be based on the Constitution and could not be changed. Insurgent Miles Poindexter of Washington suggested that a future Speaker might rule such motions out of order as being frivolous. To that Mann replied: "It may be that sometime this country will find a Speaker who will declare that a resolution in order and privileged under the Constitution is not privileged, but I hope such a man will never be found in the Speaker's chair." A Democrat asked Mann how then the Rules Committee

---

[51]Norris, *Fighting Liberal*, 131; Gwinn, *Uncle Joe Cannon*, 194–95; Brown, *Leadership of Congress*, 148; Richard Bolling, *Power in the House: A History of the Leadership of the House of Representatives* (New York: E. P. Dutton, 1968), 81.

might be changed. Mann said that it could be done, but he would not tell how.[52]

Showing the flag, Mann now turned to an unapologetic defense of the rules, the Rules Committee, and Cannon. He denied that the Rules Committee controlled House action. In the previous Congress, of 629 bills and joint resolutions enacted, the Rules Committee had involved itself with just 21. Mann described and justified these interventions. "The Committee on Rules is, in the main, a reserve power which is rarely used in the House. The truth is," he went on, "the complaint that the Speaker, under the rules, is an autocrat usually emanate from those who have urged the Speaker to use autocratic power on their behalf." The rules were not perfect, he said, but they "represent the legislative wisdom of a century." On balance, he judged, "The rules of the House are probably the best considered, most scientifically constructed and finely adjusted rules governing any parliamentary body on earth. . . . But there never has been and there never will be any set of rules devised by which each one of four hundred Members of the House can at any time bring each one of 30,000 bills before the House for immediate consideration and disposal." Public feeling against Cannon and the rules was based on misapprehension, Mann said. Cannon had not blocked progressive measures, as claimed, and Mann pointed to a number of post-1902 laws. Nor had he been an autocrat. Rather, he was "the leader and strongest influence in the House" and had been so since Speaker Reed had left the House in 1899 (including the interregnum speakership years of David Henderson, 1899–1903). Mann concluded, to Republican applause, that the years of Cannon's speakership "will stand out among the most brilliant in the history of the country."[53]

Compromise negotiations between regulars and insurgents had been going on all the while, and at 2 p.m. on 18 March insurgents joined regulars in at last approving a recess for two hours. At 4 p.m. the same group voted to adjourn until noon on 19 March, when Cannon would rule. Meanwhile, compromise efforts would continue.[54] Mann joined in conferences with Cannon and in some of the sessions with insurgents. Cannon refused to quit the Rules Committee under fire, and Mann stood with him. On that issue, principally, the intraparty negotiation failed.[55]

On 19 March Cannon duly ruled in favor of the point of order, and his ruling was overturned, 162–182. At Democratic insistence Norris offered

---

[52]*CR* 61:2, pp. 3292, 3309, 3308, 3330–32 (18 March 1910).

[53]*Ibid.*, pp. 3333–34 (18 March 1910).

[54]Geoffrey F. Morrison, "A Political Biography of Champ Clark" (Ph.D. diss., St. Louis University, 1972), 194.

[55]*Chicago Record-Herald*, 19 March 1910, and *Washington Herald*, 20 March 1910, vol. 29, Mann Papers; Bolles, *Tyrant from Illinois*, 219; Hechler, *Insurgency*, 71.

their proposal as a substitute for his own. It would exclude the Speaker from the Rules Committee and increase the size of the committee from five, appointed by the Speaker, to ten, elected by the House. Presumably, the members would really be chosen in party caucuses. The Speaker's power to appoint the members of other committees was not touched. The motion was approved, 191–156. Forty-three Republicans voted with the Democrats. That, however, was as far as most of them would go in the direction of their constituents and away from party regularity in the House. When Cannon boldly challenged the new majority to declare the chair vacant and replace him, and Democrat Albert Burleson of Texas rose to the bait, just 9 insurgents supported the motion, which failed, 155–192. Cannon had vacated the chair after Burleson's motion. Now he returned in triumph from the Speaker's room amidst uproarious applause. In the aftermath insurgents acquiesced as the Republican caucus chose six regulars headed by John Dalzell for the new Rules Committee. They wanted to control the party, not to coalesce with Democrats on the committee.[56]

The Democrats emerged from the contest still armed with the Cannon issue for the 1910 elections and remarkably united.[57] The Republicans continued divided and headed for a showdown in some states in primary elections. Taft, however, to promote his legislation, became conciliatory towards the House insurgents, whom he disliked less than some in the Senate.[58] The insurgents shared a concern for achievement and accepted the olive branch.[59] The factions disagreed as to the specifics of legislation, though, and as to who should get the credit. Such was the situation when Mann again turned his attention to the railroad bill.

For different reasons, in 1908 and 1909 both shippers and railroads called for new legislation. The Republican platform of 1908 promised increased regulation, and early in 1909 the administration began to lay the groundwork.[60] Mann was drawn in belatedly. Only in August, just after he had been

[56]CR 61:2, pp. 3428–36 (19 March 1910); Holt, *Congressional Insurgents*, 21–23.

[57]David Sarasohn, *The Party of Reform: Democrats in the Progressive Era* (Jackson: University Press of Mississippi, 1989), 77; Morrison, "Political Biography of Champ Clark," 250–51, 315.

[58]Gwinn, *Uncle Joe Cannon*, 203–5, 211–12, 219; Archie Butt to "Dear Clara," 29 May 1910, Archie Butt, *Taft and Roosevelt: The Intimate Letters of Archie Butt, Military Aide* (Garden City, N.Y.: Doubleday, Doran, and Company, 1930), 1:356–60.

[59]*Washington Times*, 11 April 1910, vol. 30, Mann Papers; Ebenezer Hill to Charles H. Clark. 19 May, 1910, series 1, box 51, Ebenezer T. Hill Papers Sterling Library, Yale University.

[60]Robert H. Wiebe, *Businessmen and Reform: A Study of the Progressive Movement* (Cambridge, Mass.: Harvard University Press, 1962), 85–86; Gabriel Kolko, *Railroads and Regulation 1877–1916* (Princeton, N.J.: Princeton University Press, 1965),

named chairman of the Committee on Interstate and Foreign Commerce, was he summoned to the White House to confer. Other conferences followed, but not agreement. Mann would not accept the keystone of the administration's emerging plan, for a special court to hear appeals from decisions of the ICC, a Commerce Court.[61] Thus Attorney General George Wickersham, in charge of drafting an administration bill, continued to rely on Charles Townsend of Michigan as his adviser from Congress, as he had since April.[62] But Mann took the administration's attentions as a mandate to draft a bill himself, at the cost of a vacation. William Stafford of Milwaukee, a member of his committee and a personal friend, assisted. On 4 January Mann introduced his bill, three days before Taft delivered a special message and six days before Townsend introduced the administration's bill. Mann's bill was the more likely to appeal to progressive Republicans and Democrats, for it had no Commerce Court section but did set out to remedy rate discrimination between long and short hauls.[63]

The administration's position was weak. To be sure, Townsend had co-sponsored the railroad bill that had passed in the House in 1905, and he was considered able and experienced. As an occasional cautious critic of the Speaker's powers, however, he had little support among Republican leaders,[64] and Democrats were probably not alone in frowning on a bill prepared in the executive branch. The Townsend bill suffered also for the fact that Taft had conferred with six railroad presidents before delivering his message or finalizing the bill. [65]

As committee chairman, Mann rarely used subcommittees and he did not resort to one for the hearings and deliberations on the railroad bill.[66] The six committee Democrats had no obligations to the administration, in contrast

---

177–79; Ari Hoogenboom and Olive Hoogenboom, *A History of the ICC: From Panacea to Palliative* (New York: W.W. Norton and Company, 1976), 60.

[61]L. Ethan Ellis, *A History of the Chicago Delegation in Congress, 1843–1952*, 52; *Chicago Record-Herald*, 23 November 1909, vol. 29, p. 52, Mann Papers; Mann in *CR* 62:2, p. 11032 (15 August 1912).

[62]Kolko, *Railroads and Regulation*, 179; Townsend in *CR* 61:2, p. 5231 (22 April 1910).

[63]Ellis, *History of the Chicago Delegation in Congress* 52; Stafford in *CR* 67:4, p. 1719 (14 January 1923); Virginia Phillips, "The Early Congressional Career of James R. Mann: A Conservative in a Progressive Era, 1897–1913" (M.A. thesis, American University, 1959), 62; Miles Poindexter to J. B. Campbell, 9 March 1910, series l, file 27, Poindexter Papers.

[64]Brown, *Leadership of Congress*, 19; Hechler, *Insurgency*, 44; *Chicago Post*, 10 January 1910, vol. 30, Mann Papers.

[65]Barfield, "Democratic Party in Congress," 141.

[66]Robert Luce, *Legislative Procedure: Parliamentary Practices and the Course of Business in the Framing of Statutes* (Boston: Houghton Mifflin, 1922), 134.

to the twelve Republicans; their votes helped substantially in bringing adoption of scores of amendments to Townsend's bill, some submitted by themselves, but many drawn by Mann from his own bill.[67] From an ideological standpoint, the amendments made the bill more progressive. In terms of the clash of interests, they reflected the aggressive involvement of shipper representatives and the passivity of railroad men, who feared that forceful efforts would boomerang, as they had in 1906.[68] Mann suffered but one major defeat, on the Commerce Court. Under strong administration pressure, ten Republicans voted for it, while only Fred Stevens of Minnesota voted with Mann and the Democrats in opposition.[69] Despite the setback, Mann decided to take charge of the bill in the House, with the prospect of his name being attached to the law, to his advantage in a tough reelection contest. He explained to the House that so many amendments had been agreed to, many suggested by Townsend, that "more as a matter of convenience than otherwise," the committee had struck from Townsend's bill all but the enabling clause and inserted the new railroad bill as an amendment. Mann's committee report made clear how different the bill was from the one that Townsend had introduced.[70] Michigan congressmen criticized Mann, but Townsend adjusted to the situation when he was offered the honor of closing debate.[71] Mann had to swallow the Commerce Court section, and defended it, but he dismissed it as unimportant.[72] Taft and Wickersham thought it highly important and adopted the revised bill as an administration measure, indeed the main one of the year. They treated it as a test of party loyalty.[73]

Mann presented the bill in a long speech begun on 12 April and completed two days later. In his remarks, and responding to hostile questions, he defended the bill against those who thought it insufficiently progressive or

---

[67]On the Democrats, Barfield, "Democratic Party in Congress," 145; William Adamson in CR 61:2, pp. 4719, 4720, 4722 (14 April 1910); and U.S. House of Representatives, 61:2, Report No. 923, "Railroad Bill," pp. 163–64, for the views of Gordon Russell and Thetus Sims, mainly agreeing with Mann's majority report. On Mann's role, see Mann in CR 63:1, p. 5027 (16 September 1913), when Mann said, "The law of 1910 I principally wrote." No one disputed the claim.

[68]Frank H. Dixon, "The Mann-Elkins Act," *Quarterly Journal of Economics* 24 (August 1910):595–96; Frank Vanderlip to James Stillman, 3 February 1910 and 11 February 1910, part B, series 1, box 3, Vanderlip Papers.

[69]*Chicago Inter-Ocean*, 27 February 1910, and *Chicago Tribune*, 1 March 1910, vol. 30, Mann Papers.

[70]CR 61:2, p. 4572 (12 April 1910); "Railroad Bill," 95–96.

[71]*Sault Ste. Marie News*, 11 April 1919, and *Grand Rapids, Michigan, Press*, 13 April 1919, vol. 30, Mann Papers.

[72]CR 61:2, p. 4578 (12 April 1910).

[73]*Chicago Examiner*, 7 March 1910, 29 March 1910, vol. 30, Mann Papers; Hechler, *Insurgency*, 163.

even retrogressive. Thus the Commerce Court, composed of judges drawn from district courts for a five-year period of specialized work, would expedite appeals from the ICC, to the advantage of shippers. Though the attorney general would represent the ICC in suits, he might use attorneys from the ICC staff, the court would control his conduct, and shippers might appear with counsel. The ICC would have many new powers, including the right to suspend rate increases for up to 120 days on its own initiative pending investigation without waiting for an appeal from a shipper. The ICC would supervise the issuance of securities, to guard against stock watering, and would oversee a ban on most forms of long- and short-haul discrimination. It could also require "just and reasonable regulations and practices." There might be rate agreements among railroads, but not pooling to the detriment of competition. While railroads could expand traffic through mergers, they could not acquire competitors, nor could competing roads have interlocking directorates. Repeatedly Mann drew contrasts between the committee's bill and the one Wickersham had drafted.[74]

William Adamson of Georgia headed a group of four committee Democrats who, though participants in making the bill, quarreled with some provisions and filed a minority report. Adamson controlled half of the time in Committee of the Whole and spoke when Mann finished. Before discussing the bill, he remarked on Mann and his speech. Mann, he said, "has long been celebrated as a rapid-fire talker. He next made a reputation as the most frequent speaker; but he has now blazed into splendor and made a new record as the longest talker who ever spoke on a commerce bill. The gentleman from Illinois made a magnificent speech."[75] In his substantive remarks Adamson criticized especially the Commerce Court provisions and the traffic agreement and stock and bond sections, the latter partly on states' rights grounds.[76]

Four days later, with some difficulty the progressive Republican freshman from Wisconsin, Irvine Lenroot, Senator La Follette's first lieutenant, got an hour from Mann. Lenroot's masterly speech established him as the leader among Republican critics of the bill. Lenroot echoed some of Adamson's themes, but added others to form the nucleus of what became a program of amendments supported with varying degrees of consistency by progressive Republicans and Democrats. When the House battle was done, on 10 May, the coalition members had significantly altered the bill. They failed on the Commerce Court, but weakened it respecting injunctions; they expanded ICC powers, to cover telephone and telegraph; they provided for physical valuation of railroad property as a basis for rate making, a cause Senator La

---

[74]CR 61:2, pp. 4571–88 (12 April 1910), 4711–19 (14 April 1910).
[75]Ibid., p. 4719 (14 April 1910).
[76]Ibid., pp. 4719–25 (14 April 1910).

Follette had championed.[77] Mann opposed most amendments and helped defeat many. Controlling the bill, he assisted with amendments that he thought were constructive. He closely guarded the bill against amendments that might jeopardize its constitutionality and gave attention, too, to expediting consideration. If the House finished before the Senate, the legislation would be the Mann-Elkins Act, not the Elkins-Mann Act. The House did finish first, and in the final vote Republicans were united and the bill passed, 201–126, though before that 12 progressive Republicans voted with Democrats to recommit with instructions, losing 157–176.[78]

In the Senate progressive Republicans benefited from an untimely railroad announcement of rate increases, to take effect on 1 June, before the new legislation strengthened the ICC. Angrily, Taft secured an injunction against the increase, while a progressive-Democratic coalition won surprising victories. Finally, Nelson Aldrich made his own deal with Democrats and regained control.[79] Even so, the Senate bill seemed sufficiently progressive to cause Lenroot to lead a strong movement of House progressive Republicans and Democrats to accept it rather than risk the hazards of a conference committee. Both Taft and Mann considered the House bill their own and prepared to defend it. Taft, whose standing had improved as the result of the injunction, consulted with Mann and then strengthened Mann's hand just before the start of debate with a message describing the surrender of the railroads on their hasty rate increase.[80]

Mann began and ended the two-hour debate, showing some belligerence when he responded to the skeptical remarks of Lenroot, Adamson, Clark, and others. He noted sloppy imperfections in the Senate bill and valuable House provisions omitted from it. He appealed to the House's proud resentment of Senate supremacy and pointed out that if balked in conference the House could reject the conference report and accept the Senate bill. But he promised that despite the conservatism of the likely Senate Republican conferees, Nelson Aldrich and Stephen Elkins of West Virginia, he would bring back a better bill than either the Senate's or the House's. By a 156–162 vote the House gave him the chance to prove it. Progressive Republicans attributed the outcome more to Taft's message than Mann's oratory. Twenty-one of them voted for Lenroot's motion, but they had counted on 26. Eight

---

[77]Herbert F. Margulies, *Senator Lenroot of Wisconsin: A Political Biography, 1900–1929* (Columbia: University of Missouri Press, 1977), 101–2.

[78]*CR* 61:2, pp. 6032–33 (10 May 1910); Hechler, *Insurgency*, 173–74.

[79]Wiebe, *Businessmen and Reform*, 86; Kolko, *Railroads and Regulation*, 190–91.

[80]Archie Butt to "Dear Clara," 8 June 1910, *Letters of Archie Butt*, 1:368; Chauncey M. Depew to Elihu Root, 23 June 1910, Chauncey M. Depew Papers, Sterling Library, Yale University; *New York Times*, 8 June 1910; *CR* 61:2, p. 7567 (7 June 1910).

progressive Republicans voted with Mann. So did 6 Democrats, 4 of them New Yorkers led by John Fitzgerald.[81]

In the conference the Democrats, Adamson and Senator Francis G. Newlands of Nevada, were ignored. Nor was Representative William Wanger a factor, except as a supporter of Mann. Decision rested with Mann for the House and Aldrich and Elkins for the Senate. Mann was able to credibly threaten House rejection of an unsatisfactory report in light of the recent close vote in the House and his own public promises. Senate progressive Republicans reinforced him by warning of protracted debate into the summer if their main amendments were dropped.[82] By rule the senators had to act jointly, but Mann pressured Aldrich through Elkins. He had worked well with Elkins over the years and again in 1910 on two railroad labor bills. Elkins, moreover, was believed to resent Aldrich's high-handed tactics in the committee that he, Elkins, chaired. Now Mann and Elkins frequently conferred outside the formal conference.[83] In consequence of his firm and informed use of a strong hand, and to a lesser extent his relationship with Elkins, Mann was able to fulfill his promise to the House. Most important, the conference adopted the Senate's provision letting the ICC suspend a rate increase for ten months pending investigation, rather than four months, as in the House bill. The House's progressive long- and short-haul provision won out. Physical valuation was dropped, but that had been expected.[84] On 18 June Mann triumphantly presented the report in the House. Adamson heaped extravagant praise on him. So did Martin Madden, Mann's old associate on the Chicago City Council, who had entered Congress in 1903. Lenroot, more grudgingly since future intraparty battles lay ahead, acknowledged that the report improved on both Senate and House bills. Mann merely answered questions, leaving speeches for others, but at the end he said, "Mr. Speaker, I stood on the floor of this House a few days ago and said to the House that if this bill went to conference and I was one of the conferees, I would not betray the confidence of the House to the best of my ability. I have kept that pledge." "Loud and continued applause" ensued, said the Congressional Record.[85]

The following month Mann's formal photograph graced the Rooseveltian *Review of Reviews*. He was identified as the chairman of the Interstate and Foreign Commerce Committee "Whose Leadership in the Debate on the

---

[81]*CR* 61:2, pp. 7569–77 (7 June 1910); *New York Times*, 8 June 1910; *Christian Science Monitor*, 8 June 1910; *Chicago Examiner*, 8 June 1910, vol 30, Mann Papers.

[82]Hechler, *Insurgency*, 176–77.

[83]*CR* 62:2, p. 692 (7 January 1912); *Detroit News*, 14 March 1910, vol. 30, Mann Papers.

[84]Barfield, "Democratic Party in Congress," 194–95.

[85]*CR* 61:2, pp. 8475–76, 8479, 8475, 8489 (18 June 1910).

Railroad Bill Has Brought Him Great Credit." [86] This token of outside recognition complemented the state of things in the House. Mann's work on the railroad bill—in committee, in the House, and in conference—had been extraordinary. It reflected well not only on him, but on the party, the House, and even the administration. Members were reminded that Mann was more than a vigilant watchdog over often trivial legislation, more than a Cannonite factionalist; he was capable of big things, too. Insurgents, calculated to be most skeptical, could take a more generous view. The most conservative Republicans, doubtful about the new law, could nevertheless credit Mann for accomplishing something that was politically helpful and realize that good features stricken in the House, including provisions for rate agreements and mergers, were lost over Mann's objections. The bill was hardly sufficient, however, to reunify the party or salvage its popularity among the electorate. [87]

Something more might be added as to Mann's position among the regulars. They could not doubt his conservatism, including strong concern for the welfare of business. On the railroad bill, not only had he sought to protect and foster the railroad system, but in advancing regulation, he had responded to important business elements among the shippers. Earlier in the session he showed the same kind of concern. In response to what proved an abortive presidential antitrust initiative, Mann fashioned a nonpunitive kind of bill. He stood in the way of a popular social welfare reform, creation of a Children's Bureau, while expressing to his constituent Jane Addams doubt as to the wisdom even of child-labor laws. [88] He also continued active for economy in appropriations. Most important, Mann remained almost hyperregular in his support of Cannon and the rules.

Congress adjourned a week after passing the railroad bill, and Mann recuperated for several weeks from what had been an exhausting session. [89] Soon he was ready to contest for renomination and reelection. In some ways the situation was ominous. Events on the national stage had local import. These same events served as political background to Mann's later actions.

"Never in my acquaintance with administrations have I seen such a change for the better as has occurred in the last four weeks for Taft," Senator Chauncey Depew of New York observed at session's end. The president's firm stand against the railroad rate increase brought a dramatic shift in press and public opinion, and congressmen responded by passing not only the railroad bill but measures respecting conservation, campaign finance, and postal

---

[86] *Review of Reviews* 42:8 (July 1910).

[87] George Wickersham condemned the main amendments to the bill, except for Mann's. Wickersham to Charles D. Hilles, 15 July 1911, series 6, file 100a, Taft Papers.

[88] Mann to Jane Addams, 6 December 1909, box 12, Parsons Papers.

[89] William Stafford in CR 67:4, p. 1720 (14 January 1923).

savings.[90] Tariff negotiations with Canada, portending action on print paper, met publisher demands.[91] Joseph Cannon, however, would not be quiet. On 18 June he denounced a new House rule drawn by Democrats and acquiesced in by John Dalzell to allow members to bypass the Speaker and bring up a bill by means of a discharge petition.[92] In July, stumping in Kansas, Cannon made it clear that, notwithstanding the hopes of many regulars and demands of insurgents, he remained a candidate for Speaker in the next Congress. [93] Further, on 19 June Roosevelt returned from abroad and diverted attention from Taft and his recent successes. Taft, still strongly antagonistic to Senators Cummins and La Follette especially, persisted in a selective antiprogressive nomination campaign. Progressive Republicans were themselves aggressive against regulars. The country watched to see where Roosevelt would stand, and the Rough Rider, though hopeful for party unification, yet spoke in August for an advanced form of progressivism at Osawatomie, Kansas, and at Denver attacked the conservative Supreme Court. Thus in the summer of 1910 intraparty battle raged, and progressive Republicans had the better of it. Forty congressional regulars lost, including one of Cannon's top lieutenants, James Tawney of Minnesota.[94]

Progressivism was strong in Illinois and Chicago, though lacking a leader comparable to La Follette or Cummins. Organized in late June by Harold Ickes, some progressive Republicans opposed Mann and other regulars. Mann benefited, though, when a popular state senator declined to run and then two progressives divided support. Mann made full use of his franking privileges and stressed his seniority, his record, and that he voted independently notwithstanding his friendship with Cannon. The progressive press scattered its attention and the *Chicago Tribune* stayed neutral. In a light vote Mann won a plurality in the new direct primary. Three regular colleagues from Chicago lost.[95]

[90]Depew to Elihu Root, 23 June 1910, Depew Papers.

[91]James C. Needham to Chester Rowell, 15 March 1910, James C. Needham Papers, Bancroft Library, University of California, Berkeley.

[92]Gwinn, *Uncle Joe Cannon*, 222.

[93]Rager, "Fall of the House of Cannon," 163; Bolles, *Tyrant from Illinois*, 227–28.

[94]Gould, *Reform and Regulation*, 131–37; Ralph Mills Sayre, "Albert Baird Cummins and the Progressive Movement in Iowa" (Ph.D. diss., Columbia University, 1958), 367; Herbert F. Margulies, *The Decline of the Progressive Movement in Wisconsin, 1890–1920* (Madison: State Historical Society of Wisconsin, 1968), 104–6; La Forte, *Leaders of Reform* 163–66, 175; George E. Mowry, *The Era of Theodore Roosevelt and the Birth of Modern America, 1900–1912* (New York: Harper and Row, 1958), 272.

[95]Ralph Arthur Straetz, "The Progressive Movement in Illinois, 1910–1916" (Ph.D. diss., University of Illinois, 1951), 35; Mann to "Dear Sir," 2 September 1910,

The progressive tide that carried progressive Republicans against regulars surged for the Democrats in the general election. Another factor also worked for them. In Cook County, as in other urban areas of the Midwest, the Democrats were in the process of winning a preponderance of ethnic voters reacting against new temperance legislation.[96] Though Mann's district was normally Republican, the head of the Democratic Congressional Campaign Committee, James C. Lloyd, tried to capture Mann's seat for John C. Vaughan, an aggressive seed dealer, who used the tariff issue along with personal attacks. Republican ranks closed, however, Senator Cummins endorsed Mann and so did the *Tribune*, and he won reelection. Mann's margin, which had been 17,673 in 1908, was reduced to 1,411. A Socialist's 2,711 votes probably hurt Vaughan more than Mann. Martin Madden's plurality was also greatly reduced, and the Republicans kept but three of their six Cook county seats.[97]

The tide was national and gave the Democrats control of the House, 228–162. The Republicans lost 47 seats in the House and 10 in the Senate, where the party's control would depend on unreliable insurgents. The Democrats also captured key governorships, including New Jersey's for Woodrow Wilson. The new House would see changes not only in the balance between the parties but within them. Of the 228 Democrats, just 95 came from the Confederate states. The "new men" would express an urban progressivism different from Bryan's agrarianism.[98] As for the Republicans, their losses were almost wholly from the ranks of regulars in such states as New York, Ohio, Illinois, and Pennsylvania. Progressive Republicans, strongest where the Democrats were weak, as in Kansas, survived. They did not make important inroads in competitive and populous two-party states.[99] Nevertheless, their relative weight in the reduced Republican ranks would be considerably increased in the new Congress.

---

7 September 1910, and to "Dear Friend," 6 September 1910, 14 September 1910, vol. 14; Mann Papers; *Chicago Tribune*, 15 September 1910, vol. 15, Mann Papers; Straetz, "Progressive Movement in Illinois," 50.

[96]William H. Harbaugh, "The Republican Party, 1893–1932," in *History of U.S. Political Parties*, vol. 3, 1910–1945: *From Square Deal to New Deal*, ed. Arthur M. Schlesinger, Jr. (New York: Chelsea House Publishers in association with R. R. Bowker Co., 1973), 2089–90.

[97]*Chicago Post*, 20 August 1910; *Chicago News*, 24 October 1910; *Chicago Record*, 6 October 1910; and *Chicago Tribune*, 4 November 1910, vol. 15, Mann Papers; John L. Moore, ed., *Congressional Quarterly's Guide to U.S. Elections* (Washington, D.C.: Congressional Quarterly, 1985), 712; Straetz, "Progressive Movement in Illinois," 64–65.

[98]Barfield, "Democratic Party in Congress," 269.

[99]Gould, *Reform and Regulation*, 140–42; Holt, *Congressional Insurgents*, 42.

Seventy-two and pessimistic, Henry Adams continued his education by closely observing the scene in Washington, where he lived. In February 1911 he wrote a friend: "In politics the Democrats have got the Republicans on the run and are whacking them over the head and shoulders with big sticks. The suppressed wail of distress is intense;—also justified. The top-heavy concern is tumbling, and on us. We are rotten as punk, all through and everywhere, and are scared blue."[100]

The fear was about 1912, when the Democrats would resume their charge and a Republican presidential candidate would cast a shadow over the full ticket. Expecting to cast that large shadow, Taft again tried conciliation. He invited progressives to consult on patronage; he proposed tariff reform through creation of a Tariff Commission to recommend on a scientific basis; and in the spring, after accepting the resignation of Richard Ballinger, long a political albatross, he named the Chicago reformer Walter Fisher as secretary of interior and the Rooseveltian Henry L. Stimson as secretary of war.

Taft's gestures were reciprocated only in part. While others accepted, La Follette declined the White House invitation. On 21 January he hosted a gathering of his own that created the National Progressive Republican League. Ostensibly dedicated to reforms such as the direct primary, recall, and referendum, the organization was actually a lightly disguised vehicle for his own candidacy for the presidential nomination. Nine senators and sixteen representatives were among the signers of the initial declaration. Men of wealth like Charles R. Crane and Rudolph Spreckles, publicists such as Norman Hapgood of *Collier's* and S. S. McClure of *McClure's*, and Rooseveltians such as James Garfield and Gifford Pinchot lent weight to the organization.[101]

James R. Mann had more than ordinary interest in these postelection events, for he would soon become his party's leader in the House. Even before the election, talk of Cannon bowing out and Mann succeeding him had caught the ear of the press, possibly by the design of the administration.[102] Cannon would not retreat under fire, but with the November victory of the Democrats, his reelection as Speaker was no longer at issue, and "Uncle Joe" could gracefully relinquish leadership to his friend and protégé with no loss of face. Cannon made no public announcement during the short session, but when he finally did make his announcement, no one was surprised, and the

---

[100]Adams to Elizabeth Cameron, 14 February 1911, Ford, *Letters of Henry Adams*, 761

[101]Belle La Follette and Fola La Follette, *Robert M. La Follette* (New York: Macmillan Company, 1953), 1:318–20, 324–25; Helene Hooker in Amos R. E. Pinchot, *The History of the Progressive Party, 1912–1916* ed. Helene Maxwell Hooker (New York: New York University Press, 1958), 20.

[102]Gwinn, *Uncle Joe Cannon*, 232; Chicago American, 20 August 1910, vol. 15, Mann Papers.

names of alternatives to Mann were no longer heard. To Mann's advantage was that though he was a loyal Cannon backer, he had also shown streaks of independence and progressivism and had voted against the Payne-Aldrich tariff. His ability to harass the Democrats also commended him.[103]

This latter trait Mann put on spectacular display in the lame-duck session, even before the Democrats took control. Deeply skeptical of rules reform as half-baked and subversive of effective party rule, Mann set out to discredit the recently adopted rule for a Discharge Calendar, a Democratic proposal, and with it the whole rules rebellion of March 1910. In the process, and with transparent enjoyment, Mann exhibited his parliamentary adroitness.

Mann had filed the first discharge petition after the rule was adopted in June. On 19 December, the first day in which the Discharge Calendar was in order, he blocked consideration of a pension bill urged by Charles Fuller, Illinois Republican, by insisting, correctly under the rule, on the priority of his motion to discharge the Post Office Committee from consideration of the post office reorganization bill. He insisted, also, again pursuant to the rule, on reading of the bill by the clerk. It contained 50,000 words and might take a week to read. Efforts to balk this dilatory scheme only worsened matters, as quorum calls and calls of the House consumed time. On 5 January, to confound those who would rectify the matter by requiring only reading of a bill's title, Mann filed 107 additional discharge petitions. Fuller, persevering, acted on a suggestion Mann had made on 19 December. He offered a motion to amend the House rules so that discharge petitions would not take priority over motions to suspend the rules, the procedure by which Fuller had tried to get consideration for his bill. Now Mann countered that Fuller's motion was not privileged. This was the very issue on which the House in March had overturned the Speaker's ruling in order to change the rules and weaken Cannon. Democratic leader Oscar Underwood of Alabama, not prepared to subordinate the new Discharge Calendar, confessed that Cannon had been correct on 19 March. Overruling him had been a revolutionary tactic, he explained. With some pleasure Cannon ruled as he had in March, and this time he was sustained by a vote of 222–53, the minority composed of 27 insurgents and 26 Democrats. Commenting on the initial rules rebellion, Mann said: "Gentlemen who voted to overrule the Speaker contributed to the unlawful enterprise, which was a violation of the Constitution, and in spite of the oath of office which they had taken." As to the discharge rule, Mann saw to it that during the session the House never got past the initial discharge motion. But, having made his several points, he did not block enactment of

---

[103]*New York Herald*, 20 August 1910, vol. 14, Mann Papers; *Boston Transcript*, 23 November 1910, vol. 15 Mann Papers.

Fuller's bill. The discharge rule would be heard of again, for the Democrats would try to patch it up.[104]

Near the end of the session Mann again used parliamentary virtuosity at the expense, chiefly, of Democrats. He opposed compensation to insurance companies for "French spoliation claims" based on seizure of American ships during the Napoleonic Wars. The provision was part of a Senate bill that also included Civil War claims of southerners. Mann's dilatory tactics resulted in rejection of the Senate bill and adoption of a separate House bill including only domestic claims. In the process Mann had occasion to deride the Democrats for incompetence and inconsistency respecting procedures, while also praising a Democratic leader, Claude Kitchin of North Carolina, for his strong speech against spoliation claims. Denunciations for conceit and high-handed arrogance he endured without response. [105]

If Mann's parliamentary legerdemain and biting words caused Democrats some discomfort, Taft's proposal for a tariff agreement with Canada more than made up for it. The president knew the political risks, but was more concerned for the possible accomplishment.[106] The agreement, completed on 21 January and submitted to Congress five days later, would reduce or eliminate tariffs on many items. It promised to lower American living costs and prevent a possible tariff war. As an executive agreement, it needed only suitable legislation in each House, not a two-thirds vote in the Senate, as with a treaty.

The bill that embodied the agreement's provisions called for free pulp and print paper, and was therefore popular with newspapers.[107] For Taft, the agreement and bill offered vindication of sorts on the vexing tariff issue. Foreseeably, some progressive Republicans might oppose it because it promised competition for the products of agrarian constituents while leaving many manufactured products better protected, but Taft, ambivalent about conciliation, did not mind exposing these critics of the Payne-Aldrich tariff as hypocritical. Much more damaging to the Republican cause was the equally foreseeable fact that most high-protectionist regulars, headed by Cannon and Payne, were opposed, and that a vote in the Senate during the short session was problematical. Strong Democratic support was promising for the legislation, but not so from a political standpoint. Taft also sacrificed

---

[104]Gwinn, *Uncle Joe Cannon*, 241–43; *CR* 61:3, pp. 498–99 (19 December 1910), 679–82 (9 January 1911); *CR* 62:1, p. 78 (5 April 1911); *CR* 61:3, pp. 733, 746 (10 January 1911)

[105]Johnson, *Oscar W. Underwood*, 131–32; *CR* 61:3, pp. 2798–2810 (17 February 1911), 2850–95 (18 February 1911), 2904–26 (19 February 1911), 2969–81 (20 February 1911).

[106]James Bryce to Sir Edward Grey, 31 January 1911, Public Records Office, London; Donald Anderson, *William Howard Taft*, 137.

[107]Ellis, *Print Paper Pendulum*, 89.

some of his newspaper support by calling for higher postal rates on newspapers and magazines.[108]

Mann had drafted the pulp and paper provisions of the treaty and the bill. Now, though Samuel McCall of Massachusetts, third-ranking Republican on Ways and Means, sponsored the legislation, Mann was in overall charge of the Taft forces.[109] But there was little he could do to reduce the political damage. The House approved the bill, 221–91, but the Republicans divided, 78 for the bill, 87 opposed. By 18 to 9 the progressive Republicans voted for the bill, but among them criticism was mounting and was now directed against Taft, not just Cannon.[110] In the Senate the bill died in committee. Taft promptly called a special session of the new Congress to meet on 4 April. The Democrats could be counted on to push the bill through, but also to cause the administration and the Republicans much embarrassment, especially with other tariff legislation.

The session ended amidst confusion, rancor, and finally a show of general good will. At issue was a bill to create a Tariff Commission that would be far stronger and longer-lived than the board created to help execute terms of the Payne-Aldrich Act. Ostensibly, Republicans favored it. More clearly, most Democrats opposed it as a protectionist scheme that could only obstruct their own tariff plans in the next Congress and beyond. The matter remained undecided as of 4 March and the last morning of the session, which under the Constitution had to end by noon. If the commission were to be created, the House had to adopt the Senate bill between 8:30, when it passed the Senate, and 12:00 while also acting on essential appropriation bills. John Fitzgerald, however, artfully killed time. Increasingly, Republicans resisted his maneuvers, abetted by rulings from Speaker Cannon. As tension mounted, Democrats whispered that the Republicans planned to turn back the clock to enact the bill. When, to clear the decks for rapid adoption of an appropriation bill, Cannon took the extraordinary step of interrupting a roll call, Mann thought that there would be a riot in the House. To forestall it, and perhaps to ensure action on the other appropriation bills, he went to the Democratic side and promised Fitzgerald and others that the clock would not be turned back for anything controversial. Then, while Fitzgerald dropped renewal of his filibuster, he went to Payne and got him to withdraw the commission bill by unanimous consent. Appropriations were duly approved, including $225,000 to continue the existing Tariff Board. Clark then offered a resolution of "high personal tribute" to Cannon, unanimously

---

[108]Coletta, *Presidency of William Howard Taft*, 142.

[109]*CR* 62:1, p. 2435 (21 June 1911); Archie Butt to "Dear Clara," 14 February 1911, *Letters of Archie Butt*, 2:594–99.

[110]Coletta, *Presidency of William Howard Taft*, 145; Hechler, *Insurgency*, 180–82; Holt, *Congressional Insurgents*, 46; *CR* 61:3, pp. 3563–64 (14 February 1911).

adopted, and Clark and Mann escorted Cannon back to the rostrum amidst cheers and waving of handkerchiefs.[111]

Mann's show of collegiality at the end seems inconsistent with his strong partisanship, his penchant for sharp, personal comments, his assertiveness, and his know-it-all attitude. Yet it accorded with a strong institutionalism that he showed in various ways during the Sixty-first Congress and before. Institutional feeling informed his concern for proper rules and scrupulous observance of all rules, his punctiliousness about the correctness in form and legitimacy in substance of all legislation, however minor, his concern for the rights and honor of the House as against the Senate, and more.

This institutional sense would be one of a number of useful attributes that in April Mann would bring to the office of minority leader. He would need them all, for the process of Republican division and decline, manifested in the last years of the Roosevelt administration and still more so during the first two years of Taft's presidency, would continue as the political context for Mann's actions in the Sixty-second Congress.

---

[111]*CR* 63:1, p. 770 (29 April 1913); *Chicago Sunday Record*, 9 November 1913, vol. 18, Mann Papers; *New York Times*, 5 March 1911. While Democrats thought that Cannon was trying to pass the commission bill, progressives thought that he, Payne, and Dalzell were trying to kill it. *La Follette's Weekly Magazine*, 3:11 (18 March 1911), and 3:12, (25 March 1911); Joseph Frederick Kenkel, "The Tariff Commission Movement: The Search for a Nonpartisan Solution of the Tariff Question" (Ph.D. diss., University of Maryland, 1962), 76.

2

Leading the Minority: Damage Control in the Sixty-second Congress, April 1911–March 1913

When the Sixty-second Congress met in special session, there was good reason to wonder whether the House Republicans, now in the minority, would wage party battles with the Democrats or among themselves. The issue related in part to the choice of Mann for party leader, and in turn to his early actions in that capacity. In both respects Mann served as a force for harmony.

Meeting on the afternoon of 3 April, hours before the party caucus, the insurgents came to no agreement. But the preordained choice of Mann was acceptable to most, and a majority of the forty-four insurgents attended the caucus, thus committing themselves to vote for Mann for Speaker. At the caucus Mann defeated the insurgents as to who should decide on committee assignments, the leader or a committee. But insurgents were accorded small courtesies, as in the choice of Nathan Kendall of Iowa as caucus secretary, and Mann diverted attention to the common enemy when he berated the Democrats for their decision to expand committee memberships without providing for additional Republican places. The caucus unanimously elected Mann as party leader.[1]

In the House the following day, seventeen insurgents withheld their votes from Mann for Speaker, but neither did they add to the winning margin of the Democratic choice, Champ Clark. Sixteen of them voted for the venerable Henry A. Cooper of Wisconsin, and Cooper voted for George Norris. The rest of the insurgents voted for Mann.[2]

---

[1]*Chicago News*, 29 March 1911; *New York Herald*, 3 April 1911, vol. 15, Mann Papers; *New York Times*, 4 April 1911.
[2]*CR* 62:1, p. 6 (4 April 1911).

Without abandoning his duties to constituents and broader obligations as a legislator, as minority floor leader Mann had special responsibilities to his party. He had to be prepared for whatever might come up on the floor through familiarity with the various calendars, pending bills, committee reports, executive-branch commentary, and what Republican committee members might tell him. Through the party whip, John W. Dwight of New York, he had to communicate with Republicans and mobilize them. On the floor he was the principal guardian of his party's parliamentary rights and the main spokesman for its positions. In fulfilling his obligation to make committee assignments, he had to know the strengths and weaknesses of his flock and their desires. Viewing his duties less formally, Mann needed to unify his discordant party to the extent possible, while smoothing over differences. At the same time, he had to expose Democratic disunity when it appeared and also take advantage of it to put a Republican stamp on measures or defeat them. Even seemingly nonpartisan matters had their partisan aspects. Collegial relationships with Democrats might foster moderation in the majority, and Mann heaped praise and courtesies on Champ Clark. Close attention to the many bills that were not party measures might bring credit to Republicans, and Mann was experienced along these lines. His responsibilities and power were all increased by the decline of the Rules Committee that resulted from enlargement and exclusion of the Speaker.[3]

Usually the floor leader was the ranking member of Ways and Means, but Mann chose not to replace Sereno Payne in that post. In fact he declined to take any committee assignment.[4] The decision was far from an act of self-abnegation. Mann wanted to be constantly vigilant and active on the floor and to use not only his evenings but also his morning hours for preparation.

---

[3]For commentary on the floor leader's duties and importance, see George B. Galloway, *History of the House of Representatives* (New York: Thomas Y. Crowell Co, 1961), 111; Randall B. Ripley, *Party Leaders in the House of Representatives* (Washington, D.C.: Brookings Institution, 1967), 66, 74; Paul DeWitt Hasbrouck, *Party Government in the House of Representatives* (New York: Macmillan Company, 1927), 103; L. Ethan Ellis, "James R. Mann, Legislator Extraordinary," *Journal of the Illinois State Historical Society* 46 (Spring 1953): 42; and Addison Smith in *CR* 67:4, p. 1721 (14 January 1923). The abundance of nonpartisan opportunity is noted in Robert Luce, *Legislative Procedure: Parliamentary Practices and the Course of Business in the Framing of Statutes* (Boston: Houghton Mifflin, 1922), quoting Representative James Good, 504, and Bascom N. Timmons, *Garner of Texas: A Personal History* (New York: Harper and Brothers, 1948), quoting Garner, 111. On Mann and Clark, see Champ Clark, *My Quarter Century of American Politics* (New York: Harper and Brothers, 1920), 1:38–39, 2:343; Champ Clark to Emma Mann, 30 December 1910, vol. 14, Mann Papers; *CR* 62:2, p. 4561 (10 April 1912), p. 3838 (26 March 1912); J. Hampton Moore, *Roosevelt and the Old Guard* (Philadelphia: Macrae Smith Co., 1925), 241; and *New York Times*, 10 December 1922.

[4]*Washington Star*, 9 April 1911, vol. 15, Mann Papers.

In that task he had the help of his longtime secretary, the highly competent Mrs. Florence Donnelley, and two clerks. As minority leader he amazed people with the extent of his knowledge, and they attributed it to his prodigious industry. But methodical ways were just as important.[5] In debate in the Sixty-second Congress and later Mann relied on allies, especially the well-spoken, quick-thinking, and conservative Frank Mondell of Wyoming and J. Hampton Moore of Pennsylvania. But to an unusual degree he played a lone hand, even at the expense of ranking committee Republicans. He thought that colleagues could more usefully devote themselves to committee work than to the preparation and delivery of speeches.

Although methodical habits harnessed to acuity were indispensable to Mann, the active floor leadership that he proposed for himself and immediately undertook required time and energy too, and some of the exertion was emotional as well as physical and intellectual. From the start, colleagues feared for his health.[6] By the end of July Vice President James Sherman reported that Mann was "working like a tiger all the time and indicates overwork by nervous twitching not merely of his face and head, but of his arms and body. I do wish he would let up."[7] Eventually Mann paid the price.

Mann's overall task in the Sixty-second Congress, and especially his role as party spokesman, must be viewed in historical context. By April of 1911 it was clear that Taft's renomination would be strongly contested and that, increasingly, the president would be unable to speak for his entire party. Mann worked in tandem with Taft, except briefly after the president refused to reappoint Edwin W. Sims as district attorney because of lax prosecution of meat packers.[8] Mann had to be more than a presidential spokesman, however. To best serve his party with respect to unity and a creditable record, he had to use his own voice and skill and judgment.

---

[5]*Ibid.*, 28 September 1913, vol. 20, Mann Papers; "James Robert Mann," *Nation* 102:618 (8 June 1916); Marvin Jones, *Memoirs* (El Paso: Texas Western Press, 1973), 42.

[6]Walter I. Smith to Mann, 4 April 1911 and J. Sloan Fassett to Mann, 5 April 1911, vol. 14, Mann Papers.

[7]Sherman to H. S. Boutell, 31 July 1911, box 67, James S. Sherman Papers, New York Public Library.

[8]White House consultation is noted in "Memorandum," 5 May 1911, series 6, reel 412, William Howard Taft Papers, Library of Congress; and Archie Butt to "Dear Clara," 18 July 1911, Archibald Butt, *Taft and Roosevelt: The Intimate Letters of Archie Butt, Military Aide* (Garden City, N.Y.: Doubleday, Doran, and Company, 1930), 2:297–98. On the Sims appointment, see especially Kenesaw Mountain Landis to Taft, 2 June 1911, and to George Wickersham, 21 July 1911, series 6, reel 418, Taft to Mann, 28 and 29 July 1911, reel 506, and Mann to Taft, 29 July 1911, series 6, reel 418, Taft Papers. Resumption of relations is indicated in *Chicago Examiner*, 15 August 1911, vol. 16, Mann Papers, and Mann to Taft, 8 September 1911, series 6, reel 387, Taft Papers.

Mann's relative weight as a party spokesman was enhanced by the situation in the Senate. With the retirement of Nelson Aldrich, leadership devolved on an uninspired party war-horse, Jacob Gallinger of New Hampshire. Gallinger's position was weakened by the aggressiveness of insurgent senators, who demanded separate, proportional recognition in committee assignments and held up his election until June. To be sure, on some matters, especially relating to foreign policy, Senators Henry Cabot Lodge and Elihu Root spoke with authority.[9]

Mann's tasks were the more important and visible because House Democrats, having gained control in the election of 1910, were in the vanguard of their party's advance. The public watched the House to see what Democrats in power could do. Building on the 1909 creation of a binding caucus by two-thirds vote, in December and January the Democrats successfully prepared to reconcile rules reform with strong leadership in the new Congress. To distance themselves from Cannonism, they agreed to reduce the powers of the Speaker and make committee assignments elective by the House. But to be effective, they proposed to make the chairman of Ways and Means a strong majority leader. Oscar Underwood, patient, serene, dignified, courteous, and skilled at parliamentary tactics, would control matters on the floor; through the Democrats on Ways and Means he would lead in making committee nominations; and through the caucus he would make it possible to please most Democrats with assignments. Underwood was moderately conservative, but assignments would be such as to let the party advance a popular progressive program. Some components of such a program were agreed to in January, to be put forth by Clark at the start of the session.[10]

Given the political weakness of Taft, the division in the GOP, and the momentum of the Democrats as reflected in the 1910 elections, the most that Mann could hope for in the Sixty-second Congress was some measure of damage control. He began the process on the second day of the session on the subject of the rules for that Congress. The proposed new rules, certain of adoption, would continue and mildly amplify reforms of the previous two years and further erode the power of the Speaker by making chairmen elec-

---

[9]James Wright, *The Progressive Yankees: Republican Reformers in New Hampshire, 1906–1916* (Hanover, N.H.: University Press of New England, 1987), 103–95; Belle La Follette and Fola La Follette, *Robert M. La Follette* (New York: Macmillan Company, 1953), 1:323–25.

[10]Ripley, *Party Leaders*, 95–96; Evans C. Johnson, *Oscar W. Underwood: A Political Biography* (Baton Rouge: Louisiana State University Press, 1980), 164; Hasbrouck, *Party Government*, 28; David Sarasohn, *The Party of Reform: Democrats in the Progressive Era* (Jackson: University Press of Mississippi, 1989), 93–94; Cordell Hull, *The Memoirs of Cordell Hull* (New York: Macmillan Company, 1948), 1:146–47; Paolo E. Coletta, *The Presidency of William Howard Taft* (Laurence: University Press of Kansas, 1973), 147.

tive and further circumscribing the recognition power through a strengthening of Calendar Wednesday and of the Unanimous Consent and Discharge calendars. The more important changes, by which the majority leader gained ascendancy, were less the product of House rules than of decisions already taken in the party caucus. Consistent with these developments, Robert L. Henry of Texas, prospective chairman of the Rules Committee, offered the rules in a highly restrictive way. There would be but four hours of debate and no amendments. One substitute might be offered, with no chance of adoption.[11]

Mann parceled out time to insurgents Norris, Lenroot, Madison, and Gardner, all of them critical especially of the ban on amendments. Regulars Dalzell, Cannon, and Marlin Olmsted of Pennsylvania spoke too and talked like insurgents against "gag rule."[12] Mann reserved his own remarks for the end of the debate, except for a preliminary jibe at the Democrats for not permitting submission of amendments, some of which he thought might have proved acceptable to the majority party.[13]

In his closing comments Mann attacked the Democrats from various standpoints. One of his themes was the hypocrisy of the Democrats. Despite all their clamor, they changed the rules only a little. They were also unwilling to vote for Mann's substitute, which was exactly what Clark had offered in 1909.[14] The Democrats were hypocritical too, Mann said, in first championing election of committee members by the House and now resorting to a committee on committees, the fourteen Democrats on Ways and Means. Furthermore, he contrasted the principled way that he promised to make Republican nominations with the horse-trading practices the Democrats had been using in advance of the session. In similar vein he chastised the majority for taking thirty-three of the thirty-five newly created committee posts, with one new one going to a Socialist and but one to a Republican.[15]

Finally, Mann went into the proposed changes in rules and criticized them as either simply stating ordinary parliamentary law or being technically flawed. He gave special attention to the discharge rule, about which there had been much Democratic boasting, and pointed to a number of loopholes in it. He warned, "I may undertake to demonstrate if I choose . . . to show the absurdity not to say idiocy of the rule as proposed. The rule that you bring in on this subject, as well as the other changes in the rules, are mainly inspired through lack of experience and knowledge."[16]

---

[11]Hasbrouck, *Party Government*, 11–12.

[12]*CR* 62:1, pp. 60–72 (5 April 1911).

[13]*Ibid.*, p. 55 (5 April 1911).

[14]*Ibid.*, pp. 75–76, 77, 79 (5 April 1911).

[15]*Ibid.*, pp. 77, 76 (5 April 1911).

[16]*Ibid.*, p. 79 (5 April 1911).

If Mann yielded nothing in defending Cannon and his rules, yet his re-marks were also calculated to appeal not only to progressives in the elector-ate but more particularly to insurgents in the House. Republicans by habit and self-interest, the insurgents were very ready to believe that their erst-while Democratic allies were not sincere reformers. How could they be while they were dedicated to a strong party, which insurgents viewed as necessarily an instrument of special interests, rather than to independent, conscience-driven action? How could they be when southerners would chair nine of the eleven main committees, control the post of majority leader, and in combi-nation with boss-ridden Tammany constitute a majority of the party cau-cus?[17] Southerners remained especially suspect among those reformers of the post–Civil War generation who lived in solid Republican areas, as most of the insurgents did. In sum, George Norris concluded in June, "The progressive and independent members are confined almost entirely to the Republican party in the House of Representatives."[18]

No doubt Mann understood, as many insurgents did not, that these reb-els would never capture the Republican party.[19] He was less fearful of them or antagonistic towards them than Cannon and far closer to them on many issues than the former Speaker. He understood, too, that a minority could tolerate more diversity than a majority. Thus Mann set out to cultivate the insurgents in order to lessen intraparty discord, to use popular and able in-surgents against the Democrats, and even to fortify them for future reelec-tion contests against Democrats. In one of many acts of conciliation, Mann deferred to insurgents in their strong objection to binding caucuses. Mann convened no caucuses at all for two sessions and then used nonbinding and open "conferences" rather than binding caucuses, except for organizational matters.[20] The insurgents' animus towards the caucus was thus diverted mainly against the Democrats and quickly proved strong, with regulars happily chiming in .[21]

---

[17]James Holt, *Congressional Insurgents and the Party System, 1909–1916* (Cambridge, Mass.: Harvard University Press, 1967), 15, 19–20. 24. 163–64; Patrick Francis Palermo, "Republicans in Revolt: The Sources of Insurgency" (Ph.D. diss., State University of New York at Stony Brook, 1973), 109–10; Claude Ercell Barfield, "The Democratic Party in Congress, 1909–1913" (Ph.D. diss.: Northwestern Uni-versity, 1965), 280; Lynn Haines, *Law Making in America: The Story of the 1911–1912 Session of the Sixty-second Congress* (Bethesda, Md.: Lynn Haines, 1912), 14.

[18]Norris to I. D. Evans, 23 June 1911, George Norris Papers, in Holt, *Congres-sional Insurgents,* 20.

[19]Holt, *Congressional Insurgents,* 20, 124.

[20]Haines, *Law Making in America,* 19; George Rothwell Brown, *The Leadership of Congress* (1922; reprint, New York: Arno Press, 1974), 178–79.

[21]Bruce L. Larson, *Lindbergh of Minnesota: A Political Biography* (New York: Harcourt Brace Jovanovich, 1973), 114; Haines, *Law Making in America,* 5, 15, 60; Chang-Wei Chiu, *The Speaker of the House of Representatives since 1896* (1928; re-

During the rules debate Mann said, with reference to committee assignments, "I shall give consideration . . . to the interests of the public as well as the desires and capabilities of the Members, their length of service in the House and on the committees, and their experience and qualifications."[22] Afterwards, he said that he had not concerned himself with balance, but with treating each Republican fairly.[23] In practice he treated insurgents very well. First, he consulted with Cooper, Nelson, Lenroot, Madison, and Iowa insurgents James Good and Gilbert Haugen as part of a large group that included many regulars. Norris he consulted privately. These men, and Victor Murdock as well, expressed surprise and pleasure at the attention. Then Mann followed through, naming Lenroot and Madison as two of the four Republicans on Rules, making Haugen ranking Republican on Agriculture, adding Norris to Judiciary, fulfilling an old ambition, and placing Good on Appropriations. Mann was not just concerned to gratify. Thus, for instance, he put Charles Pickett of Iowa on the Public Lands Committee to attend to conservation matters, a topic on which Republicans might outflank the Democrats on the left. In making these assignments, which formally he delivered to Underwood for submission to the House, Mann did not discriminate against the seventeen insurgents who had not voted for him for Speaker.[24]

Swiftly, battle with the Democrats began. Clark, on the first day of the session, spelled out the party program: downward revision of the tariff, constitutional amendment for direct election of senators, new House rules, economy, publicity of campaign contributions, and statehood for Arizona and New Mexico. A week later a party caucus added Canadian reciprocity to the list and refined the tariff program to encompass wool, cotton, and a free list on goods of interest to farmers.[25] Action on direct election and campaign funds publicity came first, and Mann gave some indication of how he would act as minority leader.

Mann took the unpopular side when direct election of senators reached the floor on 13 April, arguing that the amendment would tend to undermine the position of states in the constitutional system. He was one of 16 to vote against it, while 206 voted in favor. More successfully, Mann played on the

---

print, New York: AMS Press, 1968), 154; Luce, *Legislative Procedure*, 514. Lynn Haines's book by a Minnesota reformer based in Washington, DC. constitutes part of the progressive Republican attack on the Democrats.

[22] *CR* 62:1, p. 77 (5 April 1911).

[23] *CR* 62:2, p. 862 (11 January 1912).

[24] *Chicago Inter-Ocean*, 8 April 1911; *Washington Herald*, 8 April 1911; and *Chicago Tribune*, 12 April 1911, vol. 15, Mann Papers; George W. Norris, *Fighting Liberal: The Autobiography of George W. Norris* (New York: Macmillan Company, 1945), 131–32; Mann to Walter L. Fisher, 22 June 1911, box 14, Walter L. Fisher Papers, Library of Congress.

[25] *CR* 62:1, p. 7 (4 April 1911); Johnson, *Oscar W. Underwood*, 139.

familiar theme of Democratic incompetence, to the laughter and applause of Republicans, and his jibes at faulty wording were validated by adoption of a Mann amendment.[26]

In standing firmly and conspicuously against this democratic reform, Mann served early notice that notwithstanding his new party responsibilities, he would continue to speak his own mind. Far from lessening his effectiveness as a party leader, this trait of self-confident independence enhanced it. Not on the issue of direct election, but on other issues, such as temperance legislation, the party was divided ideologically and geographically. When issues of that sort arose, it would be convenient if Republican members and outside observers would see Mann as not attempting to speak for his party, but only for himself. Furthermore, Mann's independence eased the way for other Republicans. Were the party in the majority and responsible for legislating, his independence would have been unfortunate. As things were, however, it was a relatively harmless safety valve; the party benefited from a light hand on the reins. "There is a new atmosphere in the House of Representatives. There is more independence than there ever has been," George Norris enthused in 1912.[27] There were of course occasions when the party was reasonably unified and Mann was of a mind to speak for it, and he did so effectively. Naturally, Mann sought to unify his party when that seemed possible.

On the bill for publicity of campaign contributions, which came up the following day, Mann was able to score points for his party and perhaps build morale. The bill, an amendment to a 1910 law, called for publicity of certain contributions for general-election campaigns. Mann led regulars to the side of insurgents, and for a time even won some Democrats, in calling for an amendment to apply the regulation to primaries. Southern Democrats, fearful of federal intrusion, caused the party leadership to oppose this. After Mann won an initial victory, Democratic leaders regained control on a 157–149 vote, but Mann had tarnished their accomplishment.[28]

Next came tariff reciprocity with Canada. As in the previous Congress, House Democrats showed themselves united while Republicans divided, with Mann among those favoring the measure, which incorporated his pulp and paper suggestions. This time it passed not only in the House but in the Senate as well. But in Canada it was rejected following a September election that turned on the issue. Thus the administration failed in its effort to ap-

---

[26]CR 62:1, pp. 236, 242–43, 237–38, 242 (13 April 1911).

[27]Norris to A. C. Rankin, 21 March 1912, Norris Papers, in Holt, *Congressional Insurgents*, 19.

[28]CR 62:1, pp. 261, 266 (14 April 1911).

pease those made unhappy by Payne-Aldrich, and the tariff issue remained wide open to the Democrats.[29]

The Democrats began to develop the issue well before reciprocity failed. For many voters at that time, protective tariffs remained associated with high living costs and trusts. "We decided to put the high tariff Republicans wholly on the defensive by striking them at the tenderest points," a leading Ways and Means committee member, Cordell Hull of Tennessee, later wrote. Prospective vetoes of any bills that might go through were all to the good. Most attractive politically was wool, the notorious Schedule K. But to compensate farmers for the damage Canadian reciprocity might do to them, the Democrats acted first on the "farmer's free list" bill.[30]

Though Mann had voted against the Payne-Aldrich bill because of its pulp and print-paper features and had backed Canadian reciprocity, partly for the same reason, he was an unabashed protectionist. He realized that insurgents believed in lower rates and would vote the interests of their farmer constituents. Yet if the Republican party stood for anything, it was higher average rates than Democrats favored and more protection. Even the insurgents agreed on that, though they were readier to make exceptions. The Democrats would surely gain from the tariff bills, but Mann set out vigorously but imaginatively to oppose them all, starting with the free-list bill, in order to minimize damage and maintain Republican battle lines in the House and the nation.

Mann took the lead for his party in debate and then on amendments to the free-list bill on 25 April and 8 May. He came armed with letters he had solicited from the heads of United States Steel, International Harvester, and smaller manufacturers to fortify the standard protectionist argument that the proposed rates would cost jobs. Further, he argued that the bill was poorly drawn, to the extent that farmers would actually be hurt. Thus, for instance, the tariff was removed from flour, but put on wheat. Argentine wheat would simply be converted into flour for export to the United States, hurting American wheat growers, he said. When it came time for amendments, Mann offered many, though Democrats were committed to reject them. Some of Mann's amendments, and ultimately his motion to recommit with instructions, put forth the alternative of reciprocal trade, a moderate Republican approach urged by William McKinley, and one that Democrats embraced respecting Canada. Others of his amendments outdid the Democrats by expanding the free list. One such amendment put Underwood very much on the defensive—to put rice flour on the free list, to the disadvantage of some southerners. Balked by rulings that his amendments were not germane, Mann

---

[29]*Ibid.*, pp. 541, 558–60 (21 April 1911); Ebenezer Hill to George Cortelyou, 22 September 1911, series 1, box 52, Ebenezer J. Hill Papers, Sterling Library, Yale University.

[30]Hull, *Memoirs*, 1:64; Barfield, "Democratic Party in Congress," 310.

strongly attacked the rulings and the secret caucus that bound Democrats not only on amendments but even on parliamentary questions. Although on the final 236–109 vote 24 insurgents supported the bill, before that men like Norris, Lenroot, Kendall, and others participated with Mann in offering amendments and denouncing Democratic tactics.[31] On balance the Democrats gained from the venture, for they stood together and in August forced Taft to an unpopular veto, which the House sustained. Yet Mann had somewhat limited the damage.[32]

The story was similar respecting the wool bill. Again the Democrats united after Underwood fended off an open challenge from William Jennings Bryan, who advocated free wool instead of a revenue tariff. Mann again led the Republicans with a spirited and informed attack, and again he hit his enemies on both right and left flanks. He upheld protectionism, but also followed the lead of the Republicans on Ways and Means who, with Taft, urged delay until the Tariff Board reported in December, to give scientific basis for the bill. He attacked the rates on children's clothing as excessive and chided formerly independent Democrats like Thetus Sims for bowing to the caucus. Even some of the regulars voted with most of the insurgents for the popular bill, but before that most insurgents supported Payne's recommittal motion, which stressed the Tariff Board. Mann's vain efforts were well received by House Republicans and noted in the press.[33]

In the Senate La Follette won out, and it was he who in conference negotiated a compromise with Underwood that passed in both Houses. Although Taft's veto was sustained, most House insurgents voted to override. Mann battled to hold back the tide, on both policy and parliamentary grounds. Yet on balance the conflict on wool increased Democratic popularity and Republican division.[34]

The Democrats were again successful on cotton, putting a bill to the president that he vetoed. Along the way, however, Mann took advantage of several new opportunities to woo insurgents. He hit hard at the secret caucus, which by then had become quite galling and frustrating to insurgents, whose amendments were dismissed by the Democrats. He derided the bill as not serious, for southern senators would not permit harm to their states. So it turned out. In combination with regular Republicans, who withheld their votes, they caused the drastic House bill to pass, with intolerable amend-

---

[31]*CR* 62:1, pp. 602–12 (25 April 1911), pp. 1077–1118 (8 May 1911).

[32]*Ibid.*, p. 4174 (18 August 1911).

[33]Johnson, *Oscar W. Underwood*, 145; Ebenezer Hill to Francis T. Maxwell, 31 May 1911, 3 June 1911, series 1, box 52, Hill Papers; *CR* 62:1, pp. 1788–97 (8 June 1911), 2355–56 (20 June 1911); "No Free Wool," *Literary Digest* 42:23 (10 June 1911): 1139–40.

[34]Coletta, *Presidency of William Howard Taft*, 150; *CR* 62:1, pp. 3868–73 (12 August 1911), 3909–19, (14 August 1911), 4163, 4170 (18 August 1911).

ments, instead of again combining with insurgents on a compromise that stood some chance of surviving a veto. When Mann offered a resolution stating that the Senate, by adding provisions on steel, chemicals, and minerals, contravened the constitutional requirement that all revenue bills start in the House, his party united in support. Later he imposed a verbal toll on the Democrats for not upholding the rights of the House, an ever-popular theme. On the final vote on the Senate bill, most insurgents stood with their party in opposition.[35]

With the tariff votes of August Congress finished its business for the session. In addition to reciprocity, the tariff bills, and campaign contribution legislation, it had approved statehood for Arizona and New Mexico and creation of a committee to investigate the "sugar trust." Mann had been active on these latter two matters, as on the rest, standing with the administration in opposition to the Arizona constitutional provision for recall of judges and uniting with insurgents in opposing choice of the investigation committee members in a Democratic caucus. Once home in Chicago to farm, he said that the Democrats should have passed reciprocity and stopped at that, and that they had bungled the rest. More objective observers, however, saw the session as a triumph for Underwood in particular and the Democrats in general. Still, Mann had done some effective damage control.[36]

Between sessions, Taft spoke in twenty-eight states, but accomplished little, though his new secretary, Charles Hilles, meanwhile did effective organizational work.[37] Republicans looked for alternatives to Taft for 1912 and found La Follette active and eager and Theodore Roosevelt showing interest. The latter, unhappy with Taft over a series of personal and policy differences dating to 1909, took special umbrage when on 27 October the administration

[35]CR 62:1, pp. 3565, 3567 (3 August 1911); Haines, Law Making in America, 62–63; CR 62:1, p. 4175 (18 August 1911), pp. 4348, 4350 (21 August 1911).

[36]On statehood, see "Memorandum," 5 May 1911, series 6, reel 412, Taft Papers; Mann to Charles D. Hilles, 8 May 1911, Frederick William Lehman Papers, Washington University, St. Louis; and CR 62:1, pp. 1396–1402 (20 May 1911), p. 4230 (19 August 1911); on the sugar trust investigation, see CR 62:1, pp. 1283–86 (17 May 1911); for varying assessments of the session, see Chicago Inter-Ocean, 23 August 1911, vol. 16 Mann Papers; Frank Vanderlip to James Stillman, 24 November 1911, part B, series 1, box 4, Frank A. Vanderlip Papers, Butler Library, Columbia University; and Brown, Leadership of Congress, 178.

[37]Norman M. Wilensky, Conservatives in the Progressive Era: The Taft Republicans of 1912 (Gainesville: University of Florida Press, 1965), 12–13; Coletta, Presidency of William Howard Taft, 150–51; Robert Sherman La Forte, Leaders of Reform: Progressive Republicans in Kansas, 1900–1916 (Laurence: University Press of Kansas, 1974), 182; Spencer C. Olin, Jr., California's Prodigal Sons: Hiram Johnson and the Progressives, 1911–1917 (Berkeley: University of California Press, 1968), 58; Lewis L. Gould, Reform and Regulation: American Politics from Roosevelt to Wilson, 2nd ed. (New York: Alfred A. Knopf, 1986), 145.

began an antitrust suit against United States Steel partly because of a 1907 acquisition that Roosevelt as president explicitly approved. When Roosevelt published an article in *Outlook* on 18 November advocating a general trust policy very different from Taft's, it signaled to Republicans his possible availability. The article's favorable reception in turn told Roosevelt that his time had not passed, as he had for a while believed.[38] Thus, when Congress convened in December, House Republicans saw their own divisions mirrored on the larger presidential stage.

"There are big things to be done and big policies to be played," Taft's military aide Archie Butt wrote his sister on the eve of the session. "Of course, the Democrats have a tower of strength in Underwood, but whether he can lead and quiet them as he did last session is another question." Banker Frank Vanderlip kept in close touch with Underwood and found him disposed "to do everything he can to keep the Democrats from making fools of themselves." Congress would do little besides advance a new round of tariff bills, Vanderlip thought. To maintain discipline and unity, it behooved Underwood to continue heavy reliance on the Democrats' majority status through the caucus and "gag rules" rather than seeking coalition with insurgents, as they had done in the past. "In the present House party regularity is the supreme test," the progressive activist Lynn Haines lamented.[39]

Mann was the Republican counterpart of Underwood in seeking party unity against a common enemy and in discrediting the opposition party. The position of the Democrats simplified his task respecting the insurgents, and he exploited his opportunities. He acted in the context of the increasingly emotional battle for the Republican presidential nomination between Roosevelt, who announced in February, La Follette, who angrily persisted, and Taft. Just in advance of a 9 April presidential primary in Illinois, in which Roosevelt, greatly helped by the *Chicago Tribune*, was the strong favorite, Mann came out for Taft.[40] But Mann's political manager, Edwin W. Sims, was secretary of the National Roosevelt Committee, while also helping Mann secure an easy renomination, and the Rooseveltian press tepidly supported Mann. After Roosevelt won fifty-six of fifty-eight Illinois delegate places, Mann told the House Democrats that "if he is nominated he will beat you to death," and in June, as the contest neared its end, he chided the Democrats for making it hard for the Smithsonian Institution to display Roosevelt's gifts from his African game hunt. In sum, while Mann did not dodge the intra-

---

[38]Gould, *Reform and Regulation*, 147–50; William H. Harbaugh, *The Life and Times of Theodore Roosevelt* (New York: Oxford University Press, 1975), 375–89.

[39]Archie Butt to "Dear Clara," 3 December 1911, *Letters of Archie Butt*, 2:773; Frank Vanderlip to James Stillman, 8 December 1911, part B, series l, box 4 Vanderlip Papers; Haines, *Law Making in America*, 32.

[40]*Chicago Tribune*, 1 April 1912, vol. 11, Mann Papers.

party fight but stood with Taft, he acted more as the party man than the factionalist.[41]

One battle with the insurgents Mann could not dodge, once challenged. Insurgent Edmund Madison of Kansas died in September, and Mann chose Philip Campbell, a Kansas regular, to succeed him on the Rules Committee. On 11 January Underwood duly made the nomination, only to have George Norris move substituting the name of Victor Murdock, Kansas insurgent, for Campbell's. Norris had not quarreled with Mann's initial committee choices and considered Campbell a friend, but he still preferred a more democratic method of selection. Others said that Madison should be replaced by an insurgent. Taken by surprise, and not bound by a caucus decision, a number of Democrats, led by John Nance Garner of Texas, recommended that Democrats vote "present" or not at all, leaving the matter to Republicans to settle. But Underwood, backed by Rules chairman Henry, urged Democrats to vote, preferably for Campbell, in the interests of upholding the established selection system.[42]

Mann argued his case temperately yet forcefully. He explained the choice of Campbell partly in terms of making committee places for two other Republicans, one of them dislodged when Republican membership on Banking and Currency was reduced. After he was chosen party leader, he had told his Republican colleagues that he did not want to be a leader "of a factional party or of a faction of a party," and that as to appointments he would consider only the best interests of the country and the party. He had put Lenroot and Madison on Rules without consideration of the fact that in combination they gave insurgents representation far beyond their proportion in the party. So far as balance was concerned, Lenroot remained on the committee. In conclusion, he asked the Democrats to vote "present" or not at all, as Garner proposed. If he, Mann, did not have the confidence of his party, he wanted to know it now. Underwood, however, reiterated his earlier view. [43]

In the vote that followed, Murdock lost to Campbell, 107–167. Twenty-six insurgents voted for Murdock, 107 Republicans voted for Campbell, and 29 did not vote. Among the Democrats, 81 voted for Murdock, 59 voted for Campbell, and 67 did not vote.[44] Thus Mann was sustained not just by the assistance of Underwood but the preponderance of his own party. Both Norris and Mann had kept the contest civil—indeed, it seemed merely ritual-

---

[41]Sims to Mann, 8 April 1912, and *Chicago Examiner*, 28 April 1912, vol. 16, Mann Papers; *CR* 62:2, p. 5059 (20 April 1912), p. 7946 (10 June 1912), p. 8012 (12 June 1912). Mann had greeted Roosevelt after his return to the country and had expressed an interest in his collection. Roosevelt to Mann, 10 August 1911, vol. 14, Mann Papers. Mann was a regent of the Smithsonian Institution.

[42]*CR* 62:2, pp. 855–56 (11 January 1912).

[43]*Ibid.*, pp. 862–63 (11 January 1912).

[44]*Ibid.*, 864–65 (11 January 1912); Haines, *Law Making in America*, 31–33.

istic—and though other intraparty divisions would occur on legislative matters during the session, yet the combatants could still fight together against the Democrats.

Though Mann and the insurgents were not of one mind on some rules questions, yet it was to the general advantage of the party when Mann could discredit Democratic efforts as reflecting habitual incompetence and hypocrisy. When, two days after the Murdock-Campbell matter, Mann seized on his first opportunity to misuse the Democrats' patched-up Discharge Calendar rule, as a fringe benefit he further separated insurgents from Democrats and fortified the former against the latter for possible election contests.

Mann killed the part of the day when discharge motions were in order. The amended rule limited each member to two discharge petitions. But others had filed them besides Mann, some sincerely and some not, so Mann was able to offer in succession eleven discharge motions. These, garnished with parliamentary debate, votes, and quorum calls, consumed the time. The Democrats, blocking action on the discharge motions in order to get to suspension of the rules, thus seemed to oppose nine measures that they had campaigned for, as Philip Campbell later noted.[45]

On 3 February the Democrats in effect abandoned the Discharge Calendar reform. Chairman Henry for the Rules Committee moved a rules change by which the Discharge Calendar would lose priority to suspension of the rules. Since already it was second to the Unanimous Consent Calendar, this demotion put it in third place and almost impossible to reach on the appointed alternate Mondays. Republicans united, Norris and Lenroot more sincerely than Dalzell and Campbell, in condemning Democratic abandonment of the reform they had initiated, with Republican support, in June of 1910. Some critics argued, too, that the change would also reverse the thrust of the rules reform movement by restoring some of the Speaker's power, since he would be able to recognize or not for suspension motions. That prior Democratic caucus action hovered over the proceedings, and that a Lenroot amendment was not entertained, also brought criticism. Augustus P. Gardner, surprised and disappointed by the Democrats thought their hidden motive was to get onto the floor under suspension of the rules an anti-third term resolution directed at Theodore Roosevelt.[46] The whole episode got some press attention.[47] In similar though less spectacular vein, during the

---

[45]CR 62:2, pp. 952–56 (15 January 1912), p. 1687 (3 February 1912).

[46]Ibid., pp. 1685–90 (3 February 1912); Gardner to E. H. Abbott, 6 February 1912, Some Letters of Augustus Peabody Gardner Constance Gardner, ed., (Boston: Houghton Mifflin, 1920), 65–72. A good account of the matter is in Hasbrouck, Party Government, 145–49. Hasbrouck noted that the discharge rule was not revived until after Mann's death.

[47]Detroit News, 3 February 1912, and Philadelphia Telegram, 6 February 1912, vol. 16, Mann Papers; Superior (Wisconsin) Telegram, 3 February 1912.

session Mann scored points for a united GOP against the Democrats when he opposed putting aside Calendar Wednesday and condemned restrictive rules on certain bills.[48]

If Mann's procedural attacks were something more than mosquito bites to the Democrats, they were less than fatal stings. Of greater political consequence, and acting in the Democrat's favor, were tariff bills, investigations, headed by the "money trust" inquiry, and adoption of some progressive legislation. On the defensive still, Mann renewed the strategy of damage control and experienced general though not invariable success.

The tariff issue remained the best weapon for the Democrats, and in the House they passed bills on iron and steel, wool and woolens, cotton, sugar, and chemicals. None became law, but the first two went to the president and survived his veto in the House, though not in the Senate. The chemicals bill died in the Senate, and the cotton and sugar bills could not be reconciled in conference. Politically, the bills did their job.[49]

The Republicans, approaching the election, took yet more moderate positions than in the special session. Mann led the way. Support for the Tariff Board and its implied recommendations on wool and woolens and cotton schedules was a big part of his activity. The Democrats opposed the board and finally denied it an appropriation, so Mann could get full party advantage by defending it and by coordination his strategy with Ebenezer Hill, who drafted bills in accordance with the board's December report. The board continued to enjoy insurgent support as putting the tariff on a scientific basis, and its approach, as reflected in the Hill bills, involved the most moderate form of protectionism, the effort to compensate for cost differences between foreign and domestic production. Small and medium-sized businesses of the Midwest had since 1906 urged a Tariff Commission to secure big-business allies, and had accepted the Republicans' cost-difference formula. Thus Mann's tactic in associating the party with the board was calculated to accomplish more than simply please insurgents. Later, with the demise of the board, Mann consistently pushed for a Tariff Commission, which would be stronger than the old board.[50]

Mann was especially active and well informed on the chemicals and metal bills. He was "trying to make some record in regard to the tariff proposi-

---

[48]On Calendar Wednesday, See *CR* 62:2, pp. 7715–16 (5 June 1912) and 11890 (26 August 1912); on restrictive rules, See *Ibid.*, pp. 5893–95 (4 May 1912), p. 8717 (8 July 1912).

[49]Johnson, *Oscar W. Underwood*, 159; Haines, *Law Making in America*, 63–65; Sarasohn, *Party of Reform*, 107.

[50]*CR* 63:1, p. 1003 (2 May 1913); William S. Culbertson Diary, 27 March 1912, William S. Culbertson Papers, Library of Congress; Paul Wolman, *Most Favored Nation: The Republican Revisionists and U.S. Tariff Policy, 1897–1912* (Chapel Hill: University of North Carolina Press, 1992), 77–111, 177–92.

tion," and he objected when Gilbert Haugen innocently attempted to insert a letter in the *Record* in the middle of the tariff debate.[51] The record Mann wanted to make included sponsorship of many amendments to keep raw materials on the free list. Mann gave less attention to finished goods, whose rates the Democrats proposed to reduce.[52] He also invoked the perennial sectional issue with the charge that the Democratic levies would fall on the North, not the South. When Francis Burton Harrison of New York, floor manager for the chemicals bill, responded that there were chemical plants in his own state, Mann rejoined: "The southern Representatives have such strong control of that side of the House that they have even forced the gentleman from New York to endeavor to strike down the industries of his own state." Soon afterwards he chided Harrison for giving protection to southern peanut oil. "Peanut oil! Peanut politics!" he exclaimed, amidst laughter and applause from Republicans.[53]

Predictably, Mann was adept in often using the time-tested theme of Democratic incompetence. Thus, for instance, he pointed out that in the chemicals bill the Democrats had used a technical suggestion he had vainly made during debate on the wool bill.[54] He was able to link his own concern for competence with insurgent opposition to undemocratic Democratic practices. Mann charged that the Democrats, by deciding matters in caucuses and among their members on Ways and Means and resorting to restrictive rules on the floor, produced sloppy legislation.[55] His point was valid, as he often showed, though overstated.

On the issue of the scope of a "money trust" investigation, Democrats were deeply divided between those who wanted a broad investigation conducted by a special committee and proponents of a much narrower one by the conservative Committee on Money and Banking. Rules chairman Henry, strongly backed by William Jennings Bryan, stood for the stronger investigation, but Underwood won out in caucus for a weaker one, to be led by the chairman of Money and Banking, Arsene Pujo of Louisiana, as head of a subcommittee. When the matter reached the floor on 24 February, Mann spoke for the more conservative approach. "Mr. Speaker, the most delicate machinery in all the world is the system of financial credits. It might easily happen that the action of this House would produce an effect upon the financial credits of the county which would bring ruin and disaster in their wake." He wanted sober men to make the investigation, and within proper limits, and he

[51]*CR* 62:2, p. 2258 (20 February 1912).
[52]*Ibid.*, pp. 2214–15 (19 February 1912), 2245–46, 2250–62 (20 February 1912).
[53]*Ibid.*, pp. 2213, 2215 (19 February 1912).
[54]*Ibid.*, p. 2213 (19 February 1912).
[55]*Ibid.*, pp. 2213 (19 February 1912), 1412, 1440–42, 1458–59 (27 January 1912).

commended the Democrats on their decision.[56] Mann's congratulations proved premature, and when the issue came up again, he let the force of his convictions undermine his purposes.

After several months Henry and Samuel Untermyer, a New York lawyer, convinced Pujo of the desirability of a widened probe, more fully exposing the practices of J. P. Morgan and Company and others, and Pujo submitted the requisite resolution. In Underwood's absence, on 25 April Henry reported it, slightly revised. Mann attacked it. He said that Untermyer, recently named counsel to the committee, had drafted it in an attempt to blackmail corporations into making campaign contributions, that the committee Republicans had not been consulted, and that the whole thing was a scheme to benefit the presidential candidacy of Governor Woodrow Wilson. Minutes later the House adopted the resolution, 241–15. Frank Vanderlip, president of National City Bank in New York and experienced in Washington, deplored the outcome and blamed Mann for making the issue partisan and forcing the Democrats to unite. Vanderlip probably exaggerated, since Pujo's switch was bound to carry weight with Democrats, but certainly Mann had not helped his cause.[57] The investigation, conducted principally by Untermyer and fully reported by the press, shed harsh light on some New York banks, advanced the idea that there was a money trust, and thereby fueled progressive sentiment and further weakened conservative Republicans.

On many legislative issues during the session, Mann successfully preempted the progressive side. He achieved nothing spectacular, but his efforts helped his party. Much legislation dragged on into late August, two months after the Republicans had renominated Taft, Roosevelt had approved forming a Progressive party at another convention, and the Democrats had chosen Woodrow Wilson. Although Taft entered the convention and campaign as the conservative candidate, yet he had mildly progressive credentials too, as demonstrated in his December recommendations to Congress, appointments of Stimson and Fisher in 1911, and vigorous antitrust prosecutions. Mann's tactic, then, was in support of the administration and the party record generally. Nor was it necessary to wander very far from the party's conservative base to do this, for among the Democrats, especially the warmest supporters of Underwood, there remained a strong strain of states' rights conservatism that rendered the left flank vulnerable. Mann's approach accorded with the temper of the times and figured to benefit not only insurgents but also regulars, as well as local and state tickets, in a difficult election, while also advanc-

---

[56]Richard Todd McCulley, "The Origins of the Federal Reserve Act: Banks and Politics during the Progressive Era, 1897–1913" (Ph.D. diss., University of Texas at Austin, 1980), 418–19; *CR* 62:2, p. 2394 (24 February 1912).

[57]*CR* 62:2, p. 5345 (25 April 1912); McCulley, "Origins of the Federal Reserve Act," 421; Frank Vanderlip to James Stillman, 27 April 1912, part B, series 1, box 4, Vanderlip Papers.

ing party unity and spirit in the House. Occasionally Mann had to reverse himself in order to seem progressive, but mainly he was consistent with the moderate record he had established under Roosevelt and continued under Taft.

Parcel post was a popular reform urged by Taft, albeit on a limited scale. House Democrats preferred to dodge the issue in 1912. Underwood opposed it on states' rights grounds, and others responded to opposition from express companies, country storekeepers, salesmen, and wholesalers.[58] Finally, the Democrats brought forth within a postal appropriations bill a proposal for a purely rural service, to cater to a market that was unattractive to express companies. Mann came late to the subject, but before a final vote in the House he introduced a more thoroughgoing bill for a new fourth class mail category, as urged by Sydney Anderson, a Minnesota insurgent. Not in the hope of immediate adoption, but to make a clear record, Mann arranged to gain the floor on 2 May to move recommittal with instructions to report his bill. Speaker Clark, however, in what some considered an extraordinary action, instead recognized Martin Madden, and Madden's recommittal motion left the waters muddied. Mann denounced these proceedings to the press, and remained agitated when the issue again arose in August.[59] At issue then was a Senate bill that included a strong parcel post plan chiefly fashioned by Oregon insurgent Jonathan Bourne. Mann battled for its acceptance, but failed. However, this time he did establish a record and also put strong pressure on the House conferees, who soon yielded. Even before final adoption of the bill, *La Follette's Weekly Magazine* praised Mann for his efforts, an unexpected dividend in the interest of party unity.[60]

A Republican stamp also went on the bill to put a prohibitive tax on white phosphorus matches, which caused in workers a well-publicized disease nicknamed "phossy jaw." Taft recommended legislation, Mann submitted a bill based on use of the commerce power, and the bill on which the House acted, though managed by a Democrat, was introduced by a Republican, John J. Esch of Wisconsin. On the floor Mann helped perfect the bill. It passed the House with bipartisan support, 162–31, but 28 of those opposed were Democrats, including Underwood, who again took states' rights grounds and incurred much national criticism.[61]

---

[58]Wayne E. Fuller, *RFD: The Changing Face of Rural America* (Bloomington: Indiana University Press, 1964), 226; Haines, *Law Making in America*, 83; James M. Cox, *Journey through My Years* (New York: Simon and Schuster, 1946) 63.

[59]*CR* 62:2, p. 11486 (21 August 1912); *Chicago Tribune*, 3 May 1912, vol. 16, Mann Papers; Haines, *Law Making in America*, 83.

[60]*CR* 62:2, pp. 11039–42 (15 August 1912), 11085–89 (16 August 1912), 11486–88 (21 August 1912); *La Follette's Weekly Magazine*, 4:34 (24 August 1912), 9.

[61]Barfield, "Democratic Party in Congress," 399; Johnson, *Oscar W. Underwood*, 159–60; *CR* 62:1, p. 1122 (8 May 1911); *CR* 62:2, pp. 3966, 3977 (28 March 1912).

In the spring of 1912 the proposal for an amendment to the Constitution providing for direct election of senators was especially timely due to proceedings in the Senate to oust William Lorimer for bribing several Illinois legislators to elect him. Mann, ignoring his earlier opposition to the amendment, not only called for it but pointed up the opposition of some southern Democrats, who feared federal interference in elections.[62] In a second reversal Mann went along with creation of an information-gathering Children's Bureau, against some southern Democratic opposition.[63]

Antitrust was the biggest public issue in 1912. Much had happened in 1911 to make that so. The Supreme Court decision in the Standard Oil case in May stimulated debate because, although the government won the case, yet a court majority now accepted the test of the reasonableness of a business combination in construing the Sherman Anti-Trust Act. Congressional investigations spotlighted "trusts," especially United States Steel, and Taft's antitrust suit against that company and Roosevelt's rebuttal added to public interest. Both insurgents and Democrats set out to strengthen the Sherman Act in 1912, but Taft, while calling for a federal incorporation law, wanted no immediate change in the Sherman Act. Mann agreed to that. "Too harsh penalties make conviction harder and enforcement of law no easier," he said in advance of the regular session. "It is not easy to make the anti-trust law more certain. Such a law can only lay down a general proposition, it cannot explicitly and in terms define the many varied conditions which may arise out of changed circumstances."[64] Seemingly, Mann was on the conservative side of a powerful progressive issue. He managed, however, to create an opposite impression.

Though Taft did not seek amendment to the Sherman Act, he had a strong record on antitrust, and Mann capitalized on that. The Democrats, dedicated to economy and unfriendly to the Justice Department, proposed to appropriate for antitrust just $200,000, not the $300,000 the department requested. In a speech on 15 June favoring the higher figure, Mann noted that from 1890 to 1909 there had been sixty-two proceedings under the Sherman Act; under Taft there had already been sixty-five. Major cases were pending, he said, including the United States Steel case. The Republicans, he warned, would make a campaign issue of the Democrats' effort to deprive the government of adequate funds.[65]

---

[62]*CR* 62:2, pp. 5052 (20 April 1912), 6364 (13 May 1912).

[63]*Ibid.*, pp. 4221–23, 4226 (2 April 1912).

[64]*Chicago Tribune*, 29 November 1911, and *New York Commercial*, 24 November 1911, vol. 16, Mann Papers.

[65]*CR* 62:2, pp. 6258–59 (15 June 1912). On 25 April Mann put in the *Record* a speech by Wickersham defending administration actions and praising the Court's rule of reason. Appendix, p. 125.

On conservation issues Mann easily held ground to the left of the Democrats and in line with administration positions. No election-eve corrections were required. "As you know, we have always been able to count on him," conservation lobbyist Harry Slattery wrote Gifford Pinchot, head of the National Conservation Association, in 1919.[66] In March 1912 Mann said "I know that some gentlemen think that the public domain belongs to the people in the state where the domain is located. I do not entertain that opinion at all."[67] Instead, Mann viewed the public domain from the standpoint of his constituents and what he construed to be the national interest. Thus, on the critical general issue of the disposition of mineral lands, waterpower sites, grazing lands, and timber lands on the public domain and in the national forests, Mann agreed with Pinchot and his allies in favoring establishment of a system of leasing and permits that would yield to the government fair revenues and preserve regulatory authority against overgrazing, deforestation, or, in the case of electric utilities, excessive charges to the public. Pending establishment of such a system, on piecemeal bills Mann was less solicitous for the interests of entrepreneurs than he would have been had the public no stake in the property. Usually he took a similar position respecting dams on navigable streams outside the public domain. These issues were the subject of constant battle until they were resolved in 1920.

Most legislation relating to the public lands and navigable streams was of secondary interest to the general public and divided sections and interest groups rather than parties. Thus Mann did not have to contend with prior Democratic caucus decisions, and in the Committee of the Whole where the bills were molded by amendment, attendance was sparse and Mann, with his knowledge, thoroughness, and acuity, was able to wield a large influence. As Republican floor leader Mann had high visibility, although western Republicans headed by Frank Mondell often opposed him on lands questions, his conservationist stands associated his party with that popular issue in minor degree in the Sixty-second Congress and more fully after that. Secretary of Interior Walter Fisher, formerly head of the Municipal Voters League in Chicago and a person in whom Mann had confidence, in 1912 helped Mann legislatively. Fisher's own progressive policies, like those of Secretary of War Henry L. Stimson, whose Army Corps of Engineers was involved with navigable streams, complemented Mann's stands in the House.[68] By contrast to Mann, Underwood showed little interest in public domain questions, and on the many waterpower issues involving Alabama particularly and the South generally, he usually sided with the utilities.

---

[66]Slattery to Pinchot, 21 August 1919, box 1842, Gifford Pinchot Papers, Library of Congress.

[67]CR 62:2, p. 3705 (20 March 1912).

[68]On Mann and Fisher, see CR 62:2, pp. 3287 (13 March 1912), 3898 (27 March 1912), and Mann to Fisher, 22 June 1911, box 14, Fisher Papers.

On one conservation issue in the Sixty-second Congress, Mann disappointed Slattery. He would not oppose an omnibus dam bill authorizing seventeen private dam projects on navigable streams. In the House Mann said that he did not think that the bill went far enough in regard to restrictions, but he doubted that a majority in Congress agreed with him and meanwhile he did not want to block useful projects.[69] The bill passed in the House, but failed in the Senate.

Mann took the conservationist side on all other measures, including the Raker bill, sponsored by California Democrat John E. Raker. Although this bill was seemingly a minor measure, to give a short right-of-way over land in the Mono National Forest to the Hydro-electric Company of California, on 6 January the National Conservation Association attacked it as involving a dangerous precedent "to take and use for their own purposes what National Forest land they please" and escape from the need for a permit, which was required in national forests. The current system, with revocable permits, was unsatisfactory, the association acknowledged, but if the Raker bill passed, the effort to legislate a better system would be balked. On the previous day Mann had struck the first blow against the bill when on parliamentary grounds he prevented it being called up from the Private Calendar. The delay gave valuable time to Slattery and an associate. Finally, consideration of the bill began on a Calendar Wednesday, 6 March, and continued the following Wednesday. Mann controlled the time for the opposition, and after strong attacks by insurgents Lenroot and Pickett, he closed debate for his side, using to advantage a letter he had gotten from Walter Fisher. By a vote of 98–27, in Committee of the Whole the bill was effectively killed.[70]

On several progressive bills Mann could not outflank the Democrats, but by his assistance and support was able to reduce political damage. So it was with an agricultural extension bill sponsored by Asbury Lever of South Carolina. Mann's long-standing dedication to scientific agriculture came into play and put him at opposites with his more conservative colleagues Moore and Mondell. Disagreement between House and Senate delayed enactment

---

[69]Slattery to Gifford Pinchot, 25 July 1912, box 158, Pinchot Papers; *CR* 62:2, p. 9654 (25 July 1912).

[70]"National Conservation Association," 6 January 1912, box 2050 Pinchot Papers; M. Nelson McGeary, *Gifford Pinchot: Forester-Politician* (Princeton, N.J.: Princeton University Press, 1960), 205; *CR* 62:2, pp. 682–84 (5 January 1912), 2905–6 (6 March 1912), 3275–57, 3260, 3281–88 (13 March 1912). For a fuller account, see Herbert F. Margulies, *Senator Lenroot of Wisconsin: A Political Biography, 1900–1929* (Columbia: University of Missouri Press, 1977), 151–53. For other examples of Mann's conservatism in the second session, see *CR* 62:2, pp. 567 (20 December 1911), 3705–6 (20 March 1912), 3898 (27 March 1912), 7564 (3 June 1912).

until the next Congress.[71] Mann also helped with a noncontroversial bill to establish an eight hour day on work done under government contract.[72]

Much legislation, some of it important, did not easily fall into the categories "progressive" or "conservative." Such bills allowed Mann to demonstrate high competence, to the greater glory of his party. A Panama Canal bill was of this sort. It provided for the opening, maintenance, operation, and management of the soon-to-be-completed canal. It did not, however, include a proposal to exempt from tolls American vessels in the coastal trade, in possible violation of the Hay-Pauncefote Treaty of 1901 under which Britain surrendered to the United States the right to act alone in building the canal. In a long speech on 18 May, Mann brought to bear his expertise in reviewing the entire bill and especially in advocating addition of a tolls exemption. As a member of the Interstate and Foreign Commerce Committee he had studied the exemption issue for some time. In January 1911, following a White House conference, Mann had drafted an exemption bill. Now he was ready with an amendment. The issue pitted sections and interests against one another, but proponents of exemption were strengthened when Mann put a gloss of legitimacy on the proposal. On 21 May Mann read his amendment, but then withdrew it in favor of one by a Michigan Democrat, Frank Doremus. The Doremus amendment passed in Committee of the Whole over the opposition of Interstate and Foreign Commerce chairman Adamson, 100–90, and the following day won out in the House, 147–128.[73] The exemption survived in the Senate and became part of the new law.

Mann drew again on experience in connection with a bill to create a Department of Labor, having himself drafted the bill that established the Department of Commerce and Labor. Though doubtful about enlarging the cabinet, he helped perfect the bill with several amendments that the sponsor accepted.[74] He left his mark on appropriation bills as well. Although generally an advocate of economy, he successfully argued for testing woods as to their suitability for making paper, and for military aircraft, which he saw as the key to future success in warfare.[75]

The national political situation came into sharper focus as the session progressed. "The worst has happened," Henry Adams reported in March. "The bitterness between the wings of the Republican Party has become so great as to be irreconcilable. In spite of all the efforts of peacemakers, the

---

[71]CR 62:2, pp. 11490 (21 August 1912), 11712, 11718, 11722–23, 11731, 11742 (23 August 1912); Barfield, "Democratic Party in Congress," 400–01.

[72]CR 62:2, pp. 390–96 (11 December 1911).

[73]Ibid., pp. 6746–68 (18 May 1912), 6913, 6921 (21 May 1912), 7019 (22 May 1912).

[74]Ibid., pp. 8864–76 (10 July 1912).

[75]Ibid., pp. 3113–15 (9 March 1912), 3234 (12 March 1912), 1867, 1891–94 (9 February 1912).

split has taken huge proportions and is personal." "The 'progressives,'" he went on, "will vote for anybody rather than Taft. . . . The hatred of Theodore has become as insane as Theodore's own conduct, and the passion of the so-called progressives is red-hot." Roosevelt's advocacy of recall of judicial decisions had something to do with the intensity of the fight, as did the extravagant and extraordinary language of the candidates and their managers, which began when Taft referred to "political emotionalists or neurotics."[76]

Roosevelt demonstrated his popularity in most of the thirteen states that held presidential primaries, but Taft controlled the party machinery and commanded the support of the over-represented southern delegations. When the convention met, the outcome turned on seventy-two disputed delegates, but the Taft forces would not yield, and La Follette, still intensely bitter towards Roosevelt for subverting the La Follette candidacy in his own interest, refused to cooperate in the election of a temporary chairman.[77] Compromise was possible, but Roosevelt would not countenance it and instead encouraged his supporters to nominate him at a later convention.[78] On the first ballot Taft was nominated with 561 votes against 107 for Roosevelt, 41 for La Follette, 17 for Cummins, and 2 for Charles Evans Hughes. Three hundred forty-four Roosevelt delegates signified their future intentions by refusing to vote. Taft insisted on the renomination for vice president of standpatter James S. Sherman, but the party did adopt a moderately progressive platform.[79]

Neither Taft nor his backers had any thought of winning the election, and they were content to control the party. But how much that would be worth would depend on many things, including the outcome of legal and political battles in several states for use of the name "Republican," and the decision of insurgents between the old party and the new. That some Roosevelt delegates, together with the La Follette and Cummins delegates, participated in the balloting suggested that a substantial insurgent contingent might remain Republican. Yet the prospective new party, led by the charismatic Roosevelt and backed by politicians such as Gifford Pinchot and Governor Hiram Johnson of California, reformers such as Jane Addams, and contributors such as George Perkins and Frank Munsey, the former also a forceful manager and the latter an influential publisher, challenged the very existence

---

[76] Henry Adams to Elizabeth Cameron, 10 March 1912, *Letters of Henry Adams (1892–1918)* (Boston: Houghton Mifflin, 1938), 588–89; Harbaugh, *Life and Times of Theodore Roosevelt*, 394–401; Oscar King Davis, *Released for Publication: Some Inside Political History of Theodore Roosevelt and His Times, 1898–1918* (Boston: Houghton Mifflin, 1925), 281.

[77] Margulies, *Senator Lenroot*, 120–40.

[78] Gould, *Reform and Regulation*, 157–58; Davis, *Released for Publication*, 304.

[79] Coletta, *Presidency of William Howard Taft*, 237–38.

of the GOP as a major party, regardless of the outcome of the battles over the name "Republican."

When on 2 July the Democrats nominated the articulate progressive Woodrow Wilson, they lessened Roosevelt's chances and also strengthened themselves against the GOP at all political levels. The Wilson nomination came, however, only on the forty-sixth ballot. For a time, Speaker Champ Clark commanded a majority, though never the requisite two-thirds. Most spectacular in turning the tide for Wilson was a switch from Clark to Wilson by William Jennings Bryan, on the grounds that Clark was backed by Tammany and Wall Street.[80] For James R. Mann, there were possibilities here for future mischief, along with the more immediate need for renewed damage-control efforts.

Mann could hardly reverse party fortunes as the session continued after the Republican and Democratic conventions, but he did what he could. As action on the cotton tariff bill drew to an end on 2 August, and the Rooseveltians prepared to convene in Chicago in three days, Mann gave a half-hour speech on the Republican party calculated not only for distribution as a campaign document but to rally his forces in the House. He was not much given to lofty oratory on the floor, preferring pointed debate, but now unapologetically he boasted of and enumerated Republican accomplishments in the years of its full control, 1897–1911, and contrasted this record with that of the Democrats when they usually controlled the House, 1875–1897, and with their present policies. Implicitly he conceded defeat in the coming election, but ended with a peroration on the party's future. "The Republican Party—its memories are too sacred, its principles are too righteous, and too enduring, its record is too great, its leadership and its membership are too patriotic and too filled with hope for the country for it to be destroyed by the assault of its enemies from within or without. It will continue its organization and its work with renewed vitality, with continued loyalty, the possessor of a noble past and with a wonderful future of deeds to be accomplished." Ending amidst loud Republican applause, Mann said, plaintively yet defiantly: "It will not die. It will not cease. It will go on and on, with heroic devotion to the principles of constitutional government" (a swipe at Roosevelt and recall of judicial decisions), "and with continued faith that our right-thinking people will maintain order and preserve equality and prosperity."[81]

Often in the postconvention period Mann generated ammunition for campaign use against the Democrats. He revealed and criticized their absenteeism,[82] attacked them for exempting rivers and harbors spending from the

[80]Arthur S. Link, *Wilson: The Road to the White House* (Princeton, N.J.: Princeton University Press, 1947) 352–54. Later switches by party bosses were more important for Wilson. *Ibid.*, 458–62.

[81]*CR* 62:2, pp. 10081–82 (2 August 1912).

[82]*Ibid.*, pp. 8869 (10 July 1912), 9777–78 (27 July 1912).

new eight-hour-day requirement on government contracts,[83] chided them for the high cost of the session, contrary to their economy professions,[84] and exposed them as unwilling to vote on a politically sensitive immigration bill.[85]

After the session ended on 26 August, Mann prepared and then issued a statement attacking the Democrats for their work in the Sixty-second Congress. Though biased, Mann was able to make a comprehensive and detailed assessment. The Democrats, he said, were at once stingy and extravagant. The laws adopted were fewer and less consequential than in recent years, and some of them, such as the canal bill, "were bills prepared in previous sessions. . . or they were bills prepared by officials in President Taft's administration." In short, true to their past, the Democrats had shown themselves inefficient, disorganized, unprogressive, and inactive, Mann judged. With the fulfillment of this last obligation to his party, Mann departed for his Chicago gardens and a difficult reelection campaign.[86]

Mann faced strong opposition from Democrat John C. Vaughan, a near winner in 1910, and from Thomas D. Knight, a former president of the prestigious Hamilton Club, running as a Progressive. Vaughan had the backing of the two Hearst papers and the *Journal* and strongly attacked Mann as a standpatter, citing votes on tariff and labor bills. He benefited, too, from the Democratic surge in city and state.[87] Knight's Progressives had been energized by the Roosevelt primary campaign, the dramatic Chicago conventions, and then Roosevelt's presidential candidacy. Although most Illinois Republican politicians who supported Roosevelt prior to Taft's nomination afterwards fell away—men like Martin Madden and Edwin Sims—a group of well-known figures that included Raymond Robins and Jane Addams, assisted by practical men like Harold Ickes, organized the new party and nominated close to a full slate of candidates for Congress and state offices. The good-government, social settlement, and University of Chicago element of the party was powerful in the Hyde Park section of Mann's district.[88]

---

[83]*Ibid.*, pp. 9318, 9347 (19 July 1912).

[84]*Ibid.*, p. 9777 (27 July 1912).

[85]*Ibid.*, pp. 9249–52 (15 July 1912).

[86]*Boston Transcript*, 26 August 1912, and *New York Tribune*, 27 August 1912, vol. 16, Mann Papers.

[87]*Chicago Examiner*, 3 November 1912; *Chicago Journal*, 5 September 1912; and "The Truth about James R. Mann's Record in the 62nd Congress" (1912), vol. 33, Mann Papers.

[88]Ralph Arthur Straetz, "The Progressive Movement in Illinois, 1910–1916" (Ph.D. diss., University of Illinois, 1951), 351–95; Michael Patrick McCarthy, "Businessmen and Professionalism Municipal Reform: The Chicago Experience, 1887–1920" (Ph.D. diss., Northwestern University, 1970), 180; Allen F. Davis, *Spearheads for Reform: The Social Settlements and the Progressive Movement, 1890–1914* ((New York: Oxford University Press, 1967), 202–4.

Mann had in his favor the help of the old Jamieson machine, now led by Fred Lundin, and the backers of Governor Charles Deneen, especially national committeeman Roy O. West. Edwin Sims, who had helped cement organization support, expertly managed the campaign.[89] The Anti-Saloon League was gaining in the district but did not yet oppose Mann, as it would later.[90] In Congress Mann had given attention to local legislation and now joined interest-group support to that of influential men like President Harry Pratt Jordan of the University of Chicago. Especially gratifying to Mann, beyond its importance, was the help of reformer William Kent. In 1907 Kent, Mann's erstwhile friend turned foe, had moved from Chicago to California and in 1910 had won election to Congress. After the Progressives organized, he wired the state chairman: "Defeat of Mann would be great loss to public welfare. As hardest working Member of House, he blocks more bad legislation and promotes more good legislation than anyone else." Mann penned on his copy "I consider this quite a triumph."[91]

In his literature Mann stressed his role in enactment of progressive laws such as the Pure Food and Drug Act, the Mann Act, and railroad legislation, together with the advantage to his district of his seniority and leadership role.[92] The Victor Lawson papers supported him, and the *Tribune*, though still favoring Roosevelt, did not endorse Knight but stayed neutral, after praising Mann in a dispatch from Washington.[93]

Mann won with 37.4 percent of the vote. He got 21,374 votes to 15,827 94 for Vaughan and 15,152 for Knight.[94] Yet it was not clear that his victory was due to division among his opponents. Vaughan and Knight had very different supporters, whose combination behind one of them in the absence of the other cannot be presumed.

Safe himself, Mann was surrounded by Republican wreckage near and far. Most prominent among the congressional losers in Illinois were Cannon and

---

[89]Denison Bingham Hull, *The Legislative Life of Morton Denison Hull* (Chicago: Privately printed, 1948), 69; Sims to Mann, 26 December 1911; Roy O. West to Mann, 12 June 1912; and *Chicago Examiner*, 28 July 1912, vol. 16, Mann Papers; Edward T. Glennon to Sims, 7 November 1912, and Jim Nye to Mann, 6 November 1912, vol. 33, Mann Papers.

[90]Thomas Ray Pegram, "Progressivism and Partisanship: Reformers, Politicians, and Public Policy in Illinois, 1870–1922" (Ph.D. diss., Brandeis University, 1987), 345–47; *Chicago Herald*, 30 May 1915, vol. 22, Mann Papers.

[91]"Champion of the Calumet Region" (1912), vol. 33, Mann Papers; Kent to Chauncey Dewey, 12 August 1912, vol. 18, Mann Papers.

[92]*Chicago Tribune*, 27 September 1912, vol. 33, Mann Papers.

[93]H. H. Kohlsaat to Mann, 31 October 1912, vol. 16, Mann Papers; *Chicago Daily News*, 31 October 1912, and *Chicago Tribune*, 31 October 1912, 3 November 1912, vol. 33, Mann Papers.

[94]John L. Moore, ed., *Congressional Quarterly's Guide to U.S. Elections* (Washington, D.C.: Congressional Quarterly, 1985), 717.

William B. McKinley. McKinley had been Taft's campaign manager and was especially targeted by the Progressives.[95] Only five Republican congressmen survived, and one of them, Ira Copley, later joined the Progressive party. That party elected two others outright, and won balance of power delegations to the state assembly and the Cook County Board. In Cook County Roosevelt led the presidential candidates.[96] The Democrats were the big winners in the state. They carried Illinois for Wilson and elected twenty congressmen and a governor, defeating Charles Deneen.

National results seemed no better for the GOP. Wilson won the presidency, and the Democrats took both houses of Congress. In the House they secured 290 of 435 seats. Taft men knew that the president would lose, but some fund raisers and contributors had hoped to outdistance Roosevelt.[97] The dismaying result was that Roosevelt polled 4,119,507 popular votes and won 88 electoral votes, while Taft's totals were 3,484,956 popular votes and 8 in the electoral college. Wilson got 6,243,019 popular votes and 435 electoral votes.

Yet there were grounds for Republican hope in the congressional returns. To be sure, the Democrats were now riding high and in a position to fulfill campaign pledges and reinforce their popularity. But political tides would eventually turn, to the advantage of the opposition party in America's two-party system, and the Republicans had good reason to think that they would fend off the Progressive challenge and remain the second major party. In the Senate only Miles Poindexter stood with the new party, against forty-four Republicans. The situation in the House was not immediately clear after the election, since many insurgent Republican candidates had backed Roosevelt for president. Certainly, though, the GOP would predominate over the Bull Moosers. As it turned out, the Republican margin was 127 to 18. An astute Progressive leader, journalist Oscar K. Davis, commented in retrospect that in hopeless races, instead of running candidates, his party should have backed the Democrat to weaken the Republicans. "But very little thought was given to the Congressional election," he explained, "and thereby we lost the best chance we had to gain firm ground in the solid establishment of the Party." [98]

The Republican contingent that Mann would lead was not only reduced in number but further changed in relative composition, along the same lines as in 1910. Insurgents took only slight losses, chiefly in Kansas.[99] Regulars, however, suffered grievously, chiefly at the hands of the Democrats, but in

[95]Straetz, "Progressive Movement in Illinois," 395.

[96]Harold L. Ickes, *The Autobiography of a Curmudgeon* (New York: Reynal and Hitchcock, 1943), 163.

[97]Frank Vanderlip to James Stillman, 18 October 1912, part B, series 1, box 4, Vanderlip Papers.

[98]Davis, *Released for Publication*, 405–6.

[99]La Forte, *Leaders of Reform*, 206.

Pennsylvania and California especially, from the Progressives.[100] Among the prominent losers in addition to the Illinois men were Ebenezer Hill, Nicholas Longworth, and Edgar Crumpacker. Dalzell, too, had lost in the primaries.

"Congrats!" a Chicago political ally wrote Mann after his election. "Don't forget that you are the surviving national leader and heir apparent."[101] Mann did not greatly concern himself with future presidential possibilities, but he did take seriously his national party responsibilities. These were on his mind when, refreshed by a Panama trip, he returned to Washington for the lameduck session of the Sixty-second Congress. The legislative context was more substantive than before the elections. Democrats were ready to act on the politically ticklish immigrant and liquor issues, though on issues like the tariff, on which Wilson had campaigned, they moved warily in fear of premature policy commitments.[102] With the very survival of the Republican party in question as a result of the election and the bitterness and division that preceded and accompanied it, during the session Mann, as minority leader in the House, personally demonstrated the Republican presence and vitality. Seemingly unperturbed by political events, he acted with as much confidence, aggressiveness, and knowledge as before, and he also continued at once directly partisan and collegial.

The immigration bill, sponsored in the House by an Alabama Democrat, John Burnett, was another attempt to curtail the "new immigration" from Southern and Eastern Europe by means of a literacy test. An 1897 effort had been balked by President Cleveland's veto. Both parties were sharply divided on the measure. Thus, when Mann persistently worked against it, the partisan benefit was mainly in showing that partly through him the party was a player, not moribund.

Mann's initial efforts were twofold. Using a variety of tactics, he caused delay in the hope that the Congress might end before completing action on the bill, and he tried to add to it yet more drastic amendments to make the bill less likely to pass.[103] These efforts failed, and a bill went to the president. Taft vetoed it. The Senate overrode the veto, but by five votes the House sustained it. Chicago's city attorney congratulated Mann and said that Poles

---

[100]Holt, *Congressional Insurgents*, 72.

[101]Jim Nye to Mann, 6 November 1912, vol. 33, Mann Papers; emphasis Nye's.

[102]*St. Louis Globe-Democrat*, 30 November 1912, and *Indianapolis News*, 29 November, 1912, vol. 16, Mann Papers.

[103]*CR* 62:3, pp. 655–56 (14 December 1912), 801–4, 815, 821 (17 December 1912), 859–66 (18 December 1912).

were elated and would give Mann full credit for the result.[104] Whether or not he deserved it is not clear.

When the bill to ban the interstate shipment of liquor into dry territory reached the floor in February, the parties were again internally splintered. Perhaps mindful of the growing power of the Anti-Saloon League and the popularity of the bill, Mann did not overtly oppose it and in fact voted for it. First, though, he joined with Fitzgerald and others in objecting to consideration ahead of appropriation bills, and later he tried to block action on the Senate version of the bill.[105] The House, however, to avoid hazardous delays attending a conference so late in the session, considered and passed the Senate bill. Taft vetoed it as of doubtful constitutionality. Mann now defied a dry delegation from his district and took the floor in defense of the veto. He denied that a recent Supreme Court decision upholding the Mann Act under the commerce power was apposite, or an earlier decision on the Pure Food and Drug Act, each law his own product "in the main." The constitutional questions were best left to another Congress, he felt. The House nevertheless overrode the veto, 246–95, and the Senate overrode, 36–21, so the Webb-Kenyon Act went on the books, a harbinger of the drive for Prohibition through constitutional amendment.[106]

Certain issues that concerned Mann on their merits also had obvious party advantages. That was the case with the Panama Canal tolls exemption question, though when it came up again it was because of a 21 January anti-exemption speech by a Republican, Senator Elihu Root. Root called for repeal of the law or arbitration with Britain, which had strongly objected to the exemption as violating its treaty rights. At stake, Root felt, were relations with Britain and, since Britain's objections seemed to him valid, American national honor. Root had with him the eastern foreign policy establishment, but on balance Republicans seemed supportive of the measure. In addition to its continued popular appeal, midwestern Republicans liked it because it might increase competition with the transcontinental railroads and bring rate cuts, and regulars saw it as a party measure.[107] On 28 January Mann responded to Root. Since Mann was recognized as the House's leading authority on Panama Canal questions, his speech commanded mainly sympathetic

---

[104]John Milton Cooper, Jr., *Pivotal Decades: The United States, 1900–1920* (New York: W. W. Norton and Company, 1990), 131; N. L. Piotrowski to Mann, 21 February 1913, vol. 16, Mann Papers.

[105]*CR* 62:3, pp. 2787–90, 2817 (8 February 1913), 3013–14 (11 February 1913).

[106]*Chicago Journal*, 7 August 1916, vol. 22, Mann Papers; *CR* 62:3, pp. 4444, 4447 (1 March 1913); Peter H. Odegard, *Pressure Politics: The Story of the Anti-Saloon League* (New York: Columbia University Press, 1928), 145.

[107]Gerald D. McKnight, "Republican Leadership and the Mexican Question, 1913–1916: A Failed Bid for Party Resurgence," *Mid-America*, 62 (April–July 1980): 109–11.

attention as he restated the case he had made when the bill was enacted and blamed the transcontinentals for again raising the issue. A Senate authority, Henry Cabot Lodge, who for diplomatic reasons later supported repeal, privately believed that technically Mann was correct. The influential *New York Times* lent weight to Mann's speech by its full report on it.[108]

During the session Congress enacted a law for physical valuation of railroad property as a basis for rate making by the ICC. Tepidly supportive of the progressive measure,[109] Mann used the bill to score points on a related matter. He offered in a recommittal motion something that had been passed in the House with the railroad bill of 1910 but had been dropped in conference—federal regulation of the issuance of railroad stocks and bonds to protect innocent investors against manipulation by insiders. Southern Democrats, for constitutional and developmental reasons, opposed Mann, as they had in 1910, but after persistent efforts, mainly parliamentary battles over germaneness, the House accepted a compromise that called for an ICC report on the subject.[110] Mann's aggressive leadership for the moderate reform favorably contrasted with Democratic reluctance.

The Democrats handed Mann the issue of a Lincoln Memorial, than which nothing could better unite and invigorate anxious Republicans in the House and outside. Without waving the bloody shirt—indeed Mann talked of a Jefferson Davis Memorial—Mann took full partisan advantage of the issue. The previous Congress had authorized a Lincoln Memorial and had set up a commission to recommend specifics. These recommendations were ready for Congress when the session began, but Democrats, led by John Nance Garner, by delaying tactics on another bill late in January, tried to use up Calendar Wednesday time so the Lincoln Memorial joint resolution could not come up before the end of the Congress. In response, Mann first undertook to expose and resist the Democratic tactic. Then, to force the issue, he launched a "filibuster" of his own, not in the sense of talking at length, but by demanding the full reading of the previous day's journal, amendment to the journal, debate on the amendment, yeas and nays, and more, thus delaying the normally routine approval of the journal for three and-one-half hours. Republican battle lines closed on the issue and in support of further "filibustering," thus threatening all House business. Finally the Democrats allowed a vote on the pending and minor Garner bill to dispose of it. The following Wednesday the Lincoln Memorial resolution was in order and

---

[108]*CR* 62:3, p. 2181 (28 January 1913); McKnight, "Republican Leadership and the Mexican Question," 110; *New York Times*, 29 January 1913.

[109]*CR* 62:3, pp. 65–66 (3 December 1912).

[110]*Ibid.*, pp. 66, 74–76 (3 December 1912), 170–77 (5 December 1912); Barfield, "Democratic Party in Congress," 411.

quickly passed.[111] As Washington prepared to inaugurate a new president the following day, on 3 March woman suffrage supporters paraded while the House completed its business. The suffragists were rudely treated, and soon after the parade Richmond Hobson of Alabama protested and said that he had just been told by a lady "that her young daughter was on one of the floats and a ruffian climbed on the float and insulted her daughter." To this Mann replied: "Her daughter ought to have been at home." Within days many suffragists in his district indignantly protested. Though friends of Mann defended him, political trouble lay ahead.[112]

Mann's offhand comment came amidst a day that was for him pleasant and collegial. During a fifteen-minute recess moved by Underwood, Cannon heaped praise on Mann and then, for the House Republicans, presented his friend with a novel kind of watch that, he explained, could be used to tell its possessor when to stop or start. After further tribute, culminating in pro-longed applause, Mann responded. "I make no point of order, and I do not reserve the right to object." He confessed that he was "surprised, pleased, and touched. I am not devoid of knowledge of my many shortcomings," he continued, "and hence I appreciate more than others this kindness on the part of my friends in the House." He included Democrats among those friends, praised Underwood, who was presiding, and said that a saving grace in the House, as in the Republic, "was the possibility and practicability of remaining friends while we fight over principles." Then Clark praised Mann's industry and leadership ability and spoke of his own affection for Mann. The following morning, as the Congress came to an end, it fell to Mann to offer a resolution of thanks and praise to Clark. "Mr. Speaker," he prefaced the resolution, "with a pleasure which wells from the bottom of my heart and as a token of tribute to the splendid ability of our Speaker, and as evidence of the affectionate regard in which every Member holds him, I rise to offer the following highly privileged resolution."[113] The show of collegiality that marked the end of the Congress, while routine practice, was never devoid of significance. In March of 1913 it reinforced the abiding place of the belea-guered party that Mann led in the House. It suggested also that in the next Congress, while the victorious Democrats would be aggressive and would work closely with the first president of their party since Grover Cleveland, yet their ties to Wilson would to some degree be offset by institutional ties to the House, to the advantage of the minority.

---

[111]CR 62:3, pp. 1901–4 (22 January 1913), 1920–29 (23 January 1913), 1965–67 (24 January 1913), 2229, 2245–52 (29 January 1913).

[112]CR 62:3, pp. 4817–18 (3 March 1913); *Chicago Tribune*, 5 March 1913, 6 March 1913; *Chicago Journal*, 5 March 1913, 14 March 1913; *Chicago Examiner*, 5 March 1913; and *Chicago Inter-Ocean*, 10 March 1913, 15 March 1913, 17 March 1913, vol. 16, Mann Papers.

[113]CR 62:3, pp. 4806–7, (3 March 1913), 4853 (4 March 1913).

A preliminary caucus on 4 March made it certain that Mann would again head the House Republicans in the next Congress, though it was not yet clear how many insurgents might defect to the Progressives and how many others would deny Mann their votes for Speaker.[114] Mann would lead a group that was not entirely content with him. Complaint came especially from insurgents. Mann was not a leader at all, some said, but simply a director of routine opposition to Democratic bills; he did not try to unite Republicans on any broad, statesmanlike program, they argued. Critics complained also that he talked too much and assumed too much power in telling Republicans as well as Democrats what bills he would allow to pass. Mann's defenders rejoined that the criticism came from men who backed bills that amounted to graft, and that those who said that he talked too much could not come close to matching his knowledge of governmental affairs.[115]

Dissatisfaction would continue in the years that followed, the same complaints would be reiterated, and Mann would persist in his ways. His pattern had been set in the Sixty-second Congress. On balance, the Republican party had benefited and would continue to benefit. The charges against Mann were true, but shortsighted. He did not try to unite the party on any broad, constructive program because it was too diverse. Sniping at Democratic programs was the most that could be done. Yet in doing that, to the extent possible Mann tried to put his party on the constructive and politically tenable side. Advocacy of a Tariff Board was a good example. Mann did tend to crowd out other Republicans on the floor, and he did censor legislation, but the result was a far higher level of Republican competence and responsibility than would otherwise have obtained. Nor did Mann's tendency to dominate floor debate for his side preclude significant action in committee by capable Republicans.

Mann's talents would be challenged to the full in the next Congress. Woodrow Wilson would give aggressive leadership to a party seeking to make good. Bull Moose Progressives would be aggressive too in trying to replace the Republican party. That party needed the services of a leader like Mann, who remained "confident as a jay," and full of energy, knowledge, and talent. The goal for Mann was party survival, then revival, and, related to that revival, some movement towards a posture of moderate pro-business conservatism, updated from that of the McKinley years. Despite his party's low estate, prospects must have been exhilarating for Mann. He would be cut loose from ties to a lackluster Republican administration and free to fully vent his genius for opposition.

---

[114]*Chicago Record-Herald*, 5 March 1913, vol. 16, Mann Papers.
[115]*Chicago Daily News*, 27 February 1913, vol. 16, Mann Papers.

3

Starting Back: 1913

The 1912 election results and the emergence of the Progressive party brought a flurry of anxious proposals and some action from both regular Republicans and insurgents. Nicholas Murray Butler, president of Columbia University and Republican candidate for vice president after the death of James S. Sherman, urged a special party convention to show the flag, formulate policy proposals, and abolish southern overrepresentation at nominating conventions. Charles Hilles, the national chairman, agreed in part, but concentrated on energizing the National Committee and making it more visible and active in generating publicity. Elihu Root urged similar measures.[1]

Butler's idea of a convention to change southern representation and formulate policy represented a concession by regulars designed to win back Bull Moosers and keep the loyalty of both young Republicans and insurgents and their followers. Insurgents such as Governor Herbert Hadley of Missouri, Senators Cummins and William Kenyon of Iowa, Congressman Herbert Parsons of New York, and Secretary Stimson pressed for these measures with an eye towards the long-term goal of making the GOP the progressive party.[2]

While not disparaging proposals for party reform, when in April the new Congress met in special session to act on the tariff, Mann took a very different and far more conservative approach to the problems of Republican sur-

---

[1]Butler to Charles W. Fairbanks, 27 November 1912, Fairbanks file, Nicholas Murray Butler Papers, Butler Library, Columbia University; Charles Hilles to William Barney, 12 November 1912, series 1, box 99; H.B. Maxson to Hilles, 2 February 1913, series 1, box 82; and Root to Hilles, 20 December 1912, series 1, box 82, Charles D. Hilles Papers, Sterling Library, Yale University.

[2]Norman M. Wilensky, *Conservatives in the Progressive Era: The Taft Republicans of 1912* (Gainsville: University of Florida Press, 1965), 71–72.

vival and rejuvenation. He told reporters that the Democratic tariff bill, once passed, would hurt business and the economy and cause a swing to the Republicans. Lower prices might be achieved, he said, but at the cost of profits, wages, and purchasing power.[3] The Republicans, it followed, need only reassert their protectionism and in general position themselves as the party of business, and through it, of labor. The tariff was the key issue, and the initial one, but Mann's approach to that foreshadowed a larger strategy to which he consistently adhered in the Wilson years. While by no means abandoning progressivism on secondary issues, Mann undertook to restore Republican power by standing in conservative opposition to what he perceived as an antibusiness variant of progressivism embodied in a number of Democratic policies. While in the years of Roosevelt and Taft it had behooved regular Republicans to emphasize progressive sentiment and policies, now that Wilson had seized the progressive banner and the power to achieve his aims, the probusiness approach that Mann had always liked accorded with the interests of the party. Traditionally, it was strong with manufacturers, large and small, and relied on the conservative East as its bedrock. For a time the public had turned on business as a source of political corruption and other evils. Looking ahead, however, Mann could count on a renewal in public faith in business as essential to economic growth and prosperity. He perhaps foresaw a Republican comeback reminiscent of McKinley's victories over Bryan in 1896 and 1900 as the candidate of probity and prosperity, of protectionism and the sound dollar.

Mann was not alone among regulars in counting on the Democratic tariff to do Republican work. Yet he also differed with fellow regulars like Taft. They remained preoccupied with the factional fight that had split the GOP and saw reliance on Democratic misadventures as an alternative to making concessions either to Bull Moosers or insurgents.[4] Mann, on the other hand, was not a factionalist and remained anxious to conciliate insurgents and use such progressive appeals as were not inconsistent with the defense of business and prosperity.

If Mann seemed confident when the Congress began, even complacent, his attitude was warranted. The Bull Moose menace could not be ignored, yet it was not as serious as Roosevelt's large vote and continuing activity suggested. In local races in 1912 the Moosers ran 20 to 50 percent behind Roosevelt, elected only 250 officials, and therefore controlled few appointive offices, the stuff of grass-roots political organization. Related to that, the situation in Illinois was replicated all over—not many experienced politicians

[3] *Port Huron Michigan Times*, 15 April 1913, vol. 17, James R. Mann Papers, Library of Congress; *Chicago Inter-Ocean*, 6 April 1913, vol. 16, Mann Papers.

[4] Wilensky, *Conservatives*, 72–73; Howard Scott Greenlee, "The Republican Party in Division and Reunion, 1913–1920" (Ph.D. diss., University of Chicago, 1950), 61–62; "Rejecting Republican Reunion," *Literary Digest* 46:4 (25 January 1913): 166–68.

joined the party.[5] When in January Frank Munsey, in his newspapers and magazines, began to call for amalgamation with Republicans in a new party, the Moosers, though generally repudiating the scheme, suffered from what amounted to a major show of weakness.[6] Well-publicized internecine warfare that began right after the election, pitting a group led by Gifford and Amos Pinchot against George Perkins, wrought more damage. To Mann, the Progressives' congressional delegation posed little challenge, even after Victor Murdock agreed to lead it. "They are all well intentioned, earnest and intelligent," Washington correspondent "Cal" O'Laughlin told Roosevelt, "but the difficulty is they have not the slightest conception of their duties and what is expected of them." They needed a strong leader, "something Murdock is not."[7] Nor could Murdock come close to matching Mann in debate or as a parliamentarian. An outside Legislative Committee was being formed to draft bills, but it could hardly anticipate the ebb and flow of floor action.

Mann could be optimistic, too, about party unity. Hopefully, the Moosers invited forty-four putative insurgents to their caucus, but in vain.[8] The insurgents' districts, though temporarily scrambled in some cases, were traditionally Republican and had remained so even in 1912. The insurgents themselves had the Republican habit. Furthermore, the shadows of La Follette and Cummins hung heavily over the Wisconsin and Iowa House delegations, and to a lesser extent over other delegations of the upper Midwest. The two senators had heavy investments in the Republican party. They controlled and relied on party machinery in their states, and both men also aspired to the party's presidential nomination in 1916. For La Follette, any association with Roosevelt or his party was out of the question. On 26 March Irvine Lenroot, William Kent and Sydney Anderson announced that they would not join the Moosers, and the matter was thereby closed for virtually all insurgents.[9]

What remained to be determined was how the insurgents would relate to the regular Republicans. A number of circumstances, capitalized on by Mann through conciliation, caused the relationship to tighten in advance of the new Congress and then when Congress organized itself. Without even insisting that they vote for him for Speaker, but only that they not join the Moos-

---

[5]Wilensky, *Conservatives*, 70: William H. Harbaugh, *The Life and Times of Theodore Roosevelt* (New York: Oxford University Press, 1975), 410–11.

[6]John A. Gable, *The Bull Moose Years: Theodore Roosevelt and the Progressive Party* (Port Washington, N.Y.: Kennikat Press, 1978), 157–59.

[7]O'Laughlin to Roosevelt, 23 March 1913, series 1, box 245, Theodore Roosevelt Papers, Library of Congress.

[8]Maureen R. Romans, "Party Leadership Fights in the House of Representatives: The Cause of Conflict, 1895–1955" (Ph.D. diss., University of Massachusetts, 1976), 140.

[9]*New York Times*, 27 March 1913.

ers, Mann prepared committee lists that would satisfy insurgents. He also consulted Gardner and perhaps others.[10] Conferring together just before the party caucus, insurgents rejected the idea of a separate organization of their own. On principle, some of them would not enter the caucus, but others went, including Lenroot and Anderson, and participated in a show of harmony and spirit. Mann was the unanimous choice for Speaker and therefore minority leader and without any show of opposition was given the right to make Republican committee assignments. For his part, Mann made it clear that no one was bound on matters of legislation, meeting the expressed desire of insurgents.[11] On 7 April Mann received 111 votes for Speaker to 272 for Clark, 18 for Murdock, and just 5 for insurgents Cooper and Nelson. Two years before, 17 insurgents had defected from Mann. The emergence of the Progressive party contributed to this solidification among Republicans. Those who would not join the Moosers needed to make clear to voters and to members of the Republican Congressional Campaign Committee that they were indeed Republicans. Separate factional identification was no longer as easily understood as before, nor was it as salient, since the Republicans were outnumbered by the Democrats by more than two to one. Carefully, of course, Lenroot, Anderson, Kent, and others asserted their intention to support progressive initiatives from the president, and played down party politics.[12]

Early in the session Mann followed up on prior understandings about committees. Since the tariff bill was the only immediate business, just three committees were immediately made up. One was Ways and Means, and Mann named Anderson to it. The Minnesotan wrote in appreciation and took the assignment "as evidence of the efforts you are making to unite the party." On 3 June Mann made the rest of the assignments and gave the insurgents further grounds for gratification. They got first or second place on such important committees as Appropriations, Banking and Currency, Judiciary, Foreign Affairs, Post Office, and Immigration.[13]

---

[10]*Chicago Record-Herald*, 20 March 1913, and *New York Journal of Commerce*, 22 March 1913, vol. 16, Mann Papers.

[11]*Chicago Record-Herald*, 17 March 1913, and *Washington Post*, 6 April 1913, vol. 17, Mann Papers; Lynn Haines, *Your Congress: An Interpretation of the Political and Parliamentary Influences that Dominate Law-Making in America* (Washington, D.C.: National Voters' League, 1915), 72–73.

[12]*St. Paul Pioneer*, 8 April 1913, and *Chicago Inter-Ocean*, 6 April 1913, vol. 17, Mann Papers; *Chicago Record-Herald*, 30 March 1913, 27 March 1913, vol. 16, Mann Papers.

[13]Sydney Anderson to Mann, 11 April 1913, vol. 17, Mann Papers; *Chicago Inter-Ocean*, 1 June 1913, vol. 20, Mann Papers; *CR* 63:1, p. 1871 (3 June 1913).

By then most insurgents had been disabused of earlier illusions about progressives coming together across party lines for common purposes.[14] Wilson decided that the more prudent course was to rely on Democrats, both conservative and progressive, and use the Democratic caucus in each House to secure majorities.[15] In consequence, the "partyism" that Lynn Haines disgustedly detected in Republican organizational preliminaries he found to be persistent through the whole Congress and common to all three parties.[16] Mann, of course, contributed to Republican unity, converting possibilities into actuality.

The Underwood-Simmons Tariff Act was a triumph for the new president. In advance of the session Wilson successfully negotiated with Underwood for provisions that he could support and that would win approval among Democrats in their caucus and in the Ways and Means Committee; he dramatized the issue when, breaking a tradition dating to Jefferson, he personally addressed a joint session for the measure; he effectively wielded the patronage weapon against Senate recalcitrants; and then he went to the people with a warning against lobbyists that helped win adoption of the bill. The new law lowered average rates on dutiable goods from 41.0 to 26.8 percent, expanded the free list from 51.3 to 67.5 percent of imports, and began use of the income tax under the newly adopted Sixteenth Amendment.[17]

Curiously, the bill also well served the purposes of James R. Mann. As noted, he foresaw hard times resulting from the bill, and Republican revival on the tariff issue. In other ways, too, the bill served Mann's purposes—in fostering party unity, chiefly on a conservative, protectionist basis, yet with pleasing progressive flourishes too—and in providing many opportunities to exploit both Democratic and Progressive vulnerabilities.

At two caucuses in mid-April, Republicans set their strategy. It reflected compromise between Mann and the insurgents, chiefly represented by Lenroot, who had become de facto insurgent leader when Norris became a senator. Mann supported the insurgent idea that the caucus itself be open to the press and public, in contrast to the secret caucuses the Democrats were

---

[14]Belle La Follette and Fola La Follette, *Robert M. La Follette* (New York: Macmillan Company, 1953), 2:458; Richard Lowitt, *George W. Norris: The Making of a Progressive, 1861–1912* (Syracuse: Syracuse University Press, 1963), 275; Robert Louis Woodbury, "William Kent: Progressive Gadfly, 1864–1928" (Ph.D. diss., Yale University, 1967), 227–228; *Wisconsin State Journal*, 3 December 1912; *New York Times*, 27 March 1913.

[15]Arthur S. Link, *Wilson: The New Freedom* (Princeton, N.J.: Princeton University Press, 1956), 152-75.

[16]Haines, *Your Congress*, 62.

[17]Link, *Wilson: The New Freedom*, 179-97; David A. Lake, *Power, Protection and Free Trade: International Sources of U.S. Commercial Strategy, 1887–1939* (Ithaca, N.Y.: Cornell University Press, 1988), 154.

holding on the bill. Lenroot, in turn, moved that the caucus could be closed by majority vote. The party would propose as its alternative to the Democratic bill creation of a nonpartisan Tariff Commission (the word "Board" was abandoned), an approach strongly favored by both Mann and Lenroot, and development of specific schedules on wool and woolens and cotton, presumably based on the board's December reports. Some regulars, such as Joseph Fordney of Michigan, an arch-protectionist, preferred that the party offer no such proposals, but simply capitalize on Democratic mistakes. There was some objection, too, to the open caucus idea. The compromise held, however. Foreshadowing things to come, an Iowa insurgent, Horace Towner, criticized Wilson. He objected to a president, with the vast patronage at his disposal, recommending to the House on a revenue measure, which under the Constitution was to be initiated in the House.[18] For a united minority on Ways and Means, Sereno Payne reported on the Underwood bill and said, "In this statement we shall not attempt to analyze this bill or to criticize it in detail. Our acquaintance with it is too brief to permit this." He went on to note that the committee majority, bound by caucus action, would not consider amendments.[19] In floor debate the committee was most fully represented by J. Hampton Moore, "active, witty and caustic," as his fellow protectionist Frank Mondell later remembered him.[20] Moore spoke especially for politically important small business interests, which stood to lose the most from the bill.[21] Since the Democrats permitted amendments, but were bound by their caucus to reject them all, insurgents pitched in against caucus rule and also attacked the bill for not protecting cattle and grain and for not creating a Tariff Commission, which remained out of favor among Democrats.[22]

---

[18]*Chicago Inter-Ocean*, 12 April 1913, 18 April 1913, and *Washington Post*, 12 April 1913, vol. 17, Mann Papers; Haines, *Your Congress*, 79. Objections by some regulars are mentioned in Frank Greene to Walter H. Crockett, 26 April 1913, box 1, Greene Papers. Mann showed his interest in the tariff commission idea by introducing a bill for it on the first day of the session. *CR* 63:1, p. 8217 (7 April 1913). Lenroot had also introduced a commission bill, as he had in the previous Congress. Herbert F. Margulies, *Senator Lenroot of Wisconsin: A Political Biography, 1900–1929* (Columbia: University of Missouri Press, 1977), 165.

[19]Charles O. Jones, *The Minority Party in Congress* (Boston, Little, Brown, 1970), 62.

[20]Frank Mondell, "My Story," *Wyoming State Tribune*, 9 November 1935, 10 November 1935.

[21]Frank Burdick, "Woodrow Wilson and the Underwood Tariff," *Mid-America* 50 (October 1968): 280-86; Martin J. Sklar, *The United States as a Developing Country* (Cambridge, Eng.: Cambridge University Press, 1992), 29-30.

[22]Elston E. Roady, "Party Regularity in the Sixty-third Congress" (Ph.D. diss., University of Illinois, 1951), 40-41; Greenlee, "Republican Party," 21-22; James Holt, *Congressional Insurgents and the Party System 1909–1916* (Cambridge, Mass.: Harvard

Mann actively participated, played on all of these themes, especially that of the Tariff Commission, and added others. He gave some attention to the Progressives, whose party commitments remained soft prior to getting committee assignments from one leader or another. He indicated that the door was open, and that no three-party system was possible, while also discrediting their leader, Victor Murdock, as having stolen his Tariff Commission bill from Republicans, as having voted in the past as a free trader except where his personal or district interests were concerned, and as having dishonorably joined the Moosers after winning election as a Republican.[23] Murdock came to worry that he was not sufficiently clever in debate.[24]

In dealing with the Democrats, Mann went into matters of substance, such as the Tariff Commission, but also supervised important procedural points for his side. On the matter of securing ample time, he was successful by threatening a filibuster that would force on the Democrats a politically embarrassing "gag rule" from the Rules Committee.[25] He had trouble getting a roll-call vote on a Tariff Commission amendment or a recommittal motion embodying it, but did get a roll-call vote on Clark's ruling that it was not germane, and he directed further public attention to the popular idea.[26]

Mann's final remarks, concluding an intensive two-week consideration of the bill, were directed to his own party and the electorate. Already, he said, protests were coming in from all over, and business was slowing in fear of the bill. Ahead lay lower prices, and no party could survive that. The country had been turned over to the Democrats in good shape; they would be judged by the economic results of their legislation. Prolonged applause from the Republicans signaled their approval and, for the moment, their unity.[27] "Cal" O'Laughlin wrote ruefully to Roosevelt that while Progressives were divided on the bill, "the Republicans will vote solidly against it. This will place them in a position of standing for something definite. Their action is likely to appeal to the farmers and the small manufacturers. If hard times come, the Republicans will have the advantage, not only over the Democrats, but over the Progressives."[28] In the voting on 8 May, Mann lost just two Republicans,

---

University Press, 1967), 89; *CR* 63:1, pp. 752, 765 (29 April 1913), 820 (30 April 1913), 1006 (2 May 1913), 1046 (3 May 1913).

[23]*CR* 63:1, pp. 968 (2 May 1913), 1047 (3 May 1913), 1112-22 (5 May 1913).

[24]William S. Culbertson Diary, 3 May 1913, box 3, William S. Culbertson Papers, Library of Congress.

[25]*CR* 63:1, pp. 843 (30 April 1913), 904 (1 May 1913), 985-86 (2 May 1913).

[26]*Ibid.*, pp. 1227-34 (6 May 1913), 1370-84 (8 May 1913).

[27]*Ibid.*, p. 1368 (7 May 1913).

[28]O'Laughlin to Theodore Roosevelt, 6 May 1913, series 1, box 249, Roosevelt Papers.

while four Progressives broke ranks from their much smaller delegation.[29] Later the Republicans got their chance to press their case before the voters, for after some difficulty in the Senate, at the end of September the new tariff law was enacted.

Achievement of party unity against a Democratic tariff bill, coming so soon after the demoralizing and debilitating schism and election, did Republicans great good, but it did not settle the division between insurgents and regulars. The problem, though, was not severe. Insurgents pressed their demands on 10 May with a Chicago conference inspired by Albert Cummins. The conferees wanted a national party convention to reduce southern representation and change other procedures. After the capable Iowa insurgent Frank Woods succeeded William B. McKinley as head of the Congressional Campaign Committee, that committee threw its support behind the convention idea. Decision would be made by the National Committee in December. La Follette remained conspicuously aloof from Cummins's initiative, but creation of a new investigative-publicity organization in Washington, the National Voters' League, to be run by Lynn Haines, reflected his factional activity and hopes.[30]

For Mann, what was more significant about the insurgents in 1913 was their marked hostility towards the Democrats. This was shown most spectacularly when on 11 September, near the start of debate on Wilson's second major proposal, to reform the system of money and banking, Sydney Anderson resigned his coveted place on Ways and Means in protest against the Democrats' use of the secret caucus in preparing and acting on first the tariff bill and then the currency bill. In an emotional speech Anderson said that through the caucus the Democrats deprived his district and 140 others of representation. Making the Democratic offense the more odious to insurgents, he argued that the 129 southern Democrats were able to control the party caucus and the House itself. In the same connection he noted that southerners held all but one major committee chairmanship.[31] Frequently during the session, before and after Anderson's speech, in private as well as in public, insurgents inveighed against Democratic legislative methods. They also attacked Wilson as being dictatorial, and criticized his appointments. Nor could they abide the effort of Wilson and the Democrats to preempt the label "progressive." In the House "the undercurrent grows more like the days preceding the Cannon revolt," Harry Slattery told Pinchot in late July.

[29]Link, *Wilson: The New Freedom*, 181; Greenlee, "Republican Party," 22-23; *CR* 63:1, pp. 1386-87 (8 May 1913).

[30]Holt, *Congressional Insurgents*, 98-102; *La Follette's Weekly Magazine*, 5:28 (12 July 1913): 4, 15.

[31]*CR* 63:1, pp. 4759, 4762 (11 September 1913).

"Each day open criticisms are being made of House rules and procedures, but of course back of that lies a growing discontent with Underwoodism."[32]

Since "the enemy of my enemy is my friend," regulars and insurgents were thrown together. Unity would be to their advantage in potentially difficult reelection bids, and that fact also conduced to amity. Under these circumstances, the job for Mann in the four months between floor action on the tariff bill and the currency bill was to lead a common effort to rebuild the reputation of the party incrementally by exploiting Democratic misadventures and by demonstrating Republican competence and wisdom. Success in these efforts would automatically help Republicans against the other challengers, the Progressives.

To enhance party government, Wilson acquiesced in backward steps from the merit system by Postmaster General Albert Burleson and Secretary of State William Jennings Bryan in particular. For the most part, in 1913 Mann left it for others to develop what in the elections of 1914 and 1916 would prove a politically useful issue.[33] Occasionally Mann alluded to administration patronage policies, however, and in one instance at least he put an interesting twist to the case. Professing sympathy for Clark, he noted that the Clark people would have to suppress their hostility to Bryan, dating to the 1912 convention, in the interest of party unity and to obtain patronage. Mann was suggesting, to the delight of Republicans, that the Democrats were as divided as ever, and now many of them were forced to sacrifice their independence as legislators to curry favor with the executive branch. Only the Republicans, Mann said, were free to speak plainly.[34] In pointing to an uncomfortable truth, to an incalculable degree Mann encouraged occasional assertions of independence by Clark and his followers in 1914 and afterwards, which themselves were embarrassing to Democrats.

On 27 June a front-page headline in the sober *New York Times* said, "Mann Excoriates Wilson." The story reported on a Mann speech, and accompanying it was a more prominent article giving detail on a controversy between Wilson and a San Francisco federal district attorney, John L. McNab, who was a carryover from the Taft administration. Five days before Mann spoke, McNab had angrily and publicly resigned, charging that Attorney General James McReynolds, influenced by powerful California interests,

---

[32]Bruce L. Larson, *Lindbergh of Minnesota: A Political Biography* (New York: Harcourt Brace-Jovanovich, 1973), 53-55; Holt, *Congressional Insurgents*, 84-89; Slattery to Gifford Pinchot, 23 July 1913, box 168, Gifford Pinchot Papers, Library of Congress.

[33]Paul Van Riper, *History of the United States Civil Service* (Evanston, Ill.: Row, Peterson, 1958), 228-38; Stephen Skowronek, *Building a New American State: The Expansion of National Administrative Capacities, 1877–1920* (Cambridge, Eng.: Cambridge University Press, 1982), 194-95.

[34]*CR* 63:1, p. 287 (21 April 1913).

had improperly ordered a postponement in the case of Maury I. Diggs and
Drew Caminetti and in another, unrelated case. Wilson publicly defended
McReynolds and chastised McNab, and McNab rejoined. Embarrassingly for
the administration, Caminetti was the son of the head of the Immigration
Service in the Labor Department. McReynolds explained his postponement
request as springing from the fact that the elder Caminetti wanted to attend
his son's trial, but Secretary of Labor William Wilson could not then spare
him and had asked McReynolds for the postponement. Press attention resulted not just from the fact of the clash, but from the nature of the Diggs-
Caminetti case. Diggs and Caminetti were prominent Sacramento men in
their twenties, both married and with children, who were charged with intimidating and enticing two nineteen-year-old women of "good" families and
bringing them to Reno, Nevada, where, as McNab put it, "they were ruined
and debauched."[35]

Although when Mann entered the fray he criticized Wilson and
McReynolds, he seems to have been drawn to the matter by other considerations. He was rallying to the defense of McNab and in support of San
Francisco congressman Julius Kahn, a Republican, whose resolution to
request documents on the matter from McReynolds first raised the issue in
the House. Also, the Diggs-Caminetti case was of special interest to Mann
in that the crime alleged was a violation of his 1910 White Slave law. Whatever his principal motive, in his 26 June speech Mann did question McReynolds' action and Wilson's defense of it, and this had offensive as well as
defensive political implications. California Governor Hiram Johnson privately likened Wilson's defense of McReynolds to Taft's "whitewashing" of
Richard Ballinger.[36]

Through July Mann conducted a sporadic battle with Henry Clayton,
chairman of Judiciary, over Kahn's resolution. It began on 2 July when
Clayton moved to table the resolution, thus blocking debate, and Mann said,
"There will be no further business in the House without a quorum until we
have a chance to have some debate on this white-slave proposition." During
the summer doldrums, as the House marked time while the Senate acted on
the tariff bill, quorums were hard to get, so Mann was threatening to block
all business. Clayton had to agree to put off a vote on his motion for two
weeks. Later, Clayton did not press the motion to table, but Joseph Byrns of
Tennessee, from McReynolds' district, did and won out, 132–85. Four days
later, on 22 July, Mann warned Democrats that his party would not be
gagged and made a point of order that there was no quorum. The Democrats
surrendered and a week later, with relevant documents now available, Mann

---

[35]*New York Times*, 27 June 1913; Link, *Wilson: The New Freedom*, 117-18; *CR*
63:1, p. 2876 (29 July 1913).

[36]Johnson to George W. Perkins, 26 June 1913, box 12 general file, George W.
Perkins Papers, Butler Library, Columbia University.

got two and one half hours for his side on a new Kahn resolution. Kahn consumed an hour of it, but Mann helped Kahn with leading questions and concluded debate for the Republicans. Mann's questions brought out the noncooperation of the administration with the House's several requests for documents. In his speech Mann went into the lurid details of the crime, as a jury later judged it to be. He also stressed evidence showing that McReynolds had acted prior to the request from Secretary Wilson, a damaging fact. At the end the resolution was tabled, but by then the case and the documents had been fully aired and the administration had sustained some damage, though not enough to force McReynolds' resignation nor even prevent his elevation to the Supreme Court in 1914.[37]

Also in July Mann prepared for a 1914 battle over the Philippines, a topic that had repeatedly divided the parties since American acquisition of the islands. Mann foresaw a Democratic bill to give Filipinos a majority on a commission with legislative and administrative powers, and resultant conflict with bureaus of the American government, discontent, and rebellion. To gather ammunition, he wrote Taft, with whom he had become friendly and who had been governor in the Philippines. Anxiously he solicited a letter or letters for the use of a Republican member of the Insular Affairs Committee, Clarence Miller of Minnesota, who was to make a fact-finding trip. After prodding Taft again with a telegram, he got what he wanted. Miller, in turn, may have been the author of a letter that warned against the prospective bill that Mann released to the press in November.[38]

Much of Mann's activity during the four-month hiatus was not directly political, yet helped his party. His contributions were both substantive and institutional. The issues were either secondary for the Democrats or of an emergency nature, so caucuses were not held and Mann had opportunity for constructive involvement. His background in the House, especially through service on Interstate and Foreign Commerce, came into play, and Mann was able to speak authoritatively, at once giving sound leadership to his party followers and himself enhancing party stature as he strongly influenced events. His positions were mildly progressive on the issues of substance, without, however, sacrificing basic conservatism as expressed on the greater issues of the tariff and later the currency bill. Through his institutional contributions he represented his party creditably and fortified it as the true sec-

---

[37]CR 63:1, pp. 2311 (2 July 1913), 2539 (18 July 1913), 2624-25 (22 July 1913), 2874-88 (29 July 1913), 3006, 3023 (1 August 1913); Ellen Axson Wilson to Woodrow Wilson, 3 July 1913, Arthur S. Link, ed., *The Papers of Woodrow Wilson* (Princeton, N.J.: Princeton University Press, 1978), 28:98-99, n. 4.

[38]*Chicago Inter-Ocean*, 24 November 1913, vol. 20, Mann Papers; Mann to Taft, 21 July 1913, series 3; and Taft to Mann, 22 July 1913 series 8, reel 519, William Howard Taft Papers, Library of Congress.

ond party against the less experienced or rule-wise Murdock and the Progressives.

Intermittently after 3 June the House operated on a unanimous-consent basis while many members absented themselves. Mann agreed to this and largely acted for his party in enforcing it, so the House could deal with emergency and noncontroversial matters.[39] He took the initiative in protecting the integrity of the *Record*, so that while remarks might be extended, they should not seem as though spoken in the House.[40] When a former lobbyist for the National Association of Manufacturers (NAM) made sensational allegations of past corruption, involving such top Republicans as Cannon, Tawney, and Dalzell, as well as a leading Democrat, Swagar Sherley of Kentucky, Mann asserted his faith in Sherley and in the integrity of House members generally. Their fault, he said, was not corruption by lobbyists, but cowardice in the face of pressure from their districts. Mann urged a calm and thorough approach and helped significantly in framing the resolution that established a select committee of seven with a broad investigative mandate going beyond just the influence of the NAM over the congressmen named, and with the assistance of counsel. This last provision was contentious, but Mann won out, with heavy Republican support.[41] The investigation produced some interesting information, while not sustaining the charges of corruption.

Though no less sharp tongued than ever on occasion, Mann also attended to the bipartisan amenities that smoothed House action. He congratulated the president when he appointed two House Democrats to high executive posts, interrupted proceedings to note the fact of Underwood's birthday and to praise him, and successfully battled for a car for the Speaker. His courtesies were appreciated, and on these matters Mann showed himself not the leader of a repudiated party struggling for survival, but the confident head of a copartner in governance.[42] So it was also on matters of substance.

When a major railroad strike threatened, Mann participated in a 14 July White House conference along with two committee chairmen from the Senate and House, representatives of labor, management, and the National Civic Federation, and Secretary of Labor Wilson. Later Mann said that he was there because of his legislative background, which indeed was germane, but actually he came as representative of his party, and he was the sole representative since Senate Minority Leader Gallinger was away. Murdock of the Pro-

---

[39]*CR* 63:1, p. 1880 (3 June 1913).

[40]*Ibid.*, p. 3123 (3 August 1913).

[41]*Ibid.*, pp. 2298-2307, 2315-25 (2 July 1913), 2326-29, 2334 (5 July 1913), 2343-53 (9 July 1913); Haines, *Your Congress*, 32.

[42]*CR* 63:1, pp. 2905 (29 July 1913), 3640 (22 August 1913); Evans C. Johnson, *Oscar W. Underwood: A Political Biography* (Baton Rouge: Louisiana State University Press, 1980), 202; Genevieve Clark to Mann, 2 July 1914, vol. 19, Mann Papers; Francis Burton Harrison to Mann, 22 August 1913, vol. 20, Mann Papers.

gressives seems not to have been invited. Overriding some objections from Secretary Wilson, the conferees agreed on new legislation strengthening existing arbitration and mediation mechanisms for interstate railroads and their workers and separating mediation from the Labor Department, as unions and management wanted. On the floor the next day Mann backed Judiciary chairman Clayton in successfully urging adoption of the law in time to be signed that night, and he explained the history of the legislation, which dated to the major railroad strikes of 1894 and the Erdman Act of 1898.[43]

Mann was even more helpful in adoption of three bills directed at the opium trade. The bills, sponsored by Mississippi Democrat Pat Harrison, involved prohibitive taxation, bans on manufacturing, importation, and exportation, and the regulation of legitimate sales by pharmacists, a nettlesome matter. Some legislation was already on the books, which Mann had helped secure, but now, in advance of an international conference, stronger laws were timely. In floor debate Mann was able to call on his experience not simply with the opium problem, but with related legislation under the commerce power, especially the Pure Food and Drug Act. Mann's chief contributions were in helping perfect the bills with amendments and devising an amendment to meet the objections of Thomas Sisson of Mississippi, who feared for states' rights and threatened a potentially disastrous quorum call. The landmark Harrison Antinarcotics Act of 1914 eventuated.[44]

Mann made himself quite useful on another issue that cut across party lines, in the area of conservation. For years San Francisco had sought to ensure its water supply by means of dams and a reservoir in the Hetch Hetchy Valley, which was within Yosemite National Park and was a site of striking beauty. By 1913 the project had the support of the California delegation, including William Kent, who was active for the project, the relevant leaders of bureaus and departments, San Francisco officials, and Gifford Pinchot and his associates. Earlier opposition from irrigationists and power companies, the latter fearful of a city monopoly, had been met, but the Sierra Club spearheaded preservationist opposition. Nevertheless, the Public Lands Committee unanimously reported the bill. In the absence of Lenroot, ranking Republican on the committee, Mann provided the somewhat inexperienced chairman, Scott Ferris of Oklahoma, the fullest assistance in Committee of the Whole and vital Republican support. He had consulted often with Bay Area Republican members Kent, Kahn, and Joseph Knowland and spoke with authority. While regretting the scenic loss, and reading a letter from an opponent, Mann stressed the water needs of San Francisco, which he saw as foreshadowing similar problems elsewhere. His principal assistance to Ferris

---

[43]Arthur B. Darling, ed., *The Public Papers of Francis G. Newlands* (Boston: Houghton Mifflin, 1932), 246-49; CR 63:1, pp. 2430-33, 2438 (15 July 1913).
[44]CR 63:1, pp. 2168-69 (24 June 1913), 2194-2211 (26 June 1913).

was in perfecting the bill with a number of amendments that Ferris accepted. The bill cleared the House in September and became law in December.[45]

When at last the currency bill reached the floor on 10 September, bipartisanship ended. Already Mann had been active in defining his party as more conservative than the Democrats. In the floor debate and voting most of his colleagues followed through on that. In hard times such a posture would pay political dividends. But the specific issue of what became the Federal Reserve Act was not a good one for Republicans and not one that they afterwards used, for the legislation was much needed and proved widely popular, and Republicans were not as united against it as they had been on the tariff. Recognizing these developments, in the eight days of floor action Mann reverted to the strategy of damage control by limiting his own visibility and tempering his criticisms.

No one denied the need for money and banking reform to rectify the problems of an uncoordinated system of banking, the lack of adequate mechanisms to shift reserves from region to region, a hodgepodge of publicly and privately issued currency whose quantity was unrelated to economic tides, and more. The Aldrich Monetary Commission, created in the wake of the 1907 panic, released a plan in 1911 for a centralized, banker-controlled system, but despite strong support from the larger banks, it was heavily criticized by Democrats and not fully taken up by Republicans.[46] The plan did at least raise the major issues. How centralized should the system be, who should control it, and who should issue the currency?

Carter Glass of Virginia, Chairman of Banking and Currency, took the initiative in drafting legislation along fairly conservative lines. The bill that eventuated in late June, however, reflected pressure especially from William Jennings Bryan, along with the Bryanite chairman of the Senate Banking Committee, Robert Owen of Oklahoma, and from Brandeis, Secretary of the Treasury William Gibbs McAdoo, and ultimately President Wilson. The Federal Reserve Board, at the pinnacle of a system that would include private member banks and an intermediate layer of twelve Federal Reserve banks, would not be controlled by bankers but by presidential appointees, and Federal Reserve notes would be the obligation of the government, not the banks, and would fluctuate in quantity according to bank borrowings by businessmen and farmers.[47]

---

[45]Elmo R. Richardson, *The Politics of Conservation: Crusades and Controversies, 1897–1913* (Berkeley: University of California Press, 1962), 43-44; Elizabeth T. Kent, *William Kent, Independent: A Biography* (n.p.: Privately published, 1951), 325-27; *CR* 63:1, pp. 3118 (5 August 1913), 3897-99 (29 August 1913), 3983-84, 3990-92, 4000 (30 August 1913), 4100 (2 September 1913)

[46]Richard T. McCulley, *Banks and Politics during the Progressive Era: the Origins of the Federal Reserve System, 1897–1913* (New York: Garland, 1992), 255.

[47]Link, *Wilson: The New Freedom*, 206-18.

Wilson pressed for legislative action instead of the normal summer recess, to capitalize on momentum from the money trust investigation and the fact that most of his patronage appointments had not yet been made.[48] After addressing a joint session of Congress on 23 June, in July and August Wilson successfully promoted compromises among House Democrats in committee and in the caucus. The revised bill included concessions to the Bryanites, to benefit farmers, and to bankers, and by September the banking community, still divided, was more favorable than earlier, while manufacturers and merchants generally favored the bill. Most House Republicans remained opposed, as they had been since June, and the Democrats, having achieved a tenuous equilibrium, had little room for concessions to the Republicans.[49]

Mann said more in advance of floor action than later. He began to develop his line of criticism in a statement to the press following Wilson's 23 June speech. Mann found fault with the president for seeming to threaten use of patronage, for trying to deal with the issue on a partisan basis and for lecturing Congress like a schoolmaster with fourth graders. The Glass bill he attacked on several grounds, including partisan political control of the Federal Reserve System. This theme would remain paramount for Mann. Many bankers, including influential men from Chicago, shared the fear. It was also the main criticism offered by Frank Vanderlip of the National City Bank of New York in a twenty-three page response to Mann's request for detailed analysis of the administration's bill.[50]

In light of Vanderlip's comments, Mann published an article again stressing the danger of political control of the Reserve Board and warning of inflationary manipulation of the money supply for political purposes. After the Democratic caucus finished with the bill and it was reported, Mann issued a statement that McAdoo remembered years later. Mann warned that bankers must be reconciled to the legislation, or they would not join the system, and that businessmen generally must be supportive. He acknowledged the need

---

[48]McCulley, *Banks and Politics*, 264-68; Link, *Wilson: The New Freedom*, 213-14; Frank Vanderlip to James Stillman, 24 May 1912, 12 September 1912, part B, series 1, box 5, Frank A. Vanderlip Papers, Butler Library, Columbia University.

[49]Link, *Wilson: The New Freedom*, 214-27; McCulley, *Banks and Politics*, 297-300; Sklar, *United States as a Developing Country*, 131; James Livingston, *Origins of the Federal Reserve System: Money, Class, and Corporate Capitalism, 1890–1913* (Ithaca, N.Y.: Cornell University Press, 1986), 216-41; Frank Vanderlip to James Stillman, 15 August 1913, part B, series 1, box 5, Vanderlip Papers.

[50]*New York Times*, 24 June 1913; Livingston, *Origins of the Federal Reserve System*, 219; William G. McAdoo, *Crowded Years: The Reminiscences of William G. McAdoo* (Boston: Houghton Mifflin, 1931), 224-25, 247, 249; Vanderlip to Mann, 20 June 1913, part b, series 1, box 5, Vanderlip Papers. Vanderlip had been financial editor of the *Chicago Tribune* and from 1890 to 1901 was assistant secretary of the Treasury, so Mann surely knew him.

for legislation, and said that Republicans would gladly help write it, implicitly challenging the Democrats to permit a bipartisan approach.[51] That the Democrats would accede seemed highly unlikely, as Mann and everyone else knew. Republicans would be cast as opponents, as became evident when five of the six GOP members of Banking and Currency filed a minority report and Charles Lindbergh of Minnesota submitted a separate, critical report from a radical perspective. The five included insurgents Frank Woods and Everis Hayes.[52]

Some insurgents, including Lenroot, Cooper, and Haugen, liked the bill. But other insurgents and most regular Republicans bitterly attacked both the bill and the methods of the Democrats. Repeatedly, they depicted the currency issuing powers of the Reserve Board as akin to Bryan's free-silver schemes and blamed the currency provisions on Bryanites.[53] Mann, while still negative towards the bill, hedged his bets somewhat in recognition of the bill's growing popularity. He allowed his colleagues to do most of the talking, and in his own comments he stressed especially that the better parts of the bill were borrowed from the Aldrich bill of 1912, developed under Republican administrations by the National Monetary Commission. Defensively, too, Mann expounded on the growth and prosperity that had developed under Republican laws and administrations, even without a Federal Reserve Act.[54]

On 18 September the House passed the bill, 287–85.[55] Twenty-six Republicans voted for the bill and 81, Mann among them, opposed it. The insurgents divided almost evenly.[56] The Democratic steamroller had worked efficiently, but Senate prospects were uncertain. Whatever the outcome there, no doubt Mann was glad to be done with the bill. Republican conservatism had been affirmed in the House, but on an issue that was less auspicious politically than Mann had anticipated when he launched his attacks in June.

Soon after the currency bill cleared the House, Mann regained some of the political territory that had been lost. The Democrats gave him the opportunity. First, Wilson insisted that the House remain in session while the cur-

---

[51]*Philadelphia Public Ledger*, 12 July 1913, vol. 20, Mann Papers; McAdoo, *Crowded Years*, 248; *New York Times*, 2 September 1913.

[52]Greenlee, "Republican Party," 28.

[53]Kenneth W. Hechler, *Insurgency: Personalities and Politics of the Taft Era* (New York: Russell and Russell, 1964), 223; Gerald D. McKnight, "A Party against Itself— The Grand Old Party in the New Freedom Era, 1913–1916" (Ph.D. diss., University of Maryland, 1972), 37-38.

[54]*CR* 63:1, pp. 4993 (15 September 1913), 5064, 5100 (17 September 1913), 5659 (15 October 1913).

[55]*Ibid.*, p. 5129 (18 September 1913).

[56]Greenlee, "Republican Party," 35; Holt, *Congressional Insurgents*, 108.

rency bill was in the Senate Banking Committee, so that it could be adopted prior to the regular session in December. Keeping the House in session added to Wilson's pressure on Democratic senators, some of them dubious about the bill. Since there was only one bill requiring House action, an appropriations bill, and since the special session had already extended far beyond what was usual, most members left Washington. Under the circumstances, Underwood and his leadership colleagues would permit nothing of substance to be done, even in committee. Mann himself went home for several weeks, and in his absence Sereno Payne informally agreed that there would be no quorum calls. But when Mann returned on 7 October, refreshed in the outdoors and "feeling like a fighting cock," he quickly made a point of order that there was no quorum, in connection with the appropriations bill.[57] There was none, and a quorum call resulted, requiring the clerk to bring back absentees, a difficult and embarrassing task. As his price for lifting the quorum call, Mann forced the Democrats to capitulate on the rule governing the appropriations bill and permit debate and a vote on some of the Senate amendments. One of these would remove from the merit system deputy U.S. marshals and deputy revenue collectors, and Mann and other Republicans excoriated the Democrats for despoiling the civil service in their greed for patronage, a politically useful charge that had some basis in fact.[58]

Mann quickly made it clear what he thought should be done once the appropriations bill was disposed of. The House should adjourn for the session to allow members to refresh themselves for abundant and important legislation in the regular session. If the Democrats would not do that, but insisted on continuing, then members should return and transact real business. But if the Democrats would do neither of these things, then he proposed to put on record their absenteeism by forcing roll-call votes on daily adjournment motions, which he could force with but a one-fifth vote; and he would not agree to three day recesses or officially excusing certain members. "If the House remains in session I expect to remain here and to make it just as unpleasant as I possibly can for Democrats who go home," he warned. When it was pointed out that many Republicans were absent, Mann said "But we are not responsible for legislation."[59]

Mann acted on his threat, each day securing record votes on adjournment motions until finally, his point amply made, he relented and permitted three-day recesses. Before that, however, he embarrassed the Democrats in yet another way. Resolutions were offered on the subject of naval disarmament

[57]*Chicago Inter-Ocean*, 19 September 1913, vol. 20, Mann Papers; *Superior Telegram*, 19 September 1913; *CR* 63:1, pp. 5497 (7 October 1913), 5526 (9 October 1913).

[58]*CR* 63:1, pp. 5520-27 (9 October 1913), 5528-39 (10 October 1913).

[59]*Ibid.*, pp. 5526, 5538 (10 October 1913), 5609 (11 October 1913), 5659 (15 October 1913).

and calling for investigations of a coal strike and prisoner whippings in Delaware. Mann expressed support for the resolutions, but said that they were too important to be acted on by just a few members. Accordingly, he blocked them with points of order of no quorum, while putting the blame on Democrats for their absenteeism. Along the way Mann was also able to condemn Wilson as a dictatorial schoolmaster and chastise the House Democrats for supinely yielding by staying in session yet not working. His tactic was calculated not just for publicity but to encourage among House Democrats greater independence from the president in the future. His efforts won some newspaper attention.[60]

Mann's life was in the House chamber. He did not cultivate the press nor play to the press galleries, and he scorned those who did. Nevertheless, during and just after the special session he received increased press coverage. In a period when the GOP was struggling to recover from division and defeat, this publicity for the House minority leader benefited the party he represented. It had the further political effect of enhancing the importance of his present and future actions.

Most of the favorable publicity came from Republican newspapers and journals, which found in Mann someone to boast about. They described him physically and ran his photograph, told of his methods, praised his skills as a parliamentarian and student of all current legislation, and wrote of an affability and accessibility off the floor that made up for his occasional bitter sarcasm in debate. They noted his rapid rise from among the Cannon coterie to now stand alone at the top, his leadership unquestioned, and in one instance mentioned him as a strong presidential possibility.[61]

More important than this publicity is the fact that Mann emerged from the session with the confidence of his Republican colleagues, at least in the opinion of insurgent "Gussie" Gardner. Gardner reported that "Jim Mann is an excellent leader. More than half his followers are radical (or feel so at present). Jim is only radical in spots, and not in very many spots at that. Yet you would be surprised to know how much the boys think of him."

---

[60]For some of the adjournment votes and rejection of three-day recesses, see *CR* 63:1, pp. 5650 (13 October 1913), 5655, 5660 (15 October 1913), 5728 (21 October 1913), 5793 (22 October 1913), 5794 (23 October 1913). On the resolutions, see *CR* 63:1, pp. 5832 (13 October 1913), 5869, 5872 (6 November 1913), 5655-58 (15 October 1913), 5840 (1 November 1913). For press reports in the Mann Papers, *Pittsburgh Gazette*, 15 October 1913; *New York Post*, 17 October 1913; *Chicago Post*, 18 October 1913; and *Chicago Examiner*, 23 October 1913, vol. 20, Mann Papers.

[61]*Philadelphia Item*, 13 April 1913, vol. 17, Mann Papers; *Omaha World Herald*, 31 July 1913; *Washington National Tribune*, 7 August 1913, 11 December 1913; *Washington Star*, 28 September 1913, 26 October 1913; and *Seattle Post-Intelligencer*, 10 December 1913, vol. 20, Mann Papers; *Review of Reviews* 48:12 (July 1913): 11; *Current Opinion* 56 (January 1914): 17-18.

"Mann fights like a general who cleverly commands a beaten army in re-treat," Gardner continued. "He never unnecessarily exposes his troops on the cold hillside of a Yea and Nay vote, and he succeeds in harassing the en-emy not a little." Gardner correctly discerned Mann's conservative strategy, "to mark time until something happens," and acknowledged that such a view might be correct "if it were true that the Republican Party is a conservative party, while the Democratic Party and the Progressive Party are radical par-ties." Contentedly, Gardner thought that Mann was wrong about that, since the GOP had no appeal among southern conservatives. He would himself await developments that, he felt, would move the Republicans closer to the Democrats and Progressives in ideology, while still remaining to the right of them. Meanwhile, Mann seemed to him a skillful and useful leader.[62]

Just as Gardner was quite willing to follow the more conservative Mann, so insurgents reconciled themselves to the half a loaf proffered by the Re-publican National Committee in mid-December. Southern convention repre-sentation would be reduced as they wanted, but there would be no special convention to do it nor to put forth a program. State party conventions would be used to ratify the delegate distribution reform. Cummins and oth-ers were disappointed, but Republican election successes that summer and fall, especially in Maine in September, in a congressional district carried by Wilson in 1912, made future victories that much more likely and divisiveness that much more costly.[63]

On balance, Mann could review the first session of the Sixty-third Con-gress with satisfaction. Yet Progressives remained a threat, and Democrats still controlled in Washington and set the agenda. Ahead Mann could foresee battles on the trust question and on policies respecting Mexico, the Philip-pines, the Canal Zone, and more. What Mann could not foresee were the guns of August in Europe and a host of new issues related to war. As before, it would be Mann's task to unify his party to the extent possible, minimize the damage of such disunity as was unavoidable, and support the administra-tion as national and political necessity required, yet exploit the vulnerabilities of his enemies as they presented themselves. With the advantage of momen-tum, as the special session blended into the regular session without a break in time, Mann had grounds for optimism as to his own continuing leadership and his party's further recovery.

[62]Gardner to William H. Moody, 6 January 1914, Constance Gardner, ed., *Some Letters of Augustus Peabody Gardner* (Boston: Houghton Mifflin, 1920), 80-83.

[63]Greenlee, "Republican Party," 65-66, 70; Holt, *Congressional Insurgents, 105*; *Superior Telegram*, 9 September 1913; Hiram Johnson to George Perkins, 10 Septem-ber 1913; and Matthew Hale to Perkins, 10 September 1913, box 12, general file, Perkins Papers.

4

Election Year: 1914

Wilson addressed Congress at the start of the regular session on 2 December 1913. He called for action on twelve pieces of legislation, headed by antitrust and including repeal of the Panama Canal tolls exemption. Mann praised his speech and called it the work of a statesman, while not committing himself on specific proposals.[1] He could afford to be magnanimous and avoid major diversions, for his prediction of an economic slump was proving correct. That more than anything else would undermine the Democrats and restore the Republicans, he believed. On other matters he would have opportunity to take the offensive occasionally and at other times would play the part of constructive contributor. But these issues would be of secondary significance. Party unity would be important, but it would rest on the foundation of probusiness conservatism in the context of Democratic hard times.

Mann quickly began to make the case and exploit the economic situation. He caused something of a sensation in Washington when in mid-December he said that "the country is in the midst of a financial and industrial panic." Three days later he elaborated, citing news reports from Chicago and elsewhere of homelessness reminiscent of the 1890s. Mann attributed the situation to the tariff law, to fear of "political control of banking and currency," to other unspecified threats, and to a general lack of capacity to govern on the part of the Democrats. Speaker Clark took the floor to respond. He noted similar statements from Root, Cannon, Herbert Hadley, and Charles Hilles, chairman of the Republican National Committee, that suggested a conspiracy coinciding with the gathering of Republicans in Washington for a

---

[1]*New York Times*, 3 December 1913.

meeting of the National Committee. Undaunted, in February Mann made the case again, with fresh facts of unemployment and distress, springing, he said, from the tariff. Democrats denied his charges, but in fact gross national product did decline by 4 percent in 1914.[2]

As Mann had foreseen, the Senate did not pass the currency bill in the special session. When it did, in December, Mann continued in ritualistic opposition. He took the opportunity, as well, to talk again of unemployment, closed factories, and an absence of orders. The Democrats, he said, offered only old nostrums to inflate the currency through the new Federal Reserve System. The House nevertheless adopted the conference report, 298–60, and even the strongly Republican *New York Tribune* commended Wilson.[3]

Mann soon found what seemed a far better issue in a bill to repeal the tolls exemption in the Panama Canal for American coastal shipping, as Wilson requested. The president, mainly concerned about relations with Great Britain and other countries that objected to the exemption law of 1912, appeared before a joint session of Congress on 5 March to urge repeal. Though he talked of national honor, he did not say that the United States had violated the Hay-Pauncefote treaty, but only that there was doubt about it. Since repeal would be contrary to the 1912 Democratic platform, and for other reasons, a formidable group of Democrats quickly opposed Wilson, including the three top party leaders in the House, Underwood, Clark and Kitchin, as did the Hearst press and Irish-Americans outside Congress. Disgruntled Democrats were not prepared to break treaties, but they noted that Wilson had not made a clear case along those lines.[4]

"The issue we have been looking for so long has been sprung at last," the freshman Vermont Republican Frank Greene enthused, echoing a widespread opinion. "The President has at last forced a break with the strongest men in his party, or many of them, . . . and they have aligned themselves openly and squarely against what they publicly denounce as his un-American policy," Greene continued. "The line is clearly drawn: Wilson is charged with having

---

[2]*Ibid.*, 16 December 1913, 19 December 1913; *CR* 63:2, pp. 1169–72 (18 December 1913), 3472 (13 February 1914), 3764–68 (21 February 1914); Robert Higgs, *Crisis and Leviathan: Critical Episodes in the Growth of American Government* (New York: Oxford University Press, 1989), 107.

[3]*CR* 63:2, pp. 1463–64 (22 December 1913); Charles Seymour, ed., *The Intimate Papers of Colonel House* (Boston: Houghton, Mifflin, 1926), 1:166.

[4]Arthur S. Link, Wilson: *The New Freedom* (Princeton, N.J.: Princeton University Press, 1956), 304–14; Evans C. Johnson, *Oscar W. Underwood: A Political Biography* (Baton Rouge: Louisiana State University Press, 1980), 220; Homer Larry Ingle, "Pilgrimage to Reform: A Life of Claude Kitchin" (Ph.D. diss., University of Wisconsin, 1967), 85; John M. Blum, *Joe Tumulty and the Wilson Era* (Boston: Houghton Mifflin, 1951), 69–71; Frank Greene to Joseph Auld, 9 March 1914, box 1, Frank L. Greene Papers, Library of Congress.

been euchred by the British and with now demanding an unconditional surrender to our ancient foe and rival, and there is no telling where it will end.
The day of his domination of Congress is over, unless I am mistaken."[5]

Albert Burleson, armed with post-office patronage, swung into action
among House Democrats, abetted by Wilson's politically astute secretary,
Joseph Tumulty, and by Bryan. They had the advantage over Underwood,
who was running for the Senate and likely to win and therefore lacked the
threat of future reprisals in committee assignments.[6] Before overflowing galleries, debate began on a restrictive rule to limit debate to twenty hours and
bar amendments. The real test of strength came in votes on the question,
approved 208–177, and the rule, adopted 200–173, despite Mann's arguments.[7] Nevertheless, an atmosphere of tension and drama persisted as debate began on the repeal bill, sponsored by Thetus Sims. Champ Clark was
the object of greatest interest as he took the floor to oppose Wilson's proposal. But Mann played a significant role as the principal spokesman for Republican opponents of the bill.

Mann concluded debate for his side in a long speech. He gave main attention to America's treaty rights and exhaustively restated and amplified on
a history he had recounted before. He showed that special terms had been
granted to Panama and others and said that it was absurd to say that the
United States could grant more to Panama than to itself. He concluded with
less technical remarks, including the comment that while many Democrats
excused themselves as having to follow the president, "On our side of the
House Members of Congress may think." After a final peroration on justice,
fairness, and American rights, Mann got "loud and continued applause."[8]

The vote that followed showed the impact of administration pressure.
The bill passed, 247–162, after a recommittal motion lost by 176–231.
Democrats divided 220–52 in favor. The Republicans opposed the bill by a
margin of 93–23.[9]

As the battle shifted to the Senate, Mann continued to see great party advantage in the issue. He interpreted the results of a special election in New
Jersey and Underwood's strong victory in Alabama as repudiations of Wilson, and said, "Tolls and the tariff will be the issue from now on."[10]

---

[5]Frank Greene to Frank E. Howe, 29 March 1914, box 3, Greene Papers.

[6]John J. Broesamle, *William Gibbs McAdoo: A Passion for Change, 1863–1917*
(Port Washington, N.Y.: Kennikat Press, 1973), 213; Elston E. Roady, "Party Regularity in the Sixty-third Congress" (Ph.D. diss., University of Illinois, 1951), 179,
202; DeAlva S. Alexander, *History and Procedure of the House of Representatives*
(Boston: Houghton Mifflin, 1916), 135–36.

[7]*New York Times*, 28 March 1914; *CR* 63:2, pp. 5565–66, 5678 (26 March 1914).

[8]*CR* 63:2, pp. 5945–51 (31 March 1914).

[9]*Ibid.*, pp. 6088–89 (31 March 1914); *New York Times*, 1 April 1914.

[10]*CR* 63:2, pp. 6409–11 (8 April 1914); *New York Times*, 9 April 1914.

By June he had changed his mind. An amended bill passed the Senate, 50–35. While 22 Republicans opposed it, 13 were in favor. Among these, and highly vocal, were the well-respected foreign policy experts Lodge and Root. Furthermore, outside the Senate prestigious Republicans Henry White and Joseph Choate backed repeal, as did the Carnegie Foundation and business representatives. Taft and Philander Knox were outraged by this repudiation of their actions, and the ranks of Republican regulars split badly.[11] An administration compromise amendment, saying that no rights under the Hay-Pauncefote Treaty or from other sources were being yielded, offered a way out, and on 12 June, while still denouncing the repeal bill, Mann voted for it.[12] What initially had seemed to Mann a political bonanza proved to be no issue at all. But one political benefit for the GOP was the exposure of Democratic division and residual hard feelings towards the administration among some House Democrats.

For a time, administration policy towards Mexico looked politically promising for Republicans, but it yielded only sparse fruit in 1914. The longtime ruler Porfirio Diaz had given way to the democratic Francisco Madero in a 1911 revolution. Madero, however, was first displaced and then assassinated by General Victoriano Huerta, who in October 1913 made himself a dictator. Wilson, differing with European powers, refused to recognize Huerta because he came to power illegitimately, and he hoped that Huerta would be defeated by leaders in the north, Venustiano Carranza and his lieutenant, Francisco Villa. Wilson took no overt action for a time, instead pursuing the policy of "watchful waiting." In February, however, he revoked the arms embargo on Carranza, even though most abuses against Americans and their property occurred where he and Villa were in control.[13]

Mann in the House, like Root and Lodge in the Senate, at first treated the situation as nonpartisan.[14] In October, though, Mann began to mildly criticize the administration from seemingly opposing yet reconcilable standpoints—that it was not holding Mexico responsible for damages to Americans, but also that it was preparing for an unwise war.[15] Early in 1914 Frederick Gillett of Massachusetts and Frank Mondell stepped up the criticism of

---

[11]Gerald D. McKnight, "Republican Leadership and the Mexican Question, 1913–1916: A Failed Bid for Party Resurgence," *Mid-America* 62 (April-July 1980): 113–14.

[12]Roady, "Party Regularity," 220; Rena Mitchell, "The Congressional Career of James R. Mann" (M.A. thesis, University of Chicago, 1938), 56–57; *CR* 63:2, p. 10341 (12 June 1914).

[13]Link, *Wilson: The New Freedom*, 347–91; August Heckscher, *Woodrow Wilson* (New York: Charles Scribner's Sons, 1991), 298–300.

[14]McKnight, "Republican Leadership and the Mexican Question," 106–8; *CR* 63:1, pp. 3529 (19 August 1913), 4230 (4 September 1913).

[15]*CR* 63:2, p. 5578 (10 October 1913); *New York Times*, 4 December 1913.

Wilson, and in March Mann attracted some attention when he contrasted Roosevelt's forceful handling of the kidnapping of an American by a Moroccan bandit with Wilson's "watchful waiting" in the face of "murder, rape, and robbery" perpetrated in Mexico on Americans. His comments were well received in the House, and other Republicans followed his lead.[16]

An April incident at Tampico gave Wilson an excuse to intervene. Sailors from an American navy ship who landed without permission to get supplies were briefly arrested. Admiral Henry Mayo insisted on a formal apology, punishment of the officer responsible, and a twenty-one-gun salute. Huerta would comply, but asked for a comparable American salute, which Mayo refused. Wilson, influenced by Mayo and by news of a German ship steaming towards Veracruz with arms for Huerta, decided on an American occupation of Tampico and Veracruz. He thought that this would be bloodless and would be helpful to Carranza. Accordingly, he sent the North Atlantic battle fleet to the area. Then, after fruitless negotiations with Huerta, on 20 April Wilson came before Congress to get its backing for intervention. It was, he said, to secure Huerta's recognition of American rights and dignity and did not entail war.[17]

Observers expected swift and strong congressional support for the president, and it came. But in the House a number of Republicans led by Mann vigorously dissented. Mann insisted on ample time for debate, which he began and ended for his side. "Mr. Speaker," Mann said, "if the incident which the President narrated to us had occurred with England or Germany or France or any other great power there would be no resolution like this pending now. But because Mexico is weak," he continued, "we think that we have the moral right to declare practical war against her in the high hope that success is easily accomplished." Then he chided Wilson for not seeking advice, as he professed, but presenting Congress with a fait accompli. He criticized the Democrats for hastily supporting what he construed as a virtual declaration of war. Mann questioned the wisdom of such a declaration and said that the United States would become the ally "of the murderous crew in the north of Mexico now engaged in murdering men and outraging women." He would not condone the way Huerta had come to power, but would not go to war with him just because Wilson did not like him. "That is the real reason for the resolution," he said. Mann dodged the question as to whether he would recognize Huerta, but said that he would support action to stop the destruction of lives and property in the north.

---

[16]Howard Scott Greenlee, "The Republican Party in Division and Reunion, 1913–1920" (Ph.D. diss., University of Chicago, 1950), 42; *CR* 63:2, p. 5197 (20 March 1914); *New York Times*, 4 March 1914, 21 March 1914.

[17]Link, *Wilson: The New Freedom*, 394–98; Heckscher, *Woodrow Wilson*, 328–29; Robert E. Quirk, *An Affair of Honor: Woodrow Wilson and the Occupation of Veracruz* (Lexington: University of Kentucky Press, 1962), 73–75.

A number of Democrats set out to refute Mann, and several noted his belligerence in advance of the Spanish-American War. As debate ended, Mann responded to that. He frankly repudiated his actions in 1898, which he attributed to youth and inexperience. "I have seen the results of the Spanish War, and have seen that no one can foretell what will be the result of a war." The Philippines, Puerto Rico, and Hawaii were acquired, the army and navy greatly expanded, and partly as a result of that other nations' navies had grown. "I do not believe that it is possible for us to have a war with Mexico and ever leave Mexico," he warned, and he did not welcome the responsibility.[18]

The House approved the resolution, 337–37. Republicans divided 73–29 in favor.[19] But Mann had not isolated himself. One of the Republicans who voted to support the resolution, Frank Greene, confided that "most of us who voted to support the President . . . did so with disgust in our mouths but it came to the plain matter of fact that he had backed us into a mess by his fatuous policy of 'watchful waiting' and no matter how he got there he was there and we were there with him." Nicholas Murray Butler congratulated Mann on his speech, and in the Senate Lodge attempted to broaden the resolution to encompass the situation in northern Mexico.[20]

Neither Wilson's expectations nor Mann's were fulfilled. To Wilson's surprise, Mexicans strongly resisted at Veracruz and both sides suffered heavy casualties. But the larger war and occupation that Mann and others had foreseen did not occur either, for Wilson was able to extricate his forces by accepting the mediation of Argentina, Brazil, and Chile. For that reason the Mexican issue did not loom large in 1914.[21] The situation in Mexico was by no means settled when in July Huerta fled to Spain and Carranza took over, however, and Republicans tried to capitalize on it in 1916.

Despite his years and experience, Mann remained more authoritative on domestic economic questions than in matters of foreign policy. The twin issues of antitrust legislation and creation of a trade commission reached the floor in May and gave Mann opportunity to score political points, appeal to business, and also continue in the long-term effort to define the Republican party as constructively conservative. Some division between insurgents and regulars like Mann was inevitable on antitrust, but it was not severe enough to prove permanently disruptive. As in other important matters, Republicans benefited by not being responsible for legislating. Mann's well-known penchant for independence also softened the blow for insurgents. The impact of

---

[18]CR 63:2, pp. 6934, 6937, 6956 (20 April 1914).

[19]Ibid., p. 6957 (20 April 1914); New York Times, 21 April 1914.

[20]Greene to Luther B. Johnson, 21 April 1914, box 3, Greene Papers; Butler to Mann, 21 April 1914, James R. Mann file, Nicholas Murray Butler Papers, Butler Library, Columbia University; Link, Wilson: The New Freedom, 399.

[21]Greenlee, "Republican Party," 44.

division on antitrust was further reduced for Republicans by their general agreement in favor of the trade commission bill.

The administration's approach at the start was to push for a strong antitrust bill to amend the Sherman Act. The bill spelled out a variety of proscribed monopolistic practices and specified criminal penalties. In effect, the Supreme Court's rule of reason would be overturned. The companion bill, for a weak trade commission built on the experience of the Bureau of Corporations, was less important to the administration.[22]

The antitrust bill got full House attention in May. It was named for the chairman of Judiciary, Henry Clayton, but by then he had become a judge and on the floor the bill was managed by Edwin Y. Webb of North Carolina.[23] Although the Democrats approved the bill in a binding party caucus, they permitted submission of amendments, and Webb accepted a few. To a limited degree, therefore, such insurgents as Lenroot could participate. Since the bill descended from one largely drawn by Brandeis and Lenroot for La Follette, the Wisconsin congressman and like-minded members had reason to favor its general terms and be glad to cooperate in the bill's perfection and adoption to the extent permitted.[24]

Most Republicans stood in opposition and found themselves in a position to exploit the overextension of Democratic lines. That there should be new legislation relating to monopolistic practices no one doubted. But businessmen and journalists had great doubts as to the timing and specifics of the Clayton bill. The economy remained in the doldrums, and businessmen had not yet fully adjusted to the new tariff and banking laws. Congress and the business community should get a rest, businessmen and newspapers argued.[25] In a Chamber of Commerce national poll of businessmen, strong majorities favored a trade commission and prohibition of interlocking directorates and holding companies, which created "trusts." But respondents ever more strongly opposed prohibitions on price discrimination and exclusive contracts. In addition, over the years business organizations seeking to mold legislation had opposed criminal penalties. Small businessmen, especially,

[22]Thomas K. McCraw, *Prophets of Regulation: Charles Francis Adams, Louis D. Brandeis, James M. Landis, Alfred E. Kahn* (Cambridge, Mass.: Belknap Press of Harvard University Press, 1984), 119–28.

[23]Roady, "Party Regularity," 275.

[24]*Ibid.*, 279; Herbert F. Margulies, *Senator Lenroot of Wisconsin: A Political Biography, 1900–1929* (Columbia: University of Missouri Press, 1977), 118–19, 169; David Sarasohn, *The Party of Reform: Democrats in the Progressive Era* (Jackson: University Press of Mississippi, 1989), 169.

[25]Frank Vanderlip to James Stillman, 26 June 1914, part B, series 1, box 6 Frank A. Vanderlip Papers, Butler Library, Columbia University; "The President's Renewed Attack on the Trusts," *Literary Digest*, 48:17 (25 April 1914): 967–68; "Psychological Hard Times," *Literary Digest*, 48:24 (13 June 1914): 1420–21.

were leery of these features of the Clayton bill.[26] Many Democratic House members and leaders, headed by Underwood, themselves preferred a rest and delay and feared disturbing business, but they were driven by Wilson's pressure. Prolabor Democrats also pressed for quick action, for the bill contained provisions that unions construed as protecting them from court injunctions under antitrust law.[27]

While the bill was in Committee of the Whole, Mann limited himself to routine matters. He explained that he would not discuss a whole section "largely for physical reasons." His most pointed criticisms in this limiting context were of the labor sections and in defense of the courts. Other regulars took up the slack for him, warning especially of disturbing business.[28] Mann was one of 51 Republicans who on 5 June voted against the bill, while 44 favored it. The overall vote was 277–54.[29] On the same day, the House passed the trade commission bill and also a measure for regulation of railroad securities, which later failed in the Senate. Mann stepped to the fore with comments to the press on the bills. The *New York Times* ran his statement on page one, accompanied by shorter comments from Murdock and a Democrat.

"There is nothing in any of the Democratic anti-trust bills that will build a fire that is not out, start a factory, or in any way encourage business," Mann began. "The measures are repressive. There was a demand for legislation supplementary to the anti-trust law that would permit business to be conducted without uncertainty as to its rights. The Clayton bill adds to and does not remove any of the uncertainty that now exists. If enacted into law it will do a great deal of harm." Backtracking on the sweeping generalization with which he had begun, Mann more accurately stated his view on the trade commission bill, which had passed with little opposition and no record vote. He noted Republican origins for the idea and said, "It may serve a useful purpose by bringing business and government into closer relationship." The Clayton bill, on the other hand, he called "dangerous." "No one can do busi-

---

[26]McCraw, *Prophets of Regulation*, 120–21; Kendrick A. Clements, *The Presidency of Woodrow Wilson* (Laurence,: University Press of Kansas, 1992), 48; Martin J. Sklar, *The Corporate Reconstruction of American Capitalism, 1890–1916: The Market, The Law, and Politics* (Cambridge, Eng.: Cambridge University Press, 1988), 281; Link, *Wilson: The New Freedom*, 434.

[27]Frank Vanderlip to James Stillman, 2 May 1914, 9 May 1914, part B, series 1, box 6 Vanderlip Papers; Eileen Lorenzi McDonagh, "Electoral Bases of Policy Innovation in the Progressive Era: The Impact of Grass Roots Opinion on Roll-Call Voting in the House of Representatives, Sixty-third Congress, 1913–1915," *Journal of Policy History* 4 (1992): 170.

[28]*CR* 63:2, pp. 9669 (2 June 1914), 8839 (19 May 1914), 9653, 9668 (2 June 1914); Greenlee, "Republican Party," 38.

[29]Greenlee, "Republican Party," 39.

ness . . . without having the penitentiary facing him all the time. Every business transaction will be left liable to a criminal charge. It is sufficient to say that it is Democratic legislation."[30]

Wilson reversed course five days later. He decided to shift emphasis to a stronger trade commission bill while abandoning the Clayton bill to an unpromising fate in the Senate. He changed his mind partly in recognition of business feeling and political hazards.[31] The switch, which Democrats implemented in the Senate and in conference, staved off political disaster. Wilson further improved his position by stating in October that his economic program was now nearly done.[32] Mann, however, with his regular colleagues, had fortified the association in the public mind between the GOP and business, especially small business, and had also fortified the actual attachment. These associations were politically advantageous in the short run, especially because of the slump in the economy, and consequential in the long run, in the continuing development of the GOP.

Significant elements in the business community, represented by such organizations as the National Civic Federation, had for years sought a regulatory alternative to antitrust prosecutions, and as attention shifted to the trade commission bill, Mann renewed his and his party's association with these elements. Although Mann had supported the weak bill that passed the House on 5 June, he had no objections to a stronger measure drafted by a Brandeis associate, George Rublee, and sponsored by Democrat Ray Stevens of New Hampshire. The heart of the bill, as adopted in the Senate and embraced in the joint conference, was to outlaw "unfair methods of competition," allow a bipartisan commission of five to define that term, and then to issue cease-and-desist orders. The Federal Trade Commission (FTC) got no powers to regulate and license and thereby control prices, as some progressives had wanted. But neither could the FTC give advice and immunization from antitrust to business, as some businessmen wanted. Rublee thought that "unfair methods of competition" had clear meaning based on court decisions and legislation, but such was not the case. That and some other factors worked against the future success of the FTC. As of 1914, however, some of the vagueness of the bill added to its attractiveness, as it came to mean all things to all men.[33]

---

[30]*New York Times*, 6 June 1914.

[31]McCraw, *Prophets of Regulation*, 121–22; Heckscher, *Woodrow Wilson*, 324; Clements, *Presidency of Woodrow Wilson*, 49.

[32]Lewis L. Gould, *Reform and Regulation: American Politics from Roosevelt to Wilson*, 2nd ed. (New York: Alfred A. Knopf, 1986), 186.

[33]McCraw, *Prophets of Regulation*, 124–25; Sklar, *Corporate Reconstruction*, 330; Robert H. Wiebe, *Businessmen and Reform: A Study of the Progressive Movement* (Cambridge, Mass.: Harvard University Press, 1962), 141.

Although in the Senate the bill had encountered opposition from some Republican regulars,[34] when on 10 September the conference report reached the House, Mann was effusive in praise of the House conferees and the bill. He could afford such generous congratulations partly because his party had developed the regulatory approach over the years and had participated fully in the joint conference, as he noted. Related to that, he felt himself entitled to some of the credit for the legislation. He had pioneered in creation of the FTC's ancestor, the Bureau of Corporations; more recently he had been consulted from the inception of the bill through the conference by Democrat James Covington of Maryland, sponsor of the initial House bill and senior House conferee, and by the ranking Republican on Interstate and Foreign Commerce and in the conference, his old friend and ally Fred Stevens of Minnesota.[35]

Turning to the bill itself, Mann put his probusiness orientation in modern and moderate context. "We can not afford to destroy business. We cannot afford not to exercise some control over business," he said. The bill did not go too far, yet went "further than we have ever gone before." He recognized the vagueness of "unfair methods of competition," and that some uncertainty would result, but he believed that FTC decisions and court judgments on appeal would bring clarification. The purpose of the bill was pro-, not antibusiness. "We are moving in the direction of controlling the methods of competition, endeavoring to keep open the lines of competition so that everyone will have a fair show." He would have preferred that FTC judgment on a practice bring with it antitrust exemption, but acknowledged the legislative difficulties in that. On the surface, at least, Mann spoke for his party in the House, as the bill quickly passed without a record vote.[36]

When the somewhat emasculated Clayton bill returned from conference in October, regulars were no happier with it than before, while a number of insurgents were disgusted at its weakening, and eighteen of them joined the opposition in the voting. Mann's negative comments belong in a different context.[37]

Prior to the onset of the Great War in Europe in late July and early August, Republican political prospects seemed bright, as Republicans effectively blamed the Democrats for "the empty dinner pail," caused, they said, by the Underwood tariff and the hasty pace of reform, with consequent business uncertainty. In truth, the economic slump was worldwide. Nevertheless, in late June Frank Vanderlip was able to write, on the basis of reports from all over the country, that "the administration is losing support at an

---

[34]Link, *Wilson: The New Freedom*, 434.

[35]*CR* 63:2, pp. 14939–40 (1 September 1914); *CR* 63:3, pp. 1584–85 (14 January 1915).

[36]*CR* 63:2, pp. 14940, 14943 (10 September 1914).

[37]Greenlee, "Republican Party," 40; *CR* 63:2, p. 16340 (8 October 1914).

astonishing rate." Other observers agreed that the people were in a conservative mood, to the extent that Charles Van Hise, president of the University
of Wisconsin, correctly discerned that even in his progressive state conservatives might win in 1914.[38]

Popular disillusionment with the Democrats benefited the Republicans,
not the Progressives, and by midyear Mann and others observed that massive
Progressive defections to the GOP were in process.[39] Mann had contributed
to the tendency, for he was partly responsible for a situation that Progressive
Medill McCormick of Illinois ruefully described in January: "So far the Republicans in Washington have managed to occupy the front of the stage in
antagonism to the Democracy."[40]

Mann's probusiness stances helped put his party in a position to capitalize
on economic disturbance and dissatisfaction among businessmen, but Mann
supplemented that basic approach. On secondary though not inconsequential
issues, he took progressive stances in accordance with the Rooseveltian tradition. Both he and his party had made a moderate progressive record until
the late stages of the Roosevelt presidency and again under Taft. Adherence
to that tradition, albeit within a larger context of economic conservatism,
continued to offer political benefits by mollifying and strengthening the insurgents, both luring and embarrassing Progressives, and putting Democrats
on the defensive.

"I think I can see a very steady drift toward the rehabilitation of the
G.O.P. along lines that are more likely to be wise and truly progressive than
have been the alignment for some time," the moderate Frank Greene wrote
in April.[41] The tendency continued through the session and was especially
evident respecting conservation issues. Consistent with his record, Mann
took the lead.

Two of five conservation bills urged by Secretary of Interior Franklin K.
Lane bore upon Alaska. The first of these would authorize the government
to spend $35,000,000 to build a railroad to open up coal resources. Neither

---

[38]Heckscher, *Woodrow Wilson*, 324; George Perkins to Theodore Roosevelt, 14
April 1914, 24 April 1914, box 12 general file, George W. Perkins Papers, Butler Library, Columbia University; Vanderlip to James Stillman, 26 June 1914, part B, series
1, box 6, Vanderlip Papers.

[39]*CR* 63:2, p. 9661 (2 June 1914); Frank Greene to Howard Hindley, 31 July
1914, box 2, Greene Papers; Robert Sherman La Forte, *Leaders of Reform: Progressive
Republicans in Kansas, 1900–1916* (Lawrence: University Press of Kansas, 1974), 220,
226–27, 232–33; Martin L. Fausold, *Gifford Pinchot, Bull Moose Progressive*
(Syracuse: Syracuse University Press, 1961), 137–38; Gould, *Reform and Regulation*,
187–88.

[40]McCormick to Victor Murdock, 19 January 1914, box 52, Victor Murdock Papers, Library of Congress.

[41]Greene to Luther B. Johnson, 21 April 1914, box 3, Greene Papers.

party was united on the measure. Many westerners were wary of federal in-trusion, and Frank Mondell, former chairman of the Lands Committee, best represented that element on the Republican side. Such other Republicans as Madden, Moore, and Gillett also opposed the bill, reflecting conservative skepticism of a measure that smacked of socialism. Some Democrats shared that view and also feared stretching the Constitution. Thus, when the House began to consider the Senate's bill, Mann's strong support for it was conse-quential, since the outcome was in doubt and many Republicans would fol-low his lead.

Mann likened Democratic objections to those made to the Panama Canal, the Department of Commerce and Labor, the pure food law, and the white slave law, all measures with which he was identified. Because the government does a few things does not mean that it must do everything, he said—projects should be considered on their merits. He was not optimistic about Alaska's resources, but who could tell? Those resources, however great or little, belonged to the whole country, he argued, and should be developed.[42] Mann continued active on the bill on the following two Calendar Wednes-days until on 18 February it passed, 232–86.[43] A second bill, for leasing of Alaska coal lands, inevitably followed, and Mann took a minor supporting role in its consideration and adoption.[44]

A reclamation bill was not contentious, but the other parts of Lane's pro-gram were—one relating to the leasing and development of waterpower sites and the other to a leasing system for federal mineral lands. Following a White House negotiation presided over by Wilson, a compromise bill governing the leasing of waterpower sites on navigable streams reached the floor late in July. Though conservationists Lenroot and Kent had already gotten the bet-ter of the more development-minded Judge Adamson, who sponsored the bill, another progressive group headed by Democrat Swagar Sherley of Lou-isville, Kentucky, abetted from outside by Harry Slattery, now pushed for an amendment for annual charges on the developers, readjustable by the secre-tary of war after twenty years and every tenth year after that. The secretary of war had charge of navigable streams outside the public domain. In a nine-minute speech Mann threw his support to the Sherley amendment. He thought that it was constitutional, that it would not discourage investors, that government should conserve waterpower, and that the government could be relied on to treat investors fairly. The amendment passed, 143–45. When the House finished with the bill on 4 August, Mann continued effec-tively active. Senators were more conservative, and no legislation eventuated

[42]*CR* 63:2, pp. 2956–58 (5 February 1914).

[43]*Ibid.*, pp. 3353, 3358–59, 3362 (11 February 1914), 3617–21, 3646–47 (18 Feb-ruary 1914).

[44]*Ibid.*, pp. 14688–99 (3 September 1914), 16672–73 (15 October 1914).

that year, but the House's progressive stand was significant in the ongoing battle for legislation in a field that was of rapidly growing importance.[45]

The House took up a companion measure covering waterpower sites on public lands in Committee of the Whole for several days in August. Attendance was sparse in these "dog days." Fewer than forty members voted on many amendments, and Mann, who scrutinized each section and amendment with great care, was studiously deferred to by Public Lands Committee chairman Scott Ferris, who acknowledged of Mann that "he commands more votes on both sides of the aisle than any of the other of us." On balance, Mann was successful in defending the committee's nationalist position against the states' rights, developer-oriented westerners led by Mondell and Democrat Edward Taylor of Colorado. Like the other waterpower bill, this one passed the House, died in the Senate, yet was not inconsequential as an episode in a long story.[46]

In September the House took up and passed the last of the major conservation measures for the session. The bill set out to establish a system of leasing, with regulations and royalties, for mineral lands in the 700,000,000 acres of public domain, to replace various outmoded laws. Mann, with threats against unanimous consent agreements, forced a slower pace and closer scrutiny of the bill than Ferris wanted. Taking a very active part, Mann stood especially for adequate royalty compensation to the government, and he got his way. Though the House and Senate failed to agree, as with the waterpower bills, the House's action had long-run significance.[47] What is noteworthy politically is that on the conservation measures generally, except for Sherley in one instance, no high-level Democrat with visibility comparable to Mann's even attempted to identify himself and indirectly his party with the popular conservation cause.

Mann put his party in a more progressive and favorable light than the Democrats on several labor questions. Though he did not get the legislation, he won the approbation of the American Association for Labor Legislation when he introduced a bill to create a bureau of labor safety in the Department of Labor.[48] He was more successful legislatively, and with greater po-

[45]Margulies, *Senator Lenroot*, 178–83; *CR* 63:2, pp. 12906, 12908 (28 July 1914), 13254–55 (4 August 1914).

[46]*CR* 63:2, pp. 13677–78, 13700–13780 (13 August 1914), 13935–37 (18 August 1914), 14048–50, 14054–55, 14058–59, 14063–67 (20 August 1914), 14181–83 (24 August 1914). Ferris's remark is at p. 14064 (20 August 1914).

[47]J. Leonard Bates, *The Origins of Teapot Dome: Progressives, Parties, and Petroleum, 1909–1921* (Urbana: University of Illinois Press, 1963), 48–51; Margulies, *Senator Lenroot*, 175–78; *CR* 63:2, pp. 15170–78; (15 September 1914), 15384–85, 15291–93, 15296 (17 September 1914), 15417–18 (19 September 1914).

[48]*Chicago Record-Herald*, 1 January 1914, vol. 19, James R. Mann Papers, Library of Congress.

litical advantage, in connection with several appropriations. The most important of these was for the Children's Bureau. According to a young Democrat
from Colorado, Edward Keating, Mann was moved to take up the cause by
his admiration for the head of the bureau, Julia Lathrop, and for her Illinois
family, and by Miss Lathrop's appeal to him to win restoral of funds the Appropriations Committee proposed to cut. Whatever the case, Mann championed the bureau, battling first on several parliamentary points and then on
the substantive question of a proposed investigation of infant mortality. His
chief foe was a South Carolina Democrat, Joseph Johnson. Republicans
charged southern Democrats generally with opposing the bureau because of
their area's heavy dependence on child labor. After a two-day battle in mid-
April, the House passed an amendment offered by insurgent Republican
James Good of Iowa, a member of Appropriations, after Mann's side won a
point-of-order vote by 113–95. The Good amendment raised the appropriation to $139,000 from the $25,000 originally specified and the $50,000 that
Good initially sought.[49]

Mann was also active and successful in support of a motion by an Illinois
Democrat, Frank Buchanan, to increase the appropriation for the commis-
sioners of conciliation in the Labor Department from $25,000 to $50,000;
and Mann won adoption of his own amendment to allow the hiring of a permanent employee in place of temporary conciliators paid no more than ten
dollars a day. Mann described the recent history of conciliation and praised
the effort to head off strikes. No doubt he was not displeased when several
southern Democrats opposed him. Earlier in the session he had chided the
Democrats for having opposed the higher appropriation in August.[50]

None of these mildly progressive actions conflicted with or diverted
Mann from his preoccupation with commerce. Just before taking up the
conciliation issue, he credited the minority on Appropriations for causing
the committee to increase funds for promotion of foreign and domestic
commerce by the Commerce Department.[51]

Several of the important issues that arose early in the session bore no
clear-cut relationship to progressivism versus conservatism. First came immigration, then rural roads. On the immigration bill, although party lines were
scrambled, the role Mann played won him approbation in the House and
praise outside, to the advantage of his party. Rural roads were a popular
Democratic issue whose political importance Mann blunted by throwing his
own support to the bill.

[49]Edward Keating, *The Gentleman from Colorado: A Memoir* (Denver: Sage
Books, 1964), 358–59; *CR* 63:2, pp. 6710–13 (14 April 1914), 6811–13 (16 April
1914); *Chicago Tribune*, 16 April 1914, vol. 19, Mann Papers.
[50]*CR* 63:2, pp. 6697–6702 (14 April 1914), p. 3850 (24 February 1914).
[51]*Ibid.*, p. 6690 (14 April 1914).

Proponents of drastic restriction of immigration by means of a literacy test, having failed to override Taft's veto in 1912, now tried again. The House fiercely debated that feature of the immigration bill on the evening of 31 January. Ending the debate, Mann spoke against the literacy test in what the *New York Times* called "an eloquent plea." "The attention which the House gave Mr. Mann's speech and the applause it received rather startled the leaders," the *Times* noted, and the paper quoted Mann. He agreed with those who would exclude immigrants who could not be assimilated, but he was unwilling to judge the ability or character of a man on the basis of whether he had had the opportunity to learn to read. Such opportunity was abundant in America, he said, but not in foreign lands. "There ought to be other tests which will enable us to properly restrict immigration." America should remain the hope of the ignorant and the oppressed.[52] No one thought that the literacy test would be stricken from the bill, and it was not. The livelier question was whether the House later would override a veto, and Mann's remarks made that less likely.

Mann was more immediately successful in opposing several amendments to exclude Asians altogether, as urged by Californians of both parties. Relations with Japan were already tenuous because of discriminatory land legislation adopted in California in 1913, and Secretary Bryan had warned against offensive federal legislation prior to delicate negotiations. Culminating a spirited debate, Mann urged against all anti-Asian amendments on foreign relations grounds. He deplored anything that might invite war or interfere with American diplomacy. Mann made it clear that he was not finding fault with Everis Hayes, California Republican and author of the amendment currently before the House, but was directing his remarks to non-Californians, who were freer of constituent pressure. Swagar Sherley made a similar appeal to Democrats, and the House rejected the Hayes amendment, 54–203. The *New York Times* credited Mann for the overwhelming vote and described his "stirring appeal" as the feature of the debate.[53]

If Mann stood with the heavily immigrant cities in opposition to the emotion laden literacy test, he was willing to defer to the countryside on the matter of annual federal support for rural roads, to be accomplished constitutionally in terms of the federal postal function.[54] Mann acknowledged that the cities, which paid most of the income tax, would give more than they would get, but he saw no way to legislate for proportional benefits. The

[52]*New York Times*, 1 February 1914; *CR* 63:2, p. 7714 (31 January 1914).
[53]*CR* 63:2, pp. 2822, 2825 (3 February 1914); *New York Times*, 4 February 1914.
[54]*CR* 63:2, p. 2911 (4 February 1914).

Democrats stood to gain in fulfilling a popular platform pledge, but the overwhelming House vote, 282–42, lent the measure a bipartisan flavor.[55]

On balance, until war came in Europe, it was the Republicans who were confidently on the offensive and gaining rapidly. Then suddenly the situation changed, and the Democrats, behind Wilson, righted themselves. Those of German stock in the American population were second only to English-Americans in number, and early sentiment as between the Central Powers—Germany and Austria-Hungary—and the Allies—Great Britain, France, and Russia—roughly divided on ethnic lines. But the nearly universal popular desire to stay out of the war transcended diverse sympathies. Thus, when on 19 August President Wilson called on Americans to be neutral not only in deeds but in thought, he was easily excused for asking the impossible and gratefully applauded for his larger goal of neutrality. Even after pro-Allies sentiment gained because of Germany's invasion of Belgium and atrocity stories, through 1914 and beyond, neutrality remained the watchword for Americans. In pursuance of that goal, Wilson assumed the role of the captain of a vessel in turbulent waters, the man whose lead patriots must accept and follow. Furthermore, Democrats could now blame economic troubles on the war, rather than on the economic policies that Republicans had persistently indicted.[56]

Although the Republican party lost its momentum with the onset of war, it was not put wholly on the defensive. With Mann among the leaders, the GOP met the situation in two ways. It minimized damage by heartily agreeing to neutrality and such measures as the war required. At the same time, it found grounds for criticism of administration policies and practices that dovetailed with and broadened the strong probusiness appeal that the party had been successfully using since the start of the Sixty-third Congress.

Mann's overall outlook suited the immediate needs of his party. For years he had been on the fringe of the organized peace movement in America. Most recently, in 1913 and early 1914, he had voted to limit the increase in the battleship fleet to one vessel, and he strongly supported a resolution calling for a one-year international moratorium on naval construction. The main qualification that he advanced concerned the need for naval strength in the Pacific, where in May 1914 he saw trouble with Japan that was too delicate to discuss in Congress.[57] As the European alliance system kicked into

---

[55]*Ibid.*, p. 3284 (10 February 1914); James F. Byrnes, *Speaking Frankly* (New York: Harper and Brothers, 1947) 31–32; "Federal Millions for Good Roads," *Literary Digest*, 48 (28 February 1914): 415–18.

[56]Samuel D. Lovell, *The Election of 1916* (Carbondale: Southern Illinois University Press, 1980), 60–61; John Milton Cooper, Jr., *Pivotal Decades: The United States, 1900–1920* (New York: W. W. Norton and Company, 1990), 228–30, 251.

[57]*CR* 62:3, p. 4457 (1 March 1913); *CR* 63:2, pp. 76, 88–89 (2 December, 1913), 394–95 (6 December 1913), 8247, 8266 (5 May 1914).

place and full-scale war began in August, Mann, like most of his colleagues, thought that it would end quickly, certainly within a year.[58] Anticipating Wilson by a day, on 18 August in the House he delivered a strong, well-received, and noticed plea for American neutrality. "It seems to me that in this country at this time it is extremely important that everyone in official life, as well as those in private life, should resolve firmly that they will not be carried away with any hysterical emotion or by any partisan feeling for or against either side in this conflict abroad," Mann began. American rights would surely be violated, he warned, referring to "the ordinary courtesies or amenities." When that happened, when Americans were tempted to become partisan or "tempted in order to preserve what we may call our honor to engage in the conflict, let us make up our minds now to keep our minds firm in that determination that this country shall not become under any circumstances engaged in the war on either side." Mann expressed confidence that the administration "will be cool and calm." The danger would come when an American ship was seized or an interest affected, and the people became excited. Then it would be the duty of all to back the administration and make the administration feel that its duty to humanity, to civilization, and to the interests of the United States and her citizens is to keep out of the struggle and to make use of the opportunity which comes to us for our advance in civilization and power throughout the world."[59]

Mann's oblique reference to trade opportunities at the end of his speech was an important supplement to his peace theme and was far from a cry in the wilderness. Many newspapers in August urged the government and businessmen to take up the trade opportunities that the warring powers had forsaken.[60] In October Mann elaborated a little as he condemned the Clayton bill on final passage in the context of the war. The United States, he said, now had great opportunity to develop its domestic commerce and expand its foreign commerce. It should be encouraging production of much that had been imported, not threatening businessmen with jail sentences. "I think it would be a very good time for us, with the world conditions as they are now, to stop trying to hamper business and to legislate so that we may increase our business and add to the prosperity of our people."[61] Again and again in the next several years Mann would reiterate and elaborate this theme, which flowed from a longtime preoccupation with economic development and prosperity through business initiative and promotional governmental policies.

---

[58]*CR* 64:1, p. 1695 (28 January 1916).

[59]*CR* 63:2, p. 13931 (18 August 1914); *New York Times*, 19 August 1914.

[60]"How the War Affects America," *Literary Digest*, 49:7 (15 August 1914), 256–57; David M. Kennedy, *Over Here: The First World War and American Society* (New York: Oxford University Press, 1980), 37–38.

[61]*CR* 63:2, p 1634 (8 October 1914).

Mann's promotionalism served as a supplement to a more conventional and more frequently voiced line of criticism in which he attacked Democratic policies not in terms of lost opportunities, but simply as hurtful to existing business. With other Republicans in the period from August to the November elections, he accompanied both kinds of criticisms with support for several measures that he deemed necessary under war circumstances.

Yet the crisis of war was not yet so great, nor remedies so apparent, as to lessen party conflict. That conflict was the more intense because of the proximity of the elections, the combination among House Republicans of weariness and desire to get home to campaign, and the fact that some of the wartime dislocations related particularly to cotton and the Democratic South. Though himself weary, Mann gave vigorous leadership for his party both in supporting some measures and, more fully, in criticizing others and making a case for the GOP.

On 3 August Mann appealed to patriotism in behalf of an emergency currency bill, which was quickly passed.[62] A little later that day he gave a short speech in favor of an administration bill to liberalize terms under which foreign vessels in American ports might be transferred to American registry to facilitate the overseas shipment of American goods.[63] In October, in the face of a cotton crisis caused in part by loss of the German market to British naval intervention, Mann called for remedial legislation. He would not, however, support a new emergency currency plan.[64] Nor did he approve of a bill to create a Bureau of War Risk to insure merchant vessels.[65] On the most important of the administration's emergency measures, a bill to raise taxes, Mann was wholly negative and highly political, and he commanded the support of his party.

On a year-to-year basis, customs revenues declined by ten million dollars in August, while expenditures rose because of Mexico, the evacuation of Americans from Europe, and the establishment of the War Risk Bureau. Secretary McAdoo foresaw a possible fiscal-year deficit of $100,000,000. Democrats differed among themselves as to how to raise the money, but in mid-September they settled on a bill to impose taxes on a variety of consumer goods such as beer, chewing gum, and cosmetics, as well as on the services of bankers, brokers, and others. They hoped to raise $105,000,000 in additional revenue.[66]

Mann smelled political blood and secured agreement in the Republican caucus that there was no need for new taxes, but there was need instead for

[62]*Ibid.*, pp. 13169–70 (3 August 1914).

[63]*Ibid.*, p. 13186 (3 August 1914).

[64]*Ibid.*, pp. 16753–54 (16 October 1914), 16834 (20 October 1914), 16881, 16891 (21 October 1914), 16949–52 (22 October 1914).

[65]*Ibid.*, pp. 14409 (28 August 1914), 14449–50 (29 August 1914).

[66]Broesamle, *William Gibbs McAdoo*, 153–55.

economy. When Robert Henry presented a restrictive rule barring amendments and limiting debate to seven hours, Mann supported the extensive criticisms by Lenroot and said that the GOP was "being gagged and bound." Though the measure was called the "War Revenue Tax bill," Mann declined to treat it as a war measure, but very frankly put it in the context of the political campaign that was already under way, and he predicted Republican victory in November. Republicans united against the rule while several Democrats defected, though by a vote of 202–150 the House adopted the rule.[67]

The following day Mann delivered a long speech against the bill, keynoting his party's attack amidst repeated applause from his side. He reiterated the successful themes of 1913 and early 1914 and updated them with reference to the new situation. Mann denied the need for new taxes, urged economy instead, and decried Democratic extravagance. Without stressing the point, he suggested that if additional revenues were needed, borrowing through sale of bonds could be better modulated than could taxing and would less adversely affect investment. Mann argued, though, that fresh revenues were not needed. Using figures liberally, he said that after an August slump, shipping conditions and revenues were improving, but spending was excessive. He indicted the Democrats for using the war as an excuse to explain the dislocations in business and charged that America's economic trouble came before the war. Mann put part of the blame on the Underwood tariff, and he gave figures to show that it had brought a decline in revenues and an increase in imports, but no reduction in the cost of living. He spoke more generally of "financial fears" springing from business uncertainty associated with the tariff and the Federal Reserve Act and with fear of antitrust prosecutions and of fresh anti-business measures.

Mann held out to the electorate a better alternative. If the people would restore the GOP to control in the House, he said, "we promise the country that we will keep expenditures of the government down, avoid extravagant appropriations, and do away with the necessity for increased internal revenue taxes." Beyond that, his party would take advantage of new opportunities while "the other great commercial nations are at war with each other." Time-tested protectionism would build up such industries as dyestuffs, drugs, chemicals, silks, cottons, woolens, and others and would free America from dependence on foreign producers. The Republicans would also remove threats and restraints from business and "tell our people to get out and get the trade and . . . bless them for it." "Mr. Speaker," Mann ended to prolonged Republican applause, "you Democrats are good people, but you do not know how to run the country."[68]

---

[67]*CR* 63:2, pp. 15642, 15645–46 (24 September 1914).

[68]*Ibid.*, pp. 15697–99 (25 September 1914).

Other Republicans weighed in, taking advantage especially of the issue of extravagance. The Democrats had indeed failed to fulfill 1912 promises to cut spending, and the issue was a strong one for Republicans. Republicans also invoked the theme of Democratic incompetency, attacked the tariff and charged prosouthern bias in Democratic tariff, tax, and banking policies.[69] Though the bill became law, Mann and his colleagues correctly saw it as a vehicle to regain some of the ground lost by the fact of the war.

When on the following day the Democrats brought in a rule for consideration of a Philippines bill sponsored by William A. Jones of Virginia, Mann approached it from the standpoint of the national interest. Yet the issue divided the parties, albeit not so completely as did the war revenue bill, and it had relevance in the political campaign. The Jones bill proposed that the Philippines become independent in the indefinite future and gain fuller self-government meanwhile. Mann asked Finis J. Garrett of Tennessee, who presented the rule, about the propriety of discussing the general international situation in the Pacific, but Garrett saw no need for that in connection with the bill. Mann disagreed, and after the rule was approved over Republican objections, he prepared a speech in which he broke a self-imposed silence on the Pacific situation.[70] On 1 October Mann took twenty minutes to deliver his speech. The applause that occasionally punctuated his remarks came only from Republicans.[71]

Mann described the American presence in the Pacific—its own West Coast, Alaska, the Aleutians stretching towards Japan, the Panama Canal, Hawaii, Wake, Guam, the Philippines, and part of Samoa. "We control today to a large extent the strategic positions of the Pacific Ocean lying east of Asia and Japan," he said. Then Mann talked of the recent "marvelous growth" of Japan's influence, an unprecedented feat. Now, he went on, the same ferment was starting in China, with its vast territory and immense population. The diffusion of its people and goods would bring conflict that would last for centuries, and the same was true of Japan, Mann said. He hoped that the conflict might be purely commercial. Yet "a fight for commercial supremacy in the end leads to a fight with arms, because that is the final arbiter between nations." Under those circumstances the United States could never afford to give up the Philippines, or eventually they would be used against America. He rejected any halfway solution, a Monroe Doctrine kind of relationship. But if the Philippines were to be retained, he said, the United States had a duty "to make them our friends." That was not impossible, he felt; most people brought under the American flag wanted to stay. What was needed

---

[69]Greenlee, "Republican Party," 89–92.

[70]CR 63:2, p. 15811 (26 September 1914); Arthur S. Link, *Wilson: Confusions and Crises, 1915–1916* (Princeton, N.J.: Princeton University Press, 1964) 351.

[71]CR 63:2, pp. 16024–25 (1 October 1914).

was a more liberal policy of local self-government than was provided for in the Jones bill. He would offer amendments to accomplish that, he said, while still opposing provisions for ultimate independence.

The press gave much attention to Mann's speech. The *New York Times*'s Washington correspondent, who quoted Mann extensively, wrote: "Coming from the chosen leader of the party in the popular branch of Congress, and from a man who, in the last few weeks, frequently has been pointed out as material for the Republican Presidential nomination in 1916, the utterances of Mr. Mann were considered here tonight as the most definite Republican expression with respect to the Philippines ever made in Congress." Editorially the *Times* called the speech sound, but it felt that forecasts of future war were diplomatically unwise under present circumstances in the world. Other papers shared that view, while among still others, opinion divided along political lines.[72]

Mann fulfilled his promise of amendments. Initially, he offered them within the framework of his very serious speech, but when he came to a woman suffrage amendment, which he labeled the most important one yet, proceedings became mainly political. Then they became highly personal after Thomas Heflin of Alabama, crude and demagogic, said that Mann was "trying to save his political scalp in the November election." Mann rejoined, and words were said on both sides that the House ultimately struck from the Record, over Mann's protests. As to the Philippines bill, it won House approval, 212–60, but the Senate took no immediate action, and in the postelection lame-duck session Republicans blocked it. The bill would be heard of again in 1916.[73]

Heflin's comment respecting Mann's reelection concerns had some validity. The campaign was already under way and Mann was opposed by a group of suffragettes headed by Ruth Hanna McCormick, who caused him to be listed as one of nine congressmen on the suffragist blacklist, mainly because of his indiscreet remark at the time of the suffrage parade in March 1913. Although an Illinois woman suffrage law of 1913 did not include congressional races, the active opposition of the McCormick faction posed a challenge to Mann. Happily for him, in the campaign other influential women rallied to his defense.[74] Mann was helped also by widespread newspaper support, including that of Hearst's *Examiner*, and by a solid organization, the managerial skills of Edwin Sims, Mann's national standing and legislative ac-

---

[72]*New York Times*, 2 October 1914; "Congressional Prophet of War," *Literary Digest*, 49:16 (17 October 1914): 726–27.

[73]*CR* 63:2, pp. 16234, 16239 (6 October 1914), 16425–33 (10 October 1914); *Chicago Tribune*, 11 October 1914, vol. 21, Mann Papers; Link, *Wilson: Confusions and Crises*, 352.

[74]*Chicago Herald*, 30 August 1914, vol. 21, Mann Papers; *Chicago Tribune*, 1 October 1914, vol. 18, Mann Papers.

complishments, and division among his opponents as between Democrats, Progressives, and Socialists. For the third consecutive election, Mann won with less than a majority, yet his 48.5 percent put him well ahead of his nearest rival, Democrat Mark O'Leary, who drew 26.8 percent. John C. Vaughan, who had strongly challenged Mann in 1910 and 1912 as a Democrat, this time ran on the Progressive ticket and garnered just 19.1 percent of the vote. His poor showing was symptomatic of the Progressive party's decline in Illinois, which in part sprang from the diversion of press and public attention to the war.[75]

Although in the national elections the Republicans did not regain control of the Senate or House, their showing was nevertheless very gratifying to Mann. They scored a strong comeback after the debacle of 1912, to the extent that afterwards the Progressives no longer posed a serious challenge and Wilson and the Democrats seemed vulnerable in the 1916 elections. In the House races the GOP gained 66 seats to bring their total to 193 as against 231 for the Democrats and 8 for the Progressives, who lost 10 seats. Republicans lost 5 Senate seats to the Democrats, but more than made up for this by regaining key governorships, as in New York and Ohio. The Progressives made an all-out effort, but polled under two million votes and lost in every state but California. Notables such as Pinchot, Murdock, Albert Beveridge, and James Garfield lost in senate or governorship bids.[76]

Mann said that but for the European war, the people would have elected a Republican House majority, in reaction especially to the Underwood tariff and ensuing economic trouble. "The vote also shows," he said, "the appreciation of the fact that Wilson is in the White House, and Roosevelt is not. They do not want war. That is the only reason the Republicans did not get a majority in the House."[77] His view was reasonable in light of the campaign appeals of the major parties. "War in the East. Peace in the West! Thank God for Wilson!" the Democratic campaign book trumpeted, and cabinet officers, on the stump, anticipated the 1916 slogan "He Kept Us Out of War."[78] The

---

[75]John L. Moore, ed., *Congressional Quarterly's Guide to U.S. Elections* 2nd ed. (Washington, D.C.: Congressional Quarterly, 1985), 724; Ralph Arthur Straetz, "The Progressive Movement in Illinois, 1910–1916" (Ph.D. diss., University of Illinois, 1951), 445–518.

[76]Paul DeWitt Hasbrouck, *Party Government in the House of Representatives* (New York: Macmillan Company, 1927), 239; David Burner, "The Democratic Party, 1910–1932" in *History of U.S. Political Parties*, vol. 3, *1910–1945: From Square Deal to New Deal*, ed. Arthur M. Schlesinger, Jr. (New York: Chelsea House Publishers in association with R. R. Bowker Co., 1973), 1815; John A. Gable, *The Bull Moose Years: Theodore Roosevelt and the Progressive Party* (Port Washington, N.Y.: Kennikat Press, 1978), 182, 224.

[77]*Newark, Ohio, Weekly Tribune*, 4 November 1914, vol. 21, Mann Papers.

[78]Gould, *Reform and Regulation*, 189.

Republicans made an economic appeal against the Democrats. They stressed hard times and blamed the Democrats, especially on the issues of the tariff, business uncertainty, and the war revenue bill.[79] Mann anticipated this approach in advance of the Sixty-third Congress, and in his response to the main economic legislation of the first and second sessions he had led in sharpening the shafts hurled by Republican orators and editors in the campaign.

In some localities Republicans benefited from other arguments, including anti-Southernism[80] and a flare-up of anti-Catholicism.[81] They benefited, too, from the return of some Progressives, from Democratic factionalism in New York, Illinois, and New Jersey, and from the inability of Democratic incumbents to campaign sufficiently.[82] Most old-time Republican regulars who had been swept out of office in 1912 would not return to the House,[83] but such figures from the past as Cannon, McKinley, Longworth, and Hill were elected. Their victories suggested that Republican gains were made by conservative men running on conservative issues, and that the party would move to the right against a progressive Democratic party. The point needs to be qualified. Wilson reiterated that there would be no new disturbances of business, Mann and insurgents would not forfeit claims to progressivism. On balance, though, the election did point toward a yet more conservative Republican party and a sharper division between the major parties. GOP attacks on Democratic economic reforms resonated best in the industrial East and Midwest, where the business slump was felt most strongly, and where conservatism predominated amongst Republicans. It was in these areas that the party scored its big gains. In the West, by contrast, the Republicans lost a House seat, and Moosers were drawn to the Democrats on the basis of progressivism.[84]

The number of insurgents elected to the next Congress declined from forty-four to thirty-three, and they became but 17.19 percent of the House

[79]"The Republican Revival," *Literary Digest*, 49:20 (14 November 1914): 937–38; Greenlee, "Republican Party," 93; Arthur S. Link and William M. Leary, Jr., "Election of 1916," in *History of American Presidential Elections, 1789–1968*, vol. 3, ed. Arthur M. Schlesinger, Jr. (New York: Chelsea House Publishers in association with McGraw Hill Book Co., 1971), 2246.

[80]Greenlee, "Republican Party," 99; Ingle, "Pilgrimage to Reform," 98.

[81]Sarasohn, *Party of Reform*, 177–78.

[82]*Ibid.*, 175; Gould, *Reform and Regulation*, 187.

[83]Richard Kenneth Horner, "The House at War: The House of Representatives during World War I, 1917–1919" (Ph.D. diss., Louisiana State University, 1977), 70.

[84]Cortez A. M. Ewing, *Congressional Elections, 1896–1944* (Norman: University of Oklahoma Press, 1947), 83, 91; Sarasohn, *Party of Reform*, 175–76.

Republicans, as against 34.6 percent in the Sixty-third Congress.[85] Nor did these insurgents figure to be disruptive. In the despairing view of Lynn Haines, writing in 1915 in advance of the new Congress, the Republicans "are almost completely harmonious, with insurgency stamped out." Viewing the matter from a different angle, Taft congratulated Mann on the prospect of "heading a solid minority."[86] Mann had something to do with the posture of the insurgents, for he had gone out of his way to cultivate them. They, in turn, had made common cause with regulars, especially on the tariff and criticism of Democratic methods. With the advent of war insurgents found in the cause of peace an outlet for their progressivism, and Mann heartily agreed.

Theodore Roosevelt fulfilled his obligation to his supporters in the 1914 campaign, but he saw no long-term future for the Progressive party.[87] In 1916 he used it as a bargaining tool in seeking the Republican presidential nomination. After the 1914 returns were in, Mann anticipated the election of a Republican president in 1916 and saw the need to woo Progressives. As to Roosevelt, though, he commented: "He is not the only reformer nor the principal real reformer in the country."[88] His comment, which varied in tone and substance from a friendlier remark made in 1913, may have reflected Mann's accommodation to those regulars who hated Roosevelt for his 1912 actions and now saw no need to compromise with his weakened party; and it may have reflected Mann's own drift to the right. But taken together with his postelection statement contrasting Wilson and Roosevelt on the issue of war and peace, it indicated that he probably responded primarily to Roosevelt's comments in favor of helping Belgium and building up America's military forces—preparedness.[89] If so, Mann correctly anticipated the major issues of the next two years, the issues of American behavior in a world at war. His negative comment on Roosevelt reflected some of the ideas and attitudes he

[85]Maureen R. Romans, "Party Leadership Fights in the House of Representatives: The Causes of Conflict, 1895–1955" (Ph.D. diss., University of Massachusetts, 1976), 53.

[86]Lynn Haines, *Your Congress: An Interpretation of the Political and Parliamentary Influences that Dominate Law Making in America* (Washington, D.C.: National Voters League, 1915), 65; Taft to Mann, 14 November 1914, series 8, reel 527, William Howard Taft Papers, Library of Congress.

[87]John Milton Cooper, Jr., *The Warrior and the Priest: Woodrow Wilson and Theodore Roosevelt* (Cambridge, Mass.: Belknap Press of Harvard University Press, 1983), 248–50.

[88]*Chicago Examiner*, 5 November 1914, and *St. Louis Post-Dispatch*, 15 December 1914, vol. 21, Mann Papers.

[89]Gable, *Bull Moose Years*, 234; Joseph L. Gardner, *Departing Glory: Theodore Roosevelt as Ex-President* (New York: Charles Scribner's Sons, 1973), 325; Arthur S. Link, *Wilson: The Struggle for Neutrality 1914–1915* (Princeton, N.J.: Princeton University Press, 1960), 137.

would bring as minority leader to the foreign relations challenge, a challenge both to America's welfare and to the continuation of the Republican party's reunion and revival.

5

The Politics of Peace and Preparedness: December 1914–June 1916

Politics was in the air when on 7 December Congress convened for the lame-duck session of the Sixty-third Congress. The election of 1914 had been the qualifying bout, and the Republicans showed themselves formidable contenders. The main event would come in 1916, when the Democrats would try to reelect Wilson, retain Congress, and show that 1912 had marked a long-term transformation of American politics. The Republicans hoped to prove 1912 an aberration, born of their temporary division, and that they remained the majority party in the electorate. Swiftly, each side staked out ground on the issues of the day according to the current situation and a dimly foreseeable future.

War issues loomed large, and each party showed itself as divided as the public. Yet the outlines of majority opinion were clear. Americans wanted neutrality—to stay out of the war—and also neutral rights—especially the right to ply the seas for trade. Both sides in the war seemed to intrude on American rights. During the session what would prove the more serious and shocking violations, by Germany, took only the form of a February announcement of submarine warfare in prescribed zones, not the actuality of it. British interference came earlier, but involved only property, not lives.

Later, with the onset of submarine warfare, American defense of neutral rights would draw the nation away from neutrality and towards belligerency, but not yet. Already, however, questions arose as to how vigorously the United States should defend its neutral rights against British violations and what precautions it should take to guard neutrality. During the session side issues arose that persisted into the next Congress. The most important of these was military preparedness. In addition, Secretary McAdoo's scheme for America to buy and use German merchant vessels stuck in American ports was contentious and not immediately settled.

From the start, President Wilson was moderate and in tune with public opinion. Because of his office and prominence, he won for his party the larger measure of political capital. Mann forfeited nothing to Wilson on the war issues, but instead tried to go him one better on both neutrality and neutral rights, while positioning his party for later gains respecting preparedness. Thus Republicans kept within striking distance of the president.

Because of strong division among Republicans as the war progressed, and the fact of eventual American belligerency, Mann later suffered for some of his peace-minded positions. For the time being, they helped the GOP. During the short session the positions Mann took chiefly reflected his strong personal convictions. On preparedness, however, he began a continuing process of rationalizing in his party's interest.

In August 1914, and more expansively in October, relying for enforcement on its large cruiser fleet, Britain issued lists of absolute and conditional contraband that it would intercept and bring into naval stations in Britain and Gibraltar. It acted against neutral vessels carrying American goods such as foodstuffs, cotton, copper, and oil, even if they were headed for a neutral country like Holland, when it judged that the ultimate destination was Germany. Sir Edward Grey, British foreign secretary, went only as far as he could without provoking a severe American reaction, and Washington's response was mild.[1]

After the British seized vessels of Chicago meat packers, Mann went to the State Department and urged that it demand a stop to such practices. He was rebuffed.[2] When in his annual message to Congress on 8 December Wilson largely ignored the subject, Mann attacked the administration in an article for the *Chicago Examiner*. Britain violated American rights, Mann wrote, when it "seized and detained foodstuffs shipped in neutral vessels by Americans to neutral persons at neutral ports for consumption in neutral countries."[3] On 18 January Mann, speaking with great feeling, decried the lack of "backbone" in the State Department. A neutral ship had been detained by a British cruiser outside of New York harbor, and a reporter en route to Germany had been forced to show his passports to a British officer. Mann told of a stern letter written by Secretary of State Hamilton Fish in protest against similar French actions in 1870 during the Franco-Prussian War. "How refreshing it is to go back to the old days of Ulysses S. Grant and Hamilton Fish and learn that we had nerve to tell the French to keep their war vessels away from the entrance to our harbors with the

---

[1]Arthur S. Link, *Wilson: The Struggle for Neutrality, 1914-1915* (Princeton, N.J.: Princeton University Press, 1960), 107-8, 124-28, 171-74.

[2]*CR* 64:2, p. 4239 (24 February 1917).

[3]*Chicago Examiner*, 13 December 1914, vol. 21, James R. Mann Papers, Library of Congress.

intent to annoy the commerce of this country and keep them away. And if we would say so now," Mann concluded, to hearty cheers from both sides of the aisle, "Great Britain would keep hers away. We are a neutral power; but we have some rights, and we ought to insist upon our rights being respected."[4] Mann was far from the first Republican to talk in this way, but his statement lent weight to what were popular criticisms.[5]

On 18 August Mann had warned about allowing controversies with belligerents to bring America into the war. On that occasion, though, he had mainly referred to misplaced outrage over presumed affronts to national honor, and the abortive Veracruz intervention of June was fresh in everyone's memory. Now Mann was talking of a national interest in commerce, which he felt to be vital. Protests in defense of that interest and of America's neutral rights entailed no risk to America's neutrality, in Mann's opinion.[6] Even should American protests fail, he surely realized, the prospect of future financial compensation for lost property was available as a better remedy than war. When in March 1915 and afterwards German submarines destroyed not just property but irreplaceable lives, Mann saw a stronger danger of war and urged extreme care and a willingness to sacrifice some rights.

In connection with the ship purchase bill, Mann's caution in the interest of peace extended even to possible conflict with Great Britain. Secretary McAdoo's plan would replace the Ship Registry Act of August, which had failed to accomplish its purpose. The administration's highest priority for the session, to cope with the shortage of shipping, the new bill created a shipping corporation in which the government held at least 51 percent of the stock. The bulk of the corporation's merchant fleet would be the German vessels trapped in American ports when the war began. But what if the British stopped and detained these ships, in effect the property of the American government? That would be a much more serious matter than violation of private rights. Mann would not take the risk, and he argued against the bill on that basis. "I want to keep this country out of war and out of provocation of war," he said. A party measure buttressed by a "gag rule," the bill passed the House, but failed in the Senate.[7]

On the issue of preparedness, too, Mann took the side of those most concerned to preserve American neutrality. He understood the complexity

---

[4]*New York Times*, 19 January 1915; CR 63:3, p. 1882 (18 January 1915).

[5]John M. Blum, *Joe Tumulty and the Wilson Era* (Boston: Houghton Mifflin, 1951), 94.

[6]CR 64:2, p. 4239 (24 February 1917).

[7]John J. Broesamle; *William Gibbs McAdoo: A Passion for Change, 1863-1917* (Port Washington, N.J.: Kennikat Press, 1973), 221-28; Link, *Wilson: The Struggle for Neutrality*, 81-90, 137-57; CR 63:3, p. 3918 (16 February 1915).

and dynamism of the issue, however, and left the door open for a later change of position.

Augustus P. Gardner issued the call for preparedness on 15 October, after returning from the battlefields of Europe. He said that the United States was weak and warned that it must be able to resist expansionists flushed with victories, by which he meant Germany. Quickly, his father-in-law, Henry Cabot Lodge, Lodge's friend Roosevelt, and former Secretary of War Henry L. Stimson enlisted in the cause. The National Security League came into being to back preparedness. Wilson, distressed at these developments, looked squarely at Gardner when he addressed Congress on 8 December and defended his program of moderate military increases as quite sufficient. Anything more would show that "we had been thrown off our balance." Peace forces rallied with new organizations of their own, one of them led by Nicholas Murray Butler. In the end, Gardner and Lodge did not get the investigations of the army and navy that they called for, and no very decisive legislative battle occurred. In connection with military appropriations, congressmen had a chance to fight a minibattle.[8]

Alignments took shape that proved lasting. The isolationistic peace element in Congress was strongest among Democrats, though often in 1915 and 1916 party loyalty inhibited Democratic congressmen. Most of them came from farm districts in the South and Midwest and admired Bryan, who quit as secretary of state in June 1915 in protest at the severity of a note to Germany over the sinking of the *Lusitania*.[9]

In the Republican party three factions emerged. Isolationists in Congress, such as La Follette and Norris, represented constituencies that included old-stock agrarian progressives, who saw the war as a conflict of imperialists; German Americans; Scandinavian Americans; and some other ethnic groups that were antagonistic to one of the Allies, Russia. Isolationists were strongest in the Midwest. At the other extreme were ultranationalists, pro-Allies and willing to risk war. They were led in the Senate by Lodge and in the House by Gardner and were backed in the main by eastern Anglo-Americans, many of them businessmen and professionals. They gained strength in the wake of German submarine outrages. Between the two stood moderate internationalists such as Taft, who tended to support Wilson's policies of "differential neutrality towards the Allies."[10]

---

[8]John Milton Cooper, Jr., *The Vanity of Power: American Isolationism and the First World War, 1914-1917* (Westport, Conn.: Greenwood Publishing Corp., 1969), 21-24; Frederic L. Paxson, *American Democracy and the World War: Pre-War Years, 1913-1917* (Boston: Houghton Mifflin, 1936), 200-202.

[9]Cooper, *Vanity of Power*, 25.

[10]*Ibid.*, 22-25, 224-27; William H. Harbaugh, "The Republican Party, 1893–1932," in *History of U.S. Political Parties*, vol. 3, *1910–1945: From Square Deal to*

Although Wilson had himself repudiated preparedness, the administration's modest proposal for construction of two new battleships served as a vehicle for antipreparedness House members to express themselves by backing an amendment to limit the increase to one battleship. Democrats took the lead, and Mann joined them. In the voting he was one of 15 Republicans, mainly from the Midwest, to vote with 139 Democrats for the amendment, which lost by just 16 votes.[11] His vote was directed more in opposition to the Gardner forces than to Wilson's program. Mann even opposed a Gardner amendment to increase the aircraft appropriation from $300,000 to $1,000,000, though he had himself pioneered in the cause of military aircraft. In debate he discussed the possibility of an attack as "unprobable."[12]

In connection with the battleship amendment, Mann hedged his position. He defended the amendment as an economy measure and as part of a larger economy program being pushed by Underwood in his last House session. "As long as the Democratic policies are in control we shall have trouble about revenues and expenditures," he said. "When the Republican party again gains the ascendancy we shall have money enough and we can make the necessary expenditures."[13] What Mann could not say was that if the occasion warranted preparedness, and if a Republican preparedness program could in some fashion be disassociated from the incubus of militarism and interventionism, the party could safely and profitably offer it and take advantage of Democratic division. For the time being, Mann chose to simply emphasize his commitment to neutrality.

Mann's remarks on revenues and expenditures during debate on the battleship amendment reflected his continued adherence to the business-oriented approach to domestic affairs that he had taken in the first two sessions. The economy suffered because of the Underwood tariff, he had said, and a shortfall in federal revenues also resulted. Early in the third session Mann talked of hard times and blamed the tariff. As before, he urged a Tariff Commission as a moderate measure to ameliorate the situation. After he introduced a commission bill, he harassed the Democrats with repeated talk of slow business and unemployment and with resolutions directing Ways and Means to report his bill. When Wilson, in a Jackson Day speech, tried to show that functions of the old Tariff Board might be performed by the Federal Trade Commission and aggressively said that the Republicans had not had a new idea in thirty years, Mann responded that the provisions in ques-

New Deal, ed. Arthur M. Schlesinger, Jr., (New York: Chelsea House Publishers in association with R. R. Bowker Co., 1973), 2099.

[11]CR 63:3, p. 3131 (5 February 1915); Cooper, Vanity of Power, 225.

[12]CR 63:3, p. 2107 (22 January 1915).

[13]Ibid., pp. 3133-34 (5 February 1915).

tion in the trade commission bill had been written by a Republican, Fred Stevens, and did not in any case substitute for a Tariff Commission.[14]

In similar vein Mann warned of a large deficit that would necessitate a bond issue, and he blamed it on Democratic inability to cut appropriations. With others, he called for reform in the chaotic and archaic budget system by which departmental requests were not coordinated in the executive branch. Mann's attacks and the economic problems he exploited put the Democrats on the defensive.[15] Later, war orders boosted the economy. But economic issues survived in new forms, and Mann did not relinquish the offensive on that front.

On the occasion of a deficiency appropriations bill that included $500,000 for the American army at Veracruz, Mann renewed attacks on the administration's Mexican policies. He talked of "executions, murders, starvation, famine, rapine, throughout the land of Mexico." "We are preventing anyone else from obtaining order there," he said, "and we have not as much nerve in the present Department of State upon the subject as would supply an angle worm." The United States could end the chaos, and that without war, Mann asserted, but he declined to say how. Alternatively, "We ought to withdraw our assumed power over Mexico." Mann's remarks won attention, but his vagueness as to solutions, which reflected division among Republicans, limited the party's gain.[16]

As before, on issues not directly related to the economy, Mann often took progressive ground. Most important of these in the session was a proposed woman suffrage amendment to the Constitution, offered by Frank Mondell, whose Wyoming voting constituency already included women. To those who, during the 1914 campaign, accused Mann of a late, politically motivated conversion, he responded that he had offered a suffrage amendment to a 1912 Alaska bill well before he antagonized suffragettes, and that he agreed with his wife and mother in sincerely favoring woman suffrage. As party leader he found the issue very advantageous. The cause itself was young as far as federal action was concerned, but the movement's progress in the states and among suffrage organizations suggested that it would continue to gain in popularity. For Mann it was a useful issue by which to embarrass Democrats and appeal to Progressives and insurgents and to those women

---

[14]*Chicago Tribune*, 29 December 1914, and *Washington Star*, 31 December 1914, vol. 21, Mann Papers; *CR* 63:3, pp. 899 (2 January 1915), 1153 (7 January 1915), 1323 (9 January 1915), 2190 (23 January 1915), 1584-85 (14 January 1915).

[15]Robert C. Hilderbrand, ed., *The Papers of Woodrow Wilson: The Complete Press Conferences, 1913-1919* (Princeton, N.J.: Princeton University Press, 1985), 20 December 1914, 50:664; *New York Times*, 29 January 1915; *CR* 63:3, p. 3586 (11 February 1915).

[16]*CR* 63:3, pp. 656-57 (29 December 1914), p. 479 (21 December 1914); *New York Times*, 22 December 1914, 30 December 1914.

who already had the vote or would soon get it. (By the end of 1914 there were eleven full-suffrage states, all in the West.) Both parties were divided on the issue as members responded to constituent pressure. The result of that pressure, however, was to push the Republicans towards the reform and the Democrats away from it. For the Democrats, solid opposition in the South, because of sensitivity towards anything that might bear on Negro voting, was the major factor. Among Republicans, suffrage provisions in western state constitutions, together with midwestern progressivism, were influential factors.[17]

In advance of the voting, Mann promised the Republican Women's League of Illinois not only to vote for the amendment but to urge it on others in the Illinois delegation. On 12 January Mann spoke for it. He depicted woman suffrage as part of a worldwide, historical trend towards broadening suffrage, and he argued that women had the intellectual power to vote wisely. Submit it to the states, he said. If they did not want it, they could reject it. To no one's surprise the amendment failed of a majority, much less the necessary two-thirds. But everyone knew that the battle was just begun. In the 174-204 vote, Democrats voted "nay" by a margin of 174 to 86, while among Republicans the vote was 74 in favor and 30 against.[18] While Mann identified himself with the cause, Wilson remained committed to a states' rights approach.

Mann also positioned himself to the left of both Wilson and some southern Democrats in supporting a bill to regulate child labor under the commerce clause. It entailed a major expansion of federal regulatory authority, but on a subject that elicited the concern of many. Mann attended a Washington conference called by the National Child Labor Committee in January, and in February he helped the bill's sponsor, Democrat A. Mitchell Palmer of Pennsylvania, fight off dilatory motions and bring the bill to a vote. It passed, 233-43, with fuller support proportionally from Republicans than Democrats. The Senate killed it, but it would be heard of again in 1916.[19]

---

[17]*CR* 62:2, p. 529 (24 April 1912); *Chicago Tribune*, 1 October 1914, vol. 18, Mann Papers; Paxson, *American Democracy* 193; Eileen L. McDonagh, "Issues and Constituencies in the Progressive Era: House Roll Call Voting on the Nineteenth Amendment, 1913-1919," *Journal of Politics* 51 (February 1989): 126.

[18]*Chicago Examiner*, 31 December 1914, vol. 21, Mann Papers; *CR* 63:3, pp. 1420, 1479, 1483-84 (12 January 1915); Thomas Robert Bullard, "From Businessman to Congressman: The Careers of Martin B. Madden" (Ph.D. diss., University of Illinois at Chicago Circle, 1973), 150.

[19]*CR* 63:3, pp. 3827-36 (15 February 1915); *Jackson, Illinois, Journal*, 15 December 1915, vol. 21, Mann Papers; Arthur S. Link, *Wilson: The New Freedom* (Princeton, N.J.: Princeton University Press, 1956), 255-57.

Less conspicuously, Mann took a progressive position when he supported the full requested appropriation for physical valuation of railroads.[20]

Mann again exploited the Democrat's southern flank when the immigration bill returned from the Senate. He opposed the bill, with its literacy test, and acknowledged that an amendment to exclude Negroes, if adopted, would doom the bill. "But notwithstanding that," he said, "I am unwilling to stultify myself and do a great injustice to a race by putting myself on record in favor of such an amendment, which itself smells worse than last year's smelt." "I hope," he concluded, "the amendment will be defeated by such an overwhelming vote as will do credit to this House." The House did reject the amendment, 74-253, but among its supporters were such leading Democrats as Underwood, Kitchin, Adamson, and Sherley.[21] Later a conference report without the offending provision passed both houses, but the House sustained the president's veto.

Another emotionally explosive issue, a proposal to submit a constitutional amendment for Prohibition, had no obvious political advantages for either party. Members lined up more along rural versus urban lines than according to party. That the proposal was coming to a vote reflected the continuing rise of the Prohibition forces, headed by the Anti-Saloon League. But as yet only about a third of the House members represented strong Prohibition districts. Mann and Underwood joined in leading the opposition, which thus took on a bipartisan cast. Yet as Mann viewed it, the issue had some long-term political importance. He frankly warned that the issue itself, if it remained national, would come to dominate elections. Presumably he felt that his party would be better served if the economic issues he had been stressing remained foremost. Mann also argued against the proposal on its merits, asserting that national enforcement would be ineffective and that abuses of alcohol were more effectively dealt with locally and through taxation, with its impact on price. The amendment proposal won less than the necessary two-thirds, but the 195-190 vote encouraged the prohibitionists. In his district and nationally, Mann made important enemies by his active stand.[22]

When the final session of the Sixty-third Congress ended on 4 March, several close observers reviewed it from a political standpoint and predicted a Republican victory in 1916. Harry Slattery wrote Pinchot of "the proverbial

---

[20]CR 63:3, p. 3498 (10 February 1915).

[21]Ibid. , pp. 1137-39 (7 January 1915).

[22]Eileen Lorenzi McDonagh, "Electoral Bases of Policy Innovation in the Progressive Era: The Impact of Grass Roots Opinion on Roll-Call Voting in the House of Representatives, Sixty-third Congress, 1913-1915," Journal of Policy History 4 (1992): 175-79; "Prohibition's Day in Congress," Literary Digest, 50:1 (2 January 1915); 8; CR 63:3, pp. 530-31, 609-15 (22 December 1914); Chicago Journal, 7 August 1916, vol. 22, Mann Papers; New York Times, 7 July 1915.

inefficiency of the Democrats," for example, in passing a thirty-million-dollar rivers and harbors bill and appropriating two billion dollars in all despite the prospect of a deficit. Southerners, he said, had loaded themselves with pork and patronage, killed the child-labor bill, and attempted various anti-Negro measures. Nor had the Democrats reformed as to the caucus. In particular, they had pushed the ship purchase bill through the House in a single day. The administration was also losing ground because of the worsening Mexican situation and attacks from opposite sides respecting the war in Europe. Slattery surveyed Republican presidential possibilities and singled out three as most frequently mentioned, Governor Charles Whitman of New York, Senator Borah, and Mann, with Borah in the lead.[23]

A Mann presidential boom had been going on since mid-1914 and was serious enough to cause the Anti-Saloon League in July to warn against it. It was fueled by the activity of Edwin Sims, by the Hearst press, and by many political friends in Illinois and around the country, including the wealthy William B. McKinley. Although it continued into 1916, Mann, who never acknowledged interest in the nomination, in November 1915 explicitly denied any after Senator Lawrence Sherman had positioned himself to become the Illinois favorite-son candidate. The Mann boom, while it lasted, brought the Chicagoan a good deal of national press attention and thus further enhanced his importance as minority leader. He won renewed attention and the temporary approbation of the *New York Times*, which backed Elihu Root for the nomination, when he pricked the Sherman bubble and that of other "favorite sons" with the comment "We cannot win with a two-spot." The *Times* took the occasion to sketch Mann as a legislative leader in this period of his career.[24]

"Common sense in the degree in which Mann has it is an uncommon gift; he has common sense to such an extent that if he had any more of it it would be a vice," the *Times* editorialized. "This uncommon sense is guided by a seeing eye and that rarest of all things, a real sense of humor—which does not mean an ability to make or see jokes. He not only hates humbug, but he recognizes it under any guise." Mann, the *Times* continued, "does not look like Uncle Sam, with his aggressive square gray beard and peering eyes and

---

[23]Slattery to Pinchot, 19 March 1915, box 189, Gifford Pinchot Papers, Library of Congress. Frank Vanderlip and Charles Hilles also saw a Republican tide, and so did a number of newspapers, following a Republican victory in the Chicago mayoralty race. Vanderlip to James Stillman, 12 February 1915, part B, series 1, box 6, Frank A. Vanderlip Papers, Butler Library, Columbia University; Hilles to Samuel A. Perkins, 4 March 1915, series 1, box 99, Charles D. Hilles Papers, Sterling Library, Yale University; "Republican Victory in Chicago," *Literary Digest*, 50:16 (17 April 1915): 863-64.

[24]See especially the many articles in vols. 21 and 22, Mann Papers; *New York Times*, 31 January 1916.

staccato voice; but he is more like Uncle Sam than anybody else now prominent before the public. His joy in a fight is only equaled by his success in it. He carries a chip on his shoulder, and while he is willing to have anybody knock it off he prefers to have it knocked off by a fool or a Pharisee. He works like a steam engine," the editorial continued, "never tires, has the whole business of Congress at his finger tips and is in five places at once. . . . The public welfare is his chief consideration, modified only by a prudent eye on the permanency of his Congress seat." In his party role, the *Times* observed, "He is not only an elected leader, but a real leader, and the Republicans of the House follow him not because they elected him or because they love him, but because they have faith in his capacity, his integrity, and his insight. He is very much of a man, and he is highly different from the ruck of Congressmen; he is not a chip from a general block or a yard cut from a bolt of cloth. His blasts of common sense shiver solemnity and stupidity; he labors for the country's good as he sees it, and labors not the worse because he does not talk stiltedly or act pompously. He suggests the prairie," the *Times* concluded, "though he lives in a great city and is the most urban and knowing of men."

It was fortunate that Mann was at the height of his powers, for he was challenged by momentous and intricate problems. During the long break between Congresses, the international situation changed for the worse, and the issue of preparedness again divided Americans. In March 1915 the British imposed a stringent blockade, applicable even to noncontraband articles, in seeming violation of international law. Germany, in response, began a campaign of submarine terror against British passenger vessels. On 28 March the *Falaba* went down, and an American passenger was drowned. On 7 May, again without warning, a German submarine sank the *Lusitania*; 1,198 people lost their lives, including 128 Americans. Every American interviewed ten years later well remembered the experience of hearing the shocking news.[25] The preparedness forces sprang to life and scored gains with the public, and Wilson showed signs of responding. Bryan, however, first resigned and then went on an antipreparedness tour of the South and West.[26] Further complicating the situation, near anarchy and antiforeignism plagued Americans in Mexico.[27]

---

[25]John Milton Cooper, Jr., *Pivotal Decades: The United States, 1900-1920* (New York: W. W. Norton and Company, 1990), 233.

[26]Link, *Wilson: The Struggle for Neutrality*, 589-91; Frank Vanderlip to James Stillman, 27 August 1915, part B, series 1, box 7, Vanderlip Papers; John Patrick Finnegan, *Against the Specter of a Dragon: The Campaign for American Military Preparedness, 1914-1917* (Westport, Conn.: Greenwood Press, 1974), 93; John J. Broesamle, "The Democrats from Bryan to Wilson," in *The Progressive* Era, ed. Lewis L. Gould (Syracuse: Syracuse University Press, 1974), 109.

[27]Link, *Wilson: the Struggle for Neutrality*, 456-88.

In the first half of June, following a vacation with his wife in Hawaii, Mann toured several western states for the Republican National Committee and commented on events in speeches and interviews. Notwithstanding the *Lusitania*, he adhered to the positions he had taken earlier—stay out of war, take advantage of the war to extend trade, and be firm in defense of property rights in dealing with Britain, Mexico, and Germany. As before, he saw the tariff and resultant revenue problems as the major issue of the next election.[28] At the end of the month, back home in Chicago, he said in an interview: "I think the President was swept off his feet on the *Lusitania* case. Two men fighting in the street, and each believing the other is bent on taking his life, are not going to worry about Marquis of Queensberry rules." He dismissed extensive preparedness as financially impossible.[29]

In September several events caused Mann to shift his stand on preparedness. Germany gave the *Arabic* pledge—not to sink passenger liners without warning or providing for the rescue of passengers—and then the Kaiser called off the submarine campaign in British waters. The submarine issue remained dormant until late December.[30] Preparedness was now not as alarming as formerly to Mann personally or to fellow Republican peace advocates. Also, on 3 September Wilson released letters he had written in July to the defense secretaries that called on them to make plans to build up military forces.[31] Wilson's switch transformed the political character of the preparedness issue, for despite some evidences of belligerence towards Germany, he had established himself as an apostle of peace.

If significant numbers of Republicans led by Mann opposed preparedness, it would put the party in a bad light and divide it as well. Support for preparedness, on the other hand, might even afford large benefits to the Republican party. The matter is speculative, but Mann could hardly have been unaware of Bryanite opposition to preparedness within the Democratic party. Thus the Republicans might show themselves the better united of the major parties in upholding the national interest.

Addressing a Republican dinner in St. Louis on 28 September, Mann put his support for preparedness in a larger context with which he was familiar and comfortable. He talked first of the need for higher tariffs, even prior to creation of a Tariff Commission, to give protection and larger revenues. Then he said, "The markets of the world are ripe for our picking." Large sums were needed to spread trade at home and abroad and develop domestic

[28]H. B. Maxson to Mann, 9 July 1915, vol. 38, Mann Papers; *Sacramento Union*, 2 June 1915, vol. 22, Mann Papers; *Los Angeles Times*, 9 June 1915, *Deseret Evening News*, 16 June 1915, vol. 38, Mann Papers.

[29]*Chicago Herald*, 28 June 1915, vol. 22, Mann Papers.

[30]Arthur S. Link, *Woodrow Wilson: Revolution, War, and Peace* (Arlington Heights, Ill.: Harlan Davidson, 1979), 42.

[31]Link, *Wilson: The Struggle for Neutrality*, 591.

resources. Government should "provide the opportunity of reasonable reward for such investments." Mann saw for America a great chance for "material prosperity and intellectual and moral growth" for all. "While we are adapting means and methods for our trade and industrial development," he continued, "let us also, in view of the conditions in foreign lands, put our house in order to defend and protect itself against any foreign nation or nations. Our wealth will soon excite the envy, if not the cupidity, of the outside world. We must provide all that is necessary for our protection and we must do it soon and completely." Mann suggested that after the war was over, the high debts belligerents had incurred would provoke revolutions that would endanger American security and rights. The United States had a duty "to guarantee to American citizens whom we invite to engage in foreign trade and undertakings that so long as they follow peaceful and legitimate pursuits they will receive the attention and support of the American government and the protection of the American flag," against Mexico, for example. At the end Mann warned that "we must not become military mad." He saw little danger of that. "We may want to conquer the trade of the world, but we do not want to conquer other nations or take other lands."[32]

As the start of the Sixty-fourth Congress approached, the preparedness issue remained foremost. On 18 November Wilson invited Mann to confer with him before the session on matters that "should be entirely non-partisan . . . such as national defense." Mann told the press, "I am willing to consider preparedness in a non-partisan way, but I am not willing to take orders from the President." After Wilson provided details in his 6 December message to Congress, Mann criticized his program as at once warlike yet insufficient. Thus Mann signaled his intention that Republicans not just support preparedness, as he had indicated in his St. Louis speech, but that they should outdo the Democrats. When the two finally met, on 9 December, there was no prospect that Wilson would agree to a truly nonpartisan approach, nor that Mann would acquiesce in Wilson's program. By then, Mann had persuaded Frank Greene to abandon ambitions to be party whip in order to give full attention to his duties on the Military Affairs Committee, in his own interest and that of the party. Greene, who had fought in the Spanish-American War, was an advocate of preparedness and a man of ability and energy. He could help to develop a Republican program to expand the army more fully than Democrats would, and he could also avoid pitfalls already evident in Secretary of War Lindley Garrison's proposals. Nicholas Longworth understood Mann's position and the vulnerability of the Democrats

[32]*New York Times*, 29 September 1915; *St. Louis Post-Dispatch*, 29 September 1915, vol. 22, Mann Papers.

and he proposed that Mann and Roosevelt, the belligerent evangelist for preparedness, speak from the same platform.[33]

Mann would do nothing that would hurt his country. Nevertheless, he was very aware of the political possibilities in preparedness legislation. He could hope that Republicans might take some of the credit for the outcome. Because of special elections and a Mooser defection the Democrats held only a 31 vote margin over the Republicans when the House convened.[34] Perhaps they could help provide a majority for what emerged. At the least, they might show themselves more fully united than the Democrats in support of a program the country could approve.

Certainly, the Democrats would not be fully united. Twenty-four Tammany men were alienated from the administration.[35] More important as to preparedness, despite the administration's strenuous and partly successful efforts, Wilson could not count on some of the Bryanites. Claude Kitchin, the new majority leader succeeding Underwood, was the most important of these. A brilliant speaker and debater with a large, imposing presence, friendly manner, and reputation for high character, Kitchin had been chosen in February 1915.[36] He had a record of consistently opposing anything more than a single additional battleship and now was frank to express his fears of preparedness as being offensive rather than defensive. He agreed to oppose the program only as an individual, not as majority leader, but even so, his stand would encourage thirty to fifty like-minded Democrats to follow suit. Furthermore, Kitchin put sympathizers on the military and naval affairs committees.[37]

---

[33]Wilson to Mann, 18 November 1915, Arthur S. Link, ed., *The Papers of Woodrow Wilson* (Princeton, N.J.: Princeton University Press, 1980), 35:213; *New York Times*, 21 November 1915; *Chicago Tribune*, 8 December 1915, vol. 22, Mann Papers; Frank Greene to Walter Crockett, 12 December 1915, box 1, Frank L. Greene Papers, Library of Congress.

[34]*Congressional Directory*, Sixty-fourth Congress First Session, December 1915, p. 136.

[35]Clara Longsworth de Chambrun, *The Making of Nicholas Longworth: Annals of an American Family*, (New York: Ray Long and Richard R. Smith, 1933), 230.

[36]Arthur S. Link, *Wilson: Confusions and Crises, 1915*–1916 (Princeton N.J.: Princeton University Press, 1964), 19; Homer Larry Ingle, "Pilgrimage to Reform: A Life of Claude Kitchin" (Ph.D. diss., University of Wisconsin, 1967), 52, 94; Champ Clark, *My Quarter Century of American Politics* (New York: Harper and Brothers, 1920), 2:339; James F. Byrnes, *Speaking Frankly* (New York: Harper and Brothers, 1947), 33-34.

[37]Ingle, "Pilgrimage to Reform," 66, 103, 107; Kitchin to Victor Murdock, 18 October 1915, box 58, Victor Murdock Papers, Library of Congress; Cooper, *Vanity of Power*, 90-93.

Under the circumstances, the Democratic caucus was useless on military matters, and Wilson assumed direct legislative leadership.[38] Democrats could not afford to oppose or weaken him, for the party's success more than ever was linked to him, but privately some complained. Even earlier, a Texas member told Kitchin that Wilson "always impresses me that he feels cock sure about everything and does not need help or advice." Another southern Democrat, later asked to describe the relationship between president and Congress, responded, "the relation between master and servant. I may as well say between man and dog."[39] Animosity towards Wilson was bound to further encourage rebellion among some antipreparedness Democrats. In sum, Mann could anticipate that the Democrats would have some difficulty in developing a program, would have to settle for something weak, and might ultimately fail to rally full party support.

For Mann, there was opportunity and advantage in outdoing the Democrats on preparedness, for he could both count on and please the strong preparedness forces in his party. But he faced formidable problems. The Republican program must not alarm the country with undue bellicosity, and it must be made acceptable to some in the strong contingent of peace-minded Republicans centered in the Midwest. Revelations of sabotage and extensive politicking by German Americans, combined with Germany's continuing unwillingness to acknowledge wrongdoing in the *Lusitania* sinking, fanned an anti-Germanism that Wilson himself abetted when in his 6 December message he denounced those who had "poured the poison of disloyalty into the very arteries of our national life." [40] The Republican peace forces would not easily be reconciled to a strong preparedness bill, from either party. In approaching these problems, Mann had an unusual advantage—since he was himself part of the midwestern peace group, if he could satisfy himself, he could probably satisfy some others.

On 25 January, while the issue was in a formative stage in committee, Mann delivered a major address. Early on, he reminded his colleagues that he had never favored a large standing army and had properly been classified as "a little navy man." Then he spoke of the war among all the great powers except the United States as unique in history and possibly lasting for some time. At this point he announced himself for preparedness to meet any contingency,

---

[38]Finnegan, *Against the Specter of a Dragon*, 81; Joseph Cooper and David W. Brady, "Institutional Context and Leadership Style; The House from Cannon to Rayburn," *American Political Science Review* 75 (June 1981): 417; Randall B. Ripley, *Party Leaders in the House of Representatives* (Washington, D.C.: Brookings Institution, 1967), 72, 86; Broesamle, "Democrats," 103.

[39]Joe Eagle to Kitchin, 24 April 1915, box 1, Claude Kitchin Papers, University of North Carolina, Library, Chapel Hill, and NHPRC microfilm; *Chicago Tribune*, 28 July 1917, vol. 23, Mann Papers.

[40]Link, *Wilson: Confusions and Crises*, 36, 56-57.

and he received loud applause for that. Quickly going on, however, Mann said, "In this war I am a neutral. I think we ought to maintain peace at all hazards." Yet, he said, war might be forced upon the country. Now he spoke of the financial costs of the war to the participants and such burdens of debt as could induce revolutions later. Revolutions, he said, as he had suggested in St. Louis, "have usually led to aggression and disputes and often to war with other countries." Spending now on defense, he went on, might serve as a deterrent and make unnecessary greater spending later. Outflanking the Democrats, who in committee contemplated something less, he proposed increasing the regular army to "250,000 or 300,000, or even half a million men."

Then Mann asked for coastal defenses and for "a navy which will be able to defend us on the sea." "I have much more fear," he explained, "in the end, of war with England than I have of war with Germany." Mann did not elaborate on that remarkable declaration; its significance would not be overlooked, he knew. In one breathtakingly audacious stroke, Mann uncoupled preparedness from the danger of war with Germany, at least for the time being.

Quickly ending, he further enticed all Republicans by calling for protectionism and self-sufficiency as adjuncts to preparedness. He concluded with various pious hopes. Insofar as the prolonged applause that Mann received at the end of his speech came from the Republican side, it anticipated approval from a wide spectrum of congressmen, editors, and ethnic spokesmen in the days that followed. In remarkable degree Mann had unified Republicans behind a strong preparedness program. It was the more effective for not being extreme. Mann had made no mention, for instance, of universal military training, which many ardent preparedness men were advocating.[41]

How sincere was Mann in saying that war was more likely with England than with Germany? He was well aware that the statement, coming from the party leader, would do much to sanitize preparedness for many Republican voters, especially German Americans and Anglophobes. But the idea, though startling, was not farfetched from his standpoint. He was not forecasting war with England, but saying only that war with Germany was less likely. Indeed, the United States had endured much at the hands of German submarines without going to war. The American public, Mann knew, overwhelmingly opposed war. He could hardly have foreseen Germany's desperate decision in 1917 to sink without warning or lifesaving not only belligerent vessels but American merchantmen as well. As to England, Mann took seriously what he

---

[41]*CR* 64:1, pp. 1510-11 (25 January 1916); Harbaugh, "Republican Party," 2100; Gerald D. McKnight, "A Party against Itself—The Grand Old Party in the New Freedom Era, 1913–1916" (Ph.D. diss., University of Maryland, 1972), 245-50; *Chicago Tribune*, 26 January 1916, 27 January 1916, vol. 22, Mann Papers; "Nationwide Press Poll on Size of the Army and the Navy," *Literary Digest*, 52:11 (11 March 1916); 617-22, 647-87; Finnegan, *Against the Specter of a Dragon*, 76-77, 84.

construed as illegal interference with American shipping. He did not propose to fight about it, yet armed conflict might somehow result. Also, looking to the future, Mann envisioned the possibility of fresh war resulting from disturbed conditions produced by the present war.

The Democrats limited their political losses when they combined on a modest army reorganization bill. Wilson abandoned Secretary Garrison's plan for a large volunteer Continental Army, a proposal that antagonized the powerful National Guard, and then accepted Garrison's resignation. Soon Wilson appointed a former opponent of preparedness, Newton D. Baker, as secretary of war. Also, Wilson cultivated the small-army chairman of Military Affairs, James Hay of Virginia, and acquiesced in Hay's plans. Speaker Clark helped with soothing oil, and Kitchin quietly abandoned his opposition.[42]

On 6 March the committee reported the bill, which reached the floor on 18 March. It called for a gradual increase in the regular army from 100,000 to 140,000 and proposed to bring the National Guard, 129,000 men, under the control of the War Department. The committee reported the bill unanimously, in a show of national unity. But committee members understood that they could and would offer amendments.[43]

Mann took the offensive in favor of a stronger program. He pressed the case rhetorically and undertook to establish a record through roll-call votes. On 10 February Germany renounced the *Arabic* pledge and said that it would sink armed belligerent merchantships without warning, thus endangering American lives. Under the circumstances, members could hardly disassociate the defense bill from the possibility of war with Germany. Mann, however, remained credible as one who, while favoring preparedness, was also anxious to avoid war with Germany. In the wake of Germany's submarine announcement, Mann had renewed his neutralist credentials by backing a contentious proposal to warn Americans off belligerent ships, a matter to which we shall return. Furthermore, on 9 March Francisco (Pancho) Villa attacked Columbus, New Mexico, killing eight Americans before an army unit drove his forces into retreat, at a further cost in American lives. On 15 March Brigadier General John J. Pershing, with four thousand men, entered Mexico in pursuit. Villa, however, would not easily be caught, and President Carranza gave no clear approval to the American incursion.[44] The Mexican situation not only gave further reason for preparedness but also helped Mann

---

[42]Finnegan, *Against the Specter of a Dragon*, 74, 88-90, 140-41; August Heckscher, *Woodrow Wilson* (New York: Charles Scribner's Sons, 1991), 379; Timothy Gregory McDonald, "Southern Democratic Congressmen and the First World War, August 1914-April 1917: The Public Record of Their Support for or Opposition to Wilson's Policies," (Ph.D. diss., University of Washington, 1962), 182.

[43]Link, *Wilson: Confusions and Crises*, 327-29; Finnegan, *Against the Specter of a Dragon*, 141-42.

[44]Link, *Wilson: Confusions and Crises*, 209-17.

in at least partly separating the army bill from the question of war with Germany.

Julius Kahn of California offered the principal Republican amendment, to permit the president to immediately enlist an additional 80,000 troops to Hay's 140,000. Kahn, ranking Republican on Military Affairs, was an influential advocate for his cause. Of German-Jewish parentage, he had come to America at the age of seven. He had been an actor before entering the House in 1899. Liked and respected by his colleagues, he was a fine orator as well, and a longtime backer of preparedness.[45]

Mann gave strong support to the Kahn amendment in two speeches. He talked of Mexico, of America as a defender of neutral rights, and of its role in the postwar world. Above all, he stressed that what Wilson had called for was emergency legislation, while Hay's bill, with its authorization for a slow and limited increase, was hardly that.[46]

To the extent that Mann's purpose was to make the Republicans the party of preparedness, he was quite successful in the initial voting. In Committee of the Whole members rejected Kahn's amendment, 103-183. But on a roll-call vote in the House the amendment lost by a narrower margin, 191-213, and just 34 Republicans opposed it.[47] On three lesser amendments the Republicans showed even better cohesion and won out.[48] The House passed the amended bill by a vote of 403-2.

On 24 March a German submarine torpedoed a British channel steamer, the *Sussex*. It did not sink, and no Americans were among the eighty who died, but four were injured. The event caused a diplomatic crisis and set the stage for adoption in the Senate of a bill to increase the regular army to 250,000, authorize a national reserve army of 261,000, and federalize an expanded National Guard. The bill also provided for construction of a plant at Muscle Shoals to manufacture synthetic nitrates for munitions.[49] In the House Mann again expressed his desire to stay out of the war "except under the most extreme circumstances." His assertion rang true in light of his recent denunciation of Wilson as unduly bellicose. Yet dangers were such that he favored "preparing men who may be ready and trained to fight, if necessary, before we pour out the blood of volunteers, unprepared and untrained." What Mann urged was that House conferees be instructed to accept the main

---

[45]Alan Boxerman, "Kahn of California," *California Historical Quarterly* 55 (Winter 1976): 340–46.

[46]*CR* 64:1, pp. 4403-4 (18 March 1916), 4490 (20 March 1916).

[47]*Ibid.*, pp. 4491 (20 March 1916), 4792 (23 March 1916); Richard F. Bensel, *Sectionalism and American Political Development, 1880-1980* (Madison: University of Wisconsin Press, 1984), 125.

[48]Finnegan, *Against the Specter of a Dragon*, 144; McDonald, "Southern Democratic Congressmen," 186-88; Bensel, *Sectionalism*, 105.

[49]Link, *Wilson: Confusions and Crises*, 228, 230.

features of the Senate bill. Clark, however, blocked a record vote on that by recognizing the New York Socialist Meyer London to put a very different and objectionable recommittal motion.[50]

By 8 May the crisis with Germany had seemingly been resolved by Germany's *Sussex* pledge, and the Senate bill lost its urgency. Furthermore, the national reserve army provision seemed to the National Guard to be a new version of Garrison's Continental Army. When House conferees asked for new instructions, Mann argued for accepting the 250,000-man army and the voluntary force, but lost 141-222 and 109-251.[51] The Senate conferees now yielded somewhat. The conference report increased the regular army to 206,169, expandable to 254,000, increased the federalized National Guard to 425,000, added new army units, provided for a nitrate plant, but did not include the reserve army. The bill implemented the army's peacetime demands, but did not fully respond to the emergency.[52] Because of that, Mann cast a symbolic vote in opposition, together with untrapacifists, as the National Defense Act of 1916 passed in the House, 349-25. Despite his final vote, he had long since made his point that one could strongly oppose war while favoring an immediate military buildup. The Democrats had hardly been routed, nor had their deep internal divisions fully shown themselves, yet the Republicans had better identified themselves with the issue, in considerable part through Mann's efforts.[53]

Mann took a lesser but similar role in connection with the naval appropriations bill. In this instance, partly through historical accident, Republicans scored very clear gains at the expense of the Democrats. The latter, on 2 June, pushed through the House a bill that satisfied small-navy Democrats. First, though, on a recommittal motion, the Republicans went on record for a vastly larger program. They lost only narrowly, 189-183, and suffered just 18 defections.[54] That very day, the Battle of Jutland demonstrated the superiority of battleships over thinly armored battle cruisers. After the political conventions the Senate approved a three-year expansion bill that included ten battleships and six battle cruisers. Wilson then interceded with the House Democratic conferees, who reluctantly yielded to the Senate. When the conference report reached the House on 15 August, small-navy Democrats headed by Kitchin resisted. Mann, on the other hand, in supporting the re-

---

[50]*CR* 64:1, pp. 6815, 6819 (25 April 1916); Finnegan, *Against the Specter of a Dragon*, 152.

[51]*CR* 64:1, pp. 7599-7601 (8 May 1916).

[52]Link, *Wilson: Confusions and Crises*, 331-32; Finnegan, *Against the Specter of a Dragon*, 155.

[53]*CR* 64:1, pp. 8400, 8406 (20 May 1916).

[54]Link, *Wilson: Confusions and Crises*, 334-35; *CR* 64:1, p. 9189; Howard Scott Greenlee, "The Republican Party in Division and Reunion, 1913-1920" (Ph.D. diss., University of Chicago, 1950), 117.

port, boasted that the conferees had acquiesced in the program of the House Republicans, and that Republican votes were required to push the program through. He remained careful, though, to assert again his concern for peace, and he talked more of the postwar than the present uses of naval strength. In the 283-51 vote of approval, just 14 Republicans broke ranks.[55]

The army appropriations bill also passed after the conventions. It was not very controversial. Mann remained consistent in that while supporting the conference report, he wished that it carried more money. He continued to see danger that the United States would be dragged into the war—that when one side or another saw that it was losing, it would do all it could to drag others in. He saw a need for more ammunition and for more military training.[56]

The preparedness issue, while still important, took second place after February to the twin issues of neutrality and neutral rights. Mann acted assertively on neutral rights so long as that did not endanger his greater goal, neutrality. Thus he spoke belligerently about British violations, while taking a cautious line on German submarine warfare. Although he tried to minimize the division, he could not hope to speak for a united party, but instead led one faction. That did no serious harm. Party division on the issues of neutrality and neutral rights was not so damaging as one might suspect. Politically, these were local issues, akin to liquor and immigration, not party ones. Republicans especially, not bound to the president, divided along lines based on constituent ethnicity, ideology, and geography and set themselves up for reelection and possible party gains in their states. To be sure, in the upcoming presidential campaign, to an extent the issues would become partisan. Foreseeably, Mann's side, if it received proper emphasis in the platform and by the presidential candidate, would be popular. Furthermore, the peace element of the Republican party probably had the greater need for his leadership, especially in the Midwest, to counter the strong Democratic peace group in Congress and Wilson's own image as a man of peace. The more belligerent Republicans could do without Mann, given their strength in the East and their abundance of spokesmen in the press, the universities, and politics.

Mann's most important single action in favor of neutrality as against neutral rights was in connection with the McLemore resolution. Several statements by Wilson and Secretary of State Robert Lansing alarmed many in Congress with the fear that the administration was headed towards war with Germany over the rights of Americans on armed belligerent merchant vessels. Senator Thomas Gore, Oklahoma Democrat, and Representative Jeff

[55]Finnegan, *Against the Specter of a Dragon*, 161-63; Harold Sprout and Margaret Sprout, *The Rise of American Naval Power, 1776-1918* (Princeton, N.J.: Princeton University Press, 1966), 334-41; CR 64:1, pp. 12666, 12695-96, 12700 (15 August 1916); McDonald, "Southern Democratic Congressmen," 205.

[56]CR 64:1, p. 12399 (9 August 1916).

McLemore, Democrat of Texas, introduced resolutions to warn Americans off such ships and, in effect, disavow national responsibility for their welfare. Wilson, fearful that such action would weaken his hand diplomatically, including his secret effort to arrange for peace through American mediation, called for a congressional show of support. Because of a muddled parliamentary situation the Gore resolution came to a confused outcome, so all eyes focused on the House.[57]

The administration strategy was to report the McLemore resolution, which offended even such peace leaders as Kitchin because of its seeming defense of Germany and disrespect for the president, permit no amendments, and then vote to table it. Burleson and McAdoo came to the Capitol with a letter of appeal from Wilson, but even before that such Democratic leaders as Finis J. Garrett, Thetus Sims, Carter Glass, and Pat Harrison, moved at least as much by patriotism as by party loyalty, rallied Democrats.[58]

Mann, working in tandem with Rule Committee Republicans Campbell and Lenroot, and assisted by other leaders, surely including his peace-minded colleagues Mondell and Moore, brought pressure on Republicans for a three-step program. Mann's first goal was to keep the issue off the floor altogether. That action would conduce to party unity and would be defensible as noninterference with the executive in its conduct of diplomacy. Failing that, Mann hoped to open the way for amendments, and Campbell prepared one to simply warn Americans to stay off belligerent vessels. Such a resolution might well carry and would certainly be more appealing to Republicans than the McLemore resolution. As a last resort, however, Mann wanted Republicans to vote against tabling the McLemore resolution, for however obnoxious some of its wording might be, such a vote would put his party on the side of peace.[59]

Augustus P. Gardner, leader among Republicans who would vote down the McLemore resolution, rather belligerently and unexpectedly introduced the subject on 6 March, a day before the prospective showdown in the House. Mann replied in what the *New York Times* called "unusually fervid utterances." Members flocked in, and spectators filled the galleries. Mann explained that he had "been quite content to let the House attend to its Constitutional duties, thinking that at any time the President desired the action of the House he would come before the House or Congress and say so." He went on to suggest, however, that while few in the House liked the McLemore resolution, "a majority of this House if they expressed their

---

[57]Link, *Wilson: Confusions and Crises*, 163-89.

[58]Cooper, *Vanity of Power*, 111; McDonald, "Southern Democratic Congressmen," 137-41.

[59]Pressure on Republicans is indicated in Frank Greene to Harold Hindley, 10 March 1916, box 3, Greene Papers, and by Augustus P. Gardner in *CR* 64:1,p. 3634 (6 March 1916).

opinions, are of the opinion that American citizens at this time ought not to complicate the situation by traveling on armed merchant vessels." Prolonged applause followed this frank statement.

Gardner asked whether Americans should be protected when they did travel. Mann replied: "I think that when that question arises we ought to meet it, but I hope that our citizens may be advised that we shall not be put to the test whether we have to fight because some fool had entered upon a joy ride or voyage." Going on from that injudicious statement, Mann completed the outline of his position: "If we are forced to vote simply and solely upon the proposition to table the McLemore resolution, we have voted that we invite American citizens to travel on armed merchant vessels with the assurance that we will go to war if they do." Then Mann ridiculed the distinction Gardner had drawn between a straight vote on the McLemore resolution and a "fake" vote on something less extreme. If a vote were forced, he would amend the McLemore resolution, so the president could learn what the House truly thought. He would prefer no vote at all, he concluded, but if there were one, "I do not propose to register the will of anybody else, but to register my own judgment." Again, Mann received prolonged applause, mainly but not exclusively from Republicans.[60]

The following day the House engaged in seven hours of tense debate and took three votes. Mann left the oratory to others. He did, however, lay out the Republican program from a parliamentary standpoint. Midway in the debate, calculatedly collegial, Mann diverted attention with the announcement that it was Champ Clark's sixty-sixth birthday. Five minutes of applause, followed by words of thanks from Clark to Mann and the House, served to break some of the tension and lessen the intraparty divisiveness of the debate and of the whole affair.[61]

The crucial vote was the first, on the previous question. If it were defeated, Campbell could offer his simple warning resolution. Administration lines held, however, as the question was adopted, 256-160. Sixty-three Republicans contributed to the majority, while 132 voted with Mann.[62] Then the members approved the restrictive rule, 271-137, and four hours later they voted to table the McLemore resolution, 276-142. On that vote 93 Republicans voted to table, while 102 voted against. Among easterners, the Republican vote was 66-22 for tabling; midwesterners voted 16-62 against.[63] Although Mann failed to win any of the votes, and his party showed itself divided, yet the breakdown of Republican voting made it clear that Lodge,

[60]CR 64:1, pp. 3635-36 (6 March 1916); New York Times, 7 March 1916; Washington Post, 7 March 1916.

[61]CR 64:1, pp. 3698, 3707 (7 March 1916); New York Times, 8 March 1916.

[62]Washington Post, 8 March 1916; CR 64:1, p. 3699 (7 March 1916).

[63]CR 64:1, p. 3720 (7 March 1916); Bensel, Sectionalism, 124; McDonald, "Southern Democratic Congressmen," 151.

Gardner, Stimson, Root, and Roosevelt, who was hinting at a return to lead a "heroic" campaign, spoke for only a segment of the party, and in the House, not the largest one. Thus those congressmen and senators who needed to, and the presidential candidate as well, could credibly present themselves as defenders of neutrality and peace.

Those who were disposed to criticize Mann, especially in the press, pounced on his words about being forced into war "because some fool had entered upon a joy ride or voyage."[64] In April Mann provided his detractors with stronger ammunition. Again, however, he did so by putting himself forth as more the advocate of peace than Wilson.

Torpedoing of the *Sussex* on 24 March, seemingly a terroristic act, led Wilson into fruitless diplomacy. Finally, fearing a dangerous submarine campaign that would compel the United States to enter the war, and also in order to advance his mediation plan, Wilson decided to force the issue. On 19 April he came before Congress and read the note he had just sent to Germany. It ended with an ultimatum. Unless Germany abandoned its methods of submarine warfare on passenger and "freight-carrying vessels," the United States would break diplomatic relations.[65]

Mann, whose face flushed a "fiery red" while listening to Wilson, gave several widely reported interviews afterwards. "The truth is," he said, "the President is a Scotch Presbyterian and he hates 'the Dutch.' . . . When the McLemore resolution was up in the House I said the President wanted to involve us in war with Germany. His attitude has not been neutral in any respect. His message today shows that he expects, if he can, to force war with Germany." Mann charged that though the United States had valid complaints against Germany, Wilson had exaggerated them, while ignoring complaints against Britain. "I think this Government should be neutral. He has been on the English side all the time." Mann ended with the charge that Wilson, "as a campaign dodge, is trying to work up to a point where he can get into a war with Germany during a Presidential campaign."[66]

Mann's words were unjust, though he had no way of knowing that. They were also intemperate and injudicious, and they evoked a great wave of condemnation, as from such New York papers as the *Times*, the *Sun*, the *Evening Post*, and the *World*, and from prominent individuals headed by former Attorney General George Wickersham.[67] At the same time, though, Mann

---

[64]Rena Mitchell, "The Congressional Career of James R. Mann" (M.A. thesis, University of Chicago, 1938), 60.

[65]Link, *Woodrow Wilson: Revolution, War, and Peace*, 44-45.

[66]*Chicago Tribune*, 20 April 1916, vol. 22, Mann Papers; *New York Times*, 20 April 1916.

[67]*New York Times*, 21 April 1916, 22 April 1916, 26 April, 1916; "Our Final Word to Germany," *Literary Digest* 52:18 (29 April 1916): 201-4.

gave leadership and encouragement to Republican neutralists and virtually preempted the peace issue for those of his party who would use it.

Then Germany dramatically reversed the situation. Expecting to win on the ground that summer, and to avoid complications, on 4 May it gave the *Sussex* pledge. It would adhere to the rules of visit and search, provided the United States would bring Britain to observe international law. Wilson, and Americans generally, celebrated the announcement and still more the cessation of submarine warfare that followed, while ignoring Germany's ominous condition. As though to clinch his repossession of the peace issue, on 27 May Wilson addressed the League to Enforce Peace and outlined plans for an international organization to preserve peace when the present war ended.[68] The Republicans, however, partly through Mann's efforts, could at least say "me too" to neutrality and even dredge up instances of Wilsonian bellicosity.

Mann had little legislative opportunity to press for firm defense of neutral rights against Britain. On 6 June, however, a day before the Republican national convention, which preceded the Democratic convention by a week, Mann put in the *Record* letters testifying to British violations. "We have heard a good deal of talk about preserving the lives of Americans and how much more valuable life is than property," Mann said. "It is good talk, but it always was the talk of slaves everywhere to preserve life as against rights. What good is it to a man to have his life, if that is all he cares for? He is a slave!" Mann indicted the State Department for not doing more.[69] Although he did not himself twist the lion's tail on the subject of Ireland, the fact of Britain's recent brutal repression of the Irish rebellion augmented the political attractiveness of Mann's case.

While the issues of neutrality and neutral rights were divisive, on a vital question relating to the Philippines Mann achieved party unity and success as well during the preconvention period. In the Senate James Clarke, Democrat of Arkansas, secured adoption of an amendment to the Jones bill that would go beyond limited autonomy and the promise of self-government in the indefinite future and instead require American withdrawal within four years. With Wilson's backing, House Democratic leaders called a caucus where, despite bitter contention, the amended bill became a party measure. Mann had been fighting on the Philippines front for several years and had encouraged Republican congressmen to visit the Philippines. Three went. Now, aware that he would get help from some rebellious Democrats led by Fitzgerald, he appealed for unity to recalcitrant Republicans, including the Wisconsin congressmen who usually followed La Follette. To get it, he agreed to accept the original Jones bill. The substantial compromise, for

---

[68]Cooper, *Pivotal Decades*, 239; "President Wilson's Peace Plan," *Literary Digest* 52:24 (10 June 1916): 1683-85.

[69]*CR* 64:1, pp. 9303-4 (6 June 1916).

Mann a triumph of realism over conviction and sentiment, proved sufficient. On 1 May, by a vote of 193-151, the House rejected the Clarke amendment and instructed conferees to do likewise. Republicans voted together. They were joined by 30 Democrats, mainly Catholics who responded to the church hierarchy's fear that church property would be seized. For Mann and the Republicans, the victory was substantial. The show of unity was at once heartening to themselves and appealing to the electorate. Republicans could also hope to gain among Catholics, businessmen, and those many Americans who responded to nationalism.[70]

There were votes to be won over Mexico, too. On that, however, Mann reserved fresh denunciations of the administration's weakness for the postconvention campaign season.

During the preconvention run-up of the Sixty-fourth Congress, December to June, although the great international questions dominated, both parties gave close attention to domestic issues. The Democrats began to put forth new progressive proposals, partly to woo the remaining Moosers, whose full breakup seemed imminent, and also because agrarian and labor-minded legislators had gained in strength, and because Wilson's thinking had evolved with experience.[71]

As usual, Mann had many tasks. He needed to continue earlier efforts towards both the appearance and reality of party unification, and that required further conciliation of insurgents without alienating the rejuvenated conservative majority of House Republicans. He needed to join in the competition for Progressive voters, and that required support of some Democratic initiatives and fresh efforts to outdo the Democrats where that could be done without disrupting his own party. He needed to exploit and highlight every weakness in Democratic policy and practice, and he had to express Republican economic conservatism on basic matters.

As to that, while progressive sentiment in the electorate could hardly be ignored, yet the Progressive Movement was no longer as all-pervasive as earlier, as evidenced, for example, by the demise of muckraking. Voter attention was drawn away to international events and issues and to matters such as immigration and assimilation of immigrants, liquor, and anti-Catholicism. Economic conservatism, centered on promoting business by government and protecting business from government, was no longer in partial eclipse. It had a substantial constituency that in the North and East looked mainly to the GOP and needed to be served if the party were to regain power.

---

[70]Link, *Wilson: Confusions and Crises*, 351-54; *Chicago Tribune*, 3 May 1916, vol. 22, Mann Papers.

[71]Link, *Wilson: Confusions and Crises*, 321-22; Broesamle, "Democrats," 104, 107.

Insurgents signified their concern for party unity by their turnout at the organizing caucus in advance of the session. The caucus was better attended than any since 1907, and Mann was renominated for Speaker by acclamation. He, in turn, treated insurgents generously in committee assignments.[72]

On the domestic issues of the preconvention period, Mann achieved party unity and scored points where Democrats were weak or limited damage where they were strong. In a progressive vein, he raised rules issues against the Democrats,[73] attacked pork in the rivers and harbors bill,[74] denounced spoils politics in the Federal Farm Loan Act while backing the popular measure,[75] successfully supported a child-labor bill,[76] outdid the Democrats in appropriating for the Children's Bureau,[77] and put a Republican stamp on conservation legislation.[78] At the same time, he led his party for probusiness positions. He proposed to limit the duration of the war revenue tax,[79] raised the tariff issue through a Tariff Commission bill,[80] and attacked a bill permitting the government to buy or build ships.[81]

The parties were within weeks of their conventions when the shipping bill cleared the House. For the Republicans, completion of their rejuvenation seemed within grasp. The prospective surrender of the Progressives contributed to Republican hopes. Beyond that, although the congressional session was far from over, to that point Republicans had made a strong record. In the House Mann took the lead in advocacy of neutrality, but also of neutral

---

[72]Maureen R. Romans, "Party Leadership Fights in the House of Representatives: The Cause of Conflict, 1895-1955" (Ph.D. diss., University of Massachusetts, 1976), 141; Harry Slattery, "Memorandum for Mr. Pinchot," 15 December 1915, box 185, Pinchot Papers; *CR* 64:1, p. 241 (14 December 1915).

[73]*CR* 64:1, pp. 8 (6 December 1915), 1210 (18 January 1916).

[74]*Searchlight on Congress*, 1:4 (10 March 1916): 8; *CR* 64:1, p. 5740 (8 April 1916); James A. Frear, *Forty Years of Progressive Public Service* (Washington, D.C.: Associated Writers, 1937), 80.

[75]*CR* 64:1, pp. 7811, 7814 (9 May 1916); 7869, 7890 (12 May 1916), 7913, 7929, 7937 (13 May 1916), 7978, 8011, 8013 (15 May 1916), 10114 (27 June 1916).

[76]*CR* 64:1, pp. 7811, 7814 (9 May 1916); 7869, 7890 (12 May 1916), 7913, 7929, 7937 (13 May 1916), 7978, 8011, 8013 (15 May 1916), 10114 (27 June 1916).

[77]*Ibid.*, pp. 1593-1601 (26 January 1916), 2022-29 (2 February 1916): *Searchlight on Congress*, 1:2 (1 March 1916): 8; Arthur S. Link, *Wilson: Campaigns for Progressivism and Peace, 1916–1917* (Princeton, N.J.: Princeton University Press, 1965), 58-59.

[78]*CR* 64:1, p. 3903 (11 March 1916).

[79]*New York Times*, 21 April 1916, 22 April 1916, 26 April 1916; *CR* 64:1, pp. 358-61 (16 December 1915); *Chicago Tribune*, 17 December 1915, vol. 22, Mann Papers.

[80]Greenlee, "Republican Party," 28; *CR* 64:1, p. 249 (14 December 1915).

[81]*CR* 64:1, p. 8264 (18 May 1916); William G. McAdoo, *Crowded Years: The Reminiscences of William G. McAdoo* (Boston: Houghton Mifflin, 1931), 314-15.

rights and preparedness, together with an appealing mixture of mild progressivism, probusiness conservatism, and traditional Democrat bashing. Republicans had continued to show themselves reuniting, not on the McLemore resolution, but notably on preparedness and domestic issues.

Not all House Republicans enjoyed Mann's performance. SimeonFess, former president of Antioch College and elected from Ohio in 1912, complained of Mann's "iron rule."[82] Others, less immediately vocal, shared the disgruntlement. But it would be Mann who was ultimately hurt, not the Republican party. It benefited from the competent and astute "iron rule" Mann provided.

To what extent the Republicans would capitalize on their opportunities in the 1916 election would be determined in part by events yet to come. Much would depend on the quality of their presidential candidate and the relative effectiveness of his campaign as compared to Wilson's. Decisions by the governments of Germany, Great Britain, and Mexico would also be important. The actions of Republicans and Democrats in Congress in the postconvention season would feed into the campaigns. Mann would have ample outlet for his political and legislative energies.

---

[82]*Chicago Post*, 28 February 1916, vol. 22, Mann Papers.

6

Election: 1916; War: 1917

Not by coincidence, Republicans and Progressives convened in the same city, Chicago, on the same day, 8 June 1916. Leaders in each party were bent on reunion, though not agreed as to terms. Roosevelt wanted to be the Republican nominee, but Old Guard Republican memories of 1912 were too fresh for that, and his warlike statements clinched the case against him. The Rough Rider would settle for less because of his strong animus towards Wilson and his international policies. When on the third ballot the Republicans nominated Supreme Court justice Charles Evans Hughes, they offered a candidate Roosevelt could accept. Die-hard Progressives nominated Roosevelt, but he declined conditionally, and afterwards the Progressive National Committee voted to back Hughes.[1]

Quite apart from the Moosers, Republicans needed internal unification in the face of division on domestic and foreign policy issues. What Hughes offered was harmony and vote-getting potential. Twice governor of New York and in 1910 appointed to the Supreme Court, he had a mildly progressive background, no involvement in the 1912 schism, and no public record on the issues of the day. His attainments and presence suggested presidential stature. He would do. In furtherance of the harmony theme, the convention approved a platform that made some concessions to progressivism, blurred international questions, and meshed with the Mooser platform, which deemphasized the advanced progressivism of 1912.[2]

---

[1]James Oliver Robertson, *No Third Choice: Progressives in Republican Politics, 1916–1921* (New York: Garland, 1983), 14–21.

[2]Arthur S. Link and William M. Leary, Jr., "Election of 1916" in *History of American Presidential Elections, 1789–1968*, vol. 3, ed. Arthur M. Schlesinger, Jr. (New York: Chelsea House Publishers in association with McGraw-Hill Book Co., 1971),

Republican congressmen considered Hughes a good candidate and so did Mann. Earlier he had favored Root as the kind of strong man the times required. After the convention he praised Hughes in the same terms. "The seemingly impossible has happened. The office of President is seeking the man, not the man the office," he said. "In the greatest crisis of the world's history America should put forward its best. The American people, by general consensus of opinion, have looked to Mr. Justice Hughes as the ablest man to fill the office of President."[3]

Woodrow Wilson drafted a platform for the St. Louis convention that met on 14 June; he stressed progressivism and mature internationalism. The delegates, in their wildly enthusiastic response to speeches by former Governor Martin Glynn of New York and Senator Ollie James of Kentucky, and their very friendly greeting for Bryan, caused an addition to be made—"He kept us out of war." The peace theme would be foremost in their campaign, progressivism would come next, and prosperity would follow. Wilson, renominated, had formidable issues. In publisher Vance McCormick and banker Henry Morgenthau, recalled from the ambassadorship to Turkey, he also had able men in charge of organizing and financing the campaign.[4]

After the November elections Republican members who were unhappy with Mann over his positions or his imperious methods would try to weaken him in his leadership powers or displace him altogether. The run-up period to elections was no time for such things, and Mann continued effectively to generate campaign material.

The validity and the value of the Democratic progressivism theme, and of Republican counterclaims, would depend in part on the further actions of Congress. Mann understood that he was an important actor in the Republican campaign and quickly performed the preliminary chores of putting in the *Record* Senator Warren Harding's keynote address, the Republican platform, and Hughes's telegram of acceptance, and he defended the choice of a judge.[5] Then, aware that the Democrats would soon push ahead with mainly progressive bills, he launched a preemptive attack on the ever-attractive Mexican front.

Mann got the attention of the House when on 21 June he made the unusual announcement that he wanted to make a prepared speech. Ordinarily,

---

2249; Joseph L. Gardner, *Departing Glory: Theodore Roosevelt as Ex-President* (New York: Charles Scribner's Sons, 1973), 347.

[3]*New York Times*, 4 June 1916, 5 November 1915, 11 June 1916.

[4]Link and Leary, "Election of 1916," 2253, 2255; Arthur S. Link, *Wilson: Campaigns for Progressivism and Peace, 1916–1917* (Princeton, N.J.: Princeton University Press, 1965), 42–48; Lewis L. Gould, *Reform and Regulation: American Politics from Roosevelt to Wilson* 2nd ed. (New York: Alfred A. Knopf, 1986), 196–97; August Heckscher, *Woodrow Wilson* (New York: Charles Scribner's Sons, 1991), 397.

[5]*Searchlight on Congress*, 1:6 (10 July 1916): 2.

he spoke extemporaneously. Talking slowly but emphatically, he read a recent note from the State Department to the de facto government of Mexico reciting the situation of the three previous years, and especially the last nine months, when Mexicans had raided across American borders. "If the statements therein are true, as I believe they are," Mann concluded, "it is to the everlasting shame of the American Republic." Two days later, plausibly in light of a recent battle between American and Mexican forces, Mann predicted war resulting from America's pursuit of Villa and proposed calling up the National Guard to have men in the field and in training. When, days after that, Mann took the lead in securing an increase in army appropriations, it was to meet conditions in Mexico. Thus, for Mann, the Mexican situation did double duty—it offered opportunity to criticize the administration for weakness, and it helped in his continuing effort to minimize the association between Republican advocacy of preparedness and the possibility of war with Germany. As of September the Mexican situation remained tense, and Mann put in the Record selections from a book of letters by the wife of an American diplomat in Mexico in 1913–1914. The letters, Mann said, "throw a bright light on the blundering stupidity of the Wilson administration in dealing with Mexico."[6] In the campaign Hughes relied heavily on the issue, partly because it seemed safer than others.

In the main in the summer of 1916, Mann could only respond to Democratic initiatives. Most of these constituted continuation of the progressive program begun early in the year, but several Democratic measures were aimed at helping and wooing business. Wilson reversed himself on the Tariff Commission, and Henry Rainey of Illinois won House adoption of it as part of a new revenue act, as Mann silently approved. When the Webb bill reached the floor, to allow American manufacturers to use common selling agents abroad without fear of anti-trust prosecution, Mann gave enthusiastic support. The bill passed the House, 199–25, but did not become law until January 1918, as the Webb-Pomerene Act. [7]

Mann's response to progressive proposals was consistent with his past record. He supported a number of bills that met his approval and did no harm

[6]*Chicago Tribune*, 22 June 1916, vol. 22, James R. Mann Papers, Library of Congress; CR 64:1, pp. 9712–13 (21 June 1916); Arthur S. Link, *Wilson: Confusions and Crises, 1915–1916* (Princeton, N.J.: University Press, 1964), 303–5; CR 64:1, pp. 9873–74 (23 June 1916); *Chicago Tribune*, 27 June 1916, vol. 22, Mann Papers; CR 64:1, appendix, pp. 2161–62 (8 September 1916).

[7]John J. Broesamle, "The Democrats from Bryan to Wilson," in *The Progressive Era*, ed. Lewis L. Gould (Syracuse: Syracuse University Press, 1974), 108; Robert Alfred Waller, *Rainey of Illinois: A Political Biography, 1903–34* (Urbana: University of Illinois Press, 1977), 106, 158–63; Joseph F. Kenkel, *Progressives and Protection: The Search for a Tariff Policy, 1866–1936* (Lanham, Md.: University Press of America, 1983), 102–9; CR 64:1, pp. 13726, 13732 (2 September 1916).

to business, while strongly resisting the ones that he considered hurtful to the economy. His was a moderate approach that, viewed politically, proposed to limit Democratic gains on reform issues and establish the basis for vigorous Republican campaigning on conservative lines.

As previously noted, Mann and most House Republicans supported the child-labor and rural-credits bills that cleared the House in June. In July Mann backed a Democratic bill for workmen's compensation for federal employees. The old system, requiring special private claims bills, was cumbersome and unfair, he felt. Corporations, too, had come to favor systematizing compensation for injury, he remarked. The bill passed the House, 287–3, and in August became law.[8] Mann also supported a bill to provide federal funds on a matching basis for state vocational education. "We are going to be in competition with other nations, where they do better than we about instructing their youth in the vocations," he said. The bill cleared the House and was passed in the Senate in 1917.[9]

Claude Kitchin's new revenue bill was too progressive for Mann's taste, and he vigorously attacked it from a conservative standpoint. No friend to preparedness, and encouraged by Democrats of the South and West, Kitchin set out to impose the tax burden required for preparedness on easterners who advocated the buildup and stood to benefit financially. Blazing new paths in progressive taxation, Kitchin's Ways and Means Committee on 1 July reported a bill to double the normal income tax rate to 2 percent and raise the surtax from 6 to 10 percent. The bill also created a new tax on estates, progressively scaled, and a new tax on the gross income of munitions makers. It repealed the odious stamp taxes of 1914, created a Tariff Commission, and gave tariff protection to chemicals. The bulk of the new revenue would come from the income tax, without cutting the $3,000 exemption to expand the tax base.[10] The bill opened vote-getting prospects for Democrats, but also for Republicans. Just as it represented a further advancement in progressivism, led by Democrats, so for Mann and many of his colleagues it offered opportunity to update and renew the conservatism of the Republican party.

Mann in April 1916 had spoken of the tariff as the defining issue of the coming campaign. Now Republicans embraced the opportunity to spotlight that issue. Ways and Means member Ebenezer Hill and the ranking Ways and Means Republican, Joseph Fordney, respectively, moved that specified tariff increases be substituted for Kitchin's taxes, and that protection be afforded

---

[8]*CR* 64:1, pp. 10897, 10916 (12 July 1916).

[9]*Ibid.*, pp. 11819–20 (29 July 1916).

[10]Link, *Wilson: Campaigns for Progressivism and Peace*, 60–63; Homer Larry Ingle, "Pilgrimage to Reform: A Life of Claude Kitchin" (Ph.D. diss., University of Wisconsin, 1967), 121; John J. Broesamle, *William Gibbs McAdoo: A Passion for Change, 1863–1917* (Port Washington, N.Y.: Kennikat Press, 1973), 157.

against an anticipated postwar flood of cheap foreign products. Both men argued their cases. The House rejected the motions, 116–143 and 181–199, but the Republicans united behind their traditional issue.[11]

Mann, in a short speech, alluded to the tariff as the better way and attacked the principles underlying Kitchin's bill. "It is always easy for those who do not pay taxes to favor taxes against those who do pay taxes," Mann said. "The great problem in a republican form of government in the end will be whether the burden of taxation shall be distributed among all who receive the benefits or whether a great majority shall put the burden of taxation only upon a few." He suggested that the present system of taxes, involving income taxes, other internal revenue taxes, and customs duties should continue, "and the larger proportion of the additional revenue might well be exacted at the customhouses, equally distributing the burden and at the same time guaranteeing the American industrial independence of the world."

Then Mann gave a series of statistics. Early on, he presented figures to show that "the 11 states of Alabama, Mississippi, Arkansas, Florida, Georgia, North Carolina, Oklahoma, South Carolina, Tennessee, Louisiana, and Kentucky, with 95 Members of Congress, paid of the corporation tax last year $2,947,288, as against $5,109,164 that Chicago paid." Income tax figures were similar. Mann gave other statistics encompassing all the states and noted that New York, Pennsylvania, and Illinois, with a total membership in the House of 106 out of 435 and in the Senate of 6 of 96, paid in income and corporation taxes $69,078,981, while the other forty-five states paid $55,788,488. Concluding, Mann said, "I do believe that we may properly make wealth bear a larger proportion of taxes than poverty, that those who have accumulated fortunes may pay a larger proportion of income than those who have a small income, but the effort of the Democratic side of the House to make the few pay all of the burdens in my judgment stamps the bill as improper legislation of which we should not be guilty." Mann appended elaborate tables further detailing the statistical points he had made respecting taxation and representation, presumably as campaign material in wealthy areas.[12]

The bill passed the House by a vote of 239–142, and 39 Republicans voted for it. A few, like Gardner, wanted to be consistent with their preparedness stands but most of the 39 were midwestern insurgents who approved the bill's policy premises. Thus, though the Senate made the rates yet more progressive, the bill itself could be used by Republicans only locally. But general tax policy, especially the tariff, could be used everywhere. The anti-

[11]Fred Kelly, "Republican Floor Leader of the House of Representatives," *American Magazine* 81 (April 1916): 50–51; *CR* 64:1, pp. 10733–39, 10767 (10 July 1916).

[12]*CR* 64:1, pp. 10742–43 (10 July 1916).

southern theme, which was stressed by other Republicans besides Mann, could also be used in the campaign.[13]

The larger issue raised by Mann recalled concerns of the propertied in the revolutionary and Jacksonian eras. The new aspect was the application of conservative arguments at the start of federal progressive taxation. After America entered the war, Congress pushed rates to unheard-of levels and set the stage for a continuation of debate within the dominant Republican party in the 1920s. In the New Deal era of the 1930s the issue was between the parties, and Republicans generally adopted the position that Mann and others expressed in 1916.

On 1 September Mann again took conservative ground on a major bill, even in the face of a seeming national emergency and division in his party. A threatened strike of railroad workers had brought Wilson to try personal mediation. His effort failed, however, and on 29 August the unions announced a national strike for 4 September. Wilson came to Congress and asked for immediate legislation to head it off and also to establish long-range procedures against similar future situations. Clark hoped to win Mann's cooperation, but after Wilson's speech Mann said only that the Republicans should adopt a policy of "watchful waiting" and not commit themselves.[14]

House Democratic leaders persuaded Wilson that only part of the package could quickly be adopted, and he acquiesced. Adamson's bill of 31 August yielded to the unions' demand for an eight-hour day with no cut in wages then being paid for ten-hours, and prorated compensation for work beyond eight hours. A commission would be established to study the new arrangement and report to the president and Congress. The bill did not include presidential recommendations designed to require arbitration in future railroad disputes.[15]

As debate neared its end the next day, Mann condemned the bill. He said that while it purported to be an hours bill, actually it was a wage bill, creating a 25 percent pay increase. As such, he said, it was of doubtful constitutionality, and its effect would be to raise costs for all. He criticized Wilson for backing away from his earlier recommendations and said that as always he

---

[13]*Ibid.*, p. 10768 (10 July 1916); Gerald D. McKnight, "A Party against Itself—The Grand Old Party in the New Freedom Era, 1913–1916" (Ph.D. diss., University of Maryland, 1972), 257; Howard Scott Greenlee, "The Republican Party in Division and Reunion, 1913–1920" (Ph.D. diss., University of Chicago, 1950), 124–25; James M. Leake, "Four Years of Congress," *American Political Science Review* 11 (May 1917): 272.

[14]Link, *Wilson: Campaigns for Progressivism and Peace*, 83–89; Francis E. Newlands to Woodrow Wilson, 29 August 1916, Arthur 5. Link, ed., *The Papers of Woodrow Wilson* (Princeton, N.J.: Princeton University Press, 1982), 38:102–3; *New York Times*, 20 August 1916.

[15]Link, *Wilson: Campaigns for Progressivism and Peace*, 89–90.

"wobbled and wavered." Mann then announced that John A. Sterling of Illinois would offer an amendment and a recommittal motion that if in the future the two sides in a railroad dispute would not mediate or arbitrate, the president would appoint a commission to investigate, and pending its report there could be no strike or lockout. "If we are going to yield to the emergencies of the present moment," he said, "we ought at least to do something toward preventing disaster in the future."[16]

In the voting Republicans showed themselves reluctant to block emergency legislation, yet sympathetic to Mann's view. When Swagar Sherley ruled Sterling's amendment not germane, Mann appealed and lost by a 92–109 vote. On the same motion in the form of recommittal Mann again appealed an adverse ruling, Fitzgerald moved to table Mann's appeal, and the House voted to table, 204–87. Many Republicans evidently preferred not to cause delay. Swiftly the House passed the bill, 239–56, and Republicans divided, 54 against, Mann among them, and 70 in favor. But one of those who voted in favor, Lenroot, reflected the opinion of others in casting doubt on the wisdom of the law and deploring the administration's failure to advance legislation to inhibit emergency strikes. He excused his vote as due exclusively to the suffering that would result from a national railroad strike.[17] In the Senate Republicans attacked the bill as cowardly, and only one Republican, La Follette, voted in favor as it passed, 43–28.[18] Thus Mann's conservative position was also his party's in the election campaign.

The session ended quietly on 6 September, but not without the usual exchange of compliments. Unusual among these, however, was Fitzgerald's expressed hope that Mann would be reelected "because of his usefulness to the country."[19] He was. Anti-Saloon Leaguer A. M. Boynton, a Baptist pastor, having failed to lure a strong Republican politician into the primary election against Mann, himself ran. In addition to his dry supporters, Boynton had the backing of some women, still suspicious of Mann's position on woman suffrage, and of reform leader Charles Merriam of the University of Chicago. But publishers Robert McCormick and Victor Lawson, respectively, liked Mann's protectionist and preparedness stands, while William Randolph Hearst admired his advocacy of peace with Germany. All three, no doubt, respected his prominence, and Mann got the backing of the *Tribune*, the *Daily News*, the *Examiner*, and the *American*. Edwin Sims organized the workers and the literature, and despite heavy spending by Boynton, Mann won by a five-to-one ratio. In the general election the Democrats offered

---

[16]*CR* 64:1, p. 13597 (1 September 1916).

[17]*Ibid*., pp. 13604–8, 13582 (1 September 1916).

[18]Greenlee, "Republican Party," 187.

[19]*New York Times*, 9 September 1916.

only token opposition, and Mann, for the first time since 1908, won with a majority rather than a plurality. He got 63 percent of the vote.[20]

Part of Mann's appeal was that he might be Speaker of the House and help the administration of Charles Evans Hughes. But Hughes lost and the Democrats again organized the House and kept control of the Senate as well. Clearly, the Republican renaissance was not yet accomplished. Nevertheless, party leaders, reviewing the campaign and the election, had grounds for satisfaction and hope. The results showed continuing progress, to the point where the party was almost restored to power. The campaign, viewed in retrospect, was a source of perverse satisfaction in that Wilson's advantages and Hughes's stumblings were both ephemeral.

Presidential and House elections were very close. Wilson's victory was not confirmed for several days, until word came that he carried California by 3,773 votes and thus won in the electoral college, 277–254.[21] Both parties won 215 House seats, and the decision as to which would organize the House rested with an independent and four minor-party candidates. In the Senate, the Democrats held a twelve-seat margin, but the Republicans gained two seats.[22]

Reviewing the Hughes campaign, GOP leaders could find both encouraging successes and sources of failure that were due to correctable error or chance. A close scrutiny of the Democratic campaign, moreover, suggested that the Democratic party had reached the limits of its immediate potentiality and was very vulnerable to subsequent division and defeat.[23]

Hughes struck people as cold, excessively dignified, and an uninspired campaigner.[24] Yet, starting in mid-July, he made effective use of issues that Mann had done much to develop. He criticized the administration for waste, extravagance, "pork," sectional bias, as in the 1916 revenue law, and abuse of the civil service. These criticisms fell short only in that they were not supplemented by discussion of bigger issues. When Hughes tried to meet that

---

[20]*Chicago Tribune*, 21 July 1916, 2 October 1916, vol. 22, Mann Papers; Rena Mitchell, "The Congressional Career of James R. Mann" (M.A. thesis, University of Chicago, 1938), 18; Robert R. McCormick to Mann, 18 September 1916; Victor Lawson to Mann, 20 October 1916; and R. H. Keehn to Mann, 17 October 1916, vol. 34, Mann Papers; *Chicago Tribune*, 14 September 1916; John L. Moore, ed., *Congressional Quarterly's Guide to U.S. Elections*, 2nd ed. (Washington, D.C.: Congressional Quarterly, 1985), 730.

[21]Heckscher, *Woodrow Wilson*, 215; Gould, *Reform and Regulation*, 205–6; Gardner, *Departing Glory*, 358.

[22]Seward W. Livermore, *Politics Is Adjourned: Woodrow Wilson and the War Congress, 1916–1918* (Middletown, Conn.: Wesleyan University Press, 1966), 10.

[23]Gould, *Reform and Regulation*, 206.

[24]Samuel D. Lovell, *The Election of 1916* (Carbondale: Southern Illinois, University Press, 1980), 146.

criticism and talked of the war in Europe and the situation in Mexico, he lapsed into understandable but hurtful vagueness.[25] Then in September Hughes took up the Adamson Act and energized his campaign.[26] He also turned to the tariff, but found that issue temporarily blunted by prosperity and the fact that the danger from imports lay in the future more than the present. He forfeited progressivism without a fight, at some cost, but unified conservatives of the East and Midwest and largely swept these areas. He also won the backing of Roosevelt and about 80 percent of the Moosers and held the insurgents as well, and though fatally weak in the West, he carried such strong insurgent states as Wisconsin, Iowa, Minnesota, South Dakota, and Oregon. Progressives and insurgents embraced his attack on "class legislation."[27]

The Democrats managed their campaign better than did the Republicans, who were led by the politically inexperienced friend of Hughes's, William R. Willcox.[28] Capitalizing on their recently adopted laws, they forged a progressive coalition of labor, farmers, publicists, intellectuals, and such disaffected Progressives as Victor Murdock. It represented a union of South and West, with just enough other support, notably from Ohio, to bring victory.[29]

The preparedness issue had been sufficiently blunted legislatively, and Democrats did not stress it.[30] Instead, they exploited the peace theme fully, and Wilson cooperated. Roosevelt campaigned belligerently, so that at the end Democrats used the slogan "Wilson and Peace with Honor? Hughes with Roosevelt and War?"[31] Many German-Americans, who had grown suspicious of Wilson, were won to this appeal less by Wilson's record than by Roosevelt's speeches. News of terrible carnage on the western front brought a surge of peace sentiment, and overtures from Carranza added to the effectiveness of the Democratic appeal.[32] Fortunately for the Democrats, Germany desisted from submarine attacks and thus did not challenge Wilson's

---

[25]*Ibid.*, 130–31; Livermore, *Politics is Adjourned*, 242–43.

[26]Link and Leary, "Election of 1916," 2262–63; Lovell, *Presidential Election of 1916*, 133.

[27]James Holt, *Congressional Insurgents and the Party System, 1909–1916* (Cambridge, Mass.: Harvard University Press, 1967), 161; John Milton Cooper, Jr., *The Warrior and the Priest: Woodrow Wilson and Theodore Roosevelt* (Cambridge, Mass.: Belknap Press of Harvard University Press, 1983), 357.

[28]Lovell, *Presidential Election of 1916*, 89; Link and Leary, "Election of 1916," 2255.

[29]Link and Leary, "Election of 1916," 2265–76; Broesamle, "Democrats," 111–12.

[30]John Patrick Finnegan, *Against the Specter of a Dragon: The Campaign for American Military Preparedness, 1914–1917* (Westport, Conn.: Greenwood Press, 1974), 164.

[31]Gould, *Reform and Regulation*, 200, 202.

[32]Heckscher, *Woodrow Wilson*, 409; Arthur S. Link, *Woodrow Wilson: Revolution, War, and Peace* (Arlington Heights, Ill.: Harlan Davidson, 1979), 51–53.

still-standing ultimatum during the campaign period, so the president seemed after all to be the peace candidate.

Despite all that, Hughes still might have won. Although he included Moosers in his organization, regulars froze them out of the campaign. When Hughes campaigned in California, it was regulars who surrounded him, to the exclusion of the Progressives. Hughes's failure to call on Governor and Senate candidate Hiram Johnson when they were briefly stopping at the same hotel was only the most publicized of the slights that Hughes unwittingly dealt the California Progressives. Their more active campaign help could easily have delivered the state and the election to Hughes.[33]

Looking to the future, Republicans could hope for stronger campaigners, better managers, and better luck. They could rejoice in the return of Roosevelt and most of his followers and the virtual demise of the Progressive party and anticipate gradual reconciliation. To be sure, in the short run the reabsorption process might be bumpy and add to some division on domestic issues and conflict over positions of authority. Differences within the party on the great issues of peace and war posed an even greater challenge. Republicans could take comfort, though, in the more serious divisions in the Democratic party, which were only temporarily papered over in 1916. Northern and western farmers were not firmly and traditionally in the Democratic camp, and the further rise of such issues as immigration, temperance, and anti-Catholicism would put an intolerable strain on a party made up of rural, old-stock, "dry" Protestants and urban, immigrant, "wet" Catholics. Thus patient Republicans had reason to view the 1916 elections as a further important step towards the resumption of power.

Indeed, for months Republicans hoped to organize the recently elected House, where neither party had a majority. In preparation for that possibility, House Republicans negotiated and battled among themselves in an intricate contest over power and policy. This unusual situation intertwined with something equally unusual—turbulent international events. At the same time, politics of the ordinary sort continued in the short session that began in December. Mann, though occasionally inhibited by unspecified health problems, gave leadership of a familiar sort. He supported mildly progressive legislation, sometimes to the embarrassment of Democrats; he exploited Democratic procedural blunders; and he took conservative ground on fundamental economic questions. Though some progressive Republicans (as the insurgents had come to be called) asked for a program that would be active as well as reactive, on the issues he took up Mann spoke for a reasonably united party.

---

[33]Link and Leary, "Election of 1916," 2257; Lovell, *Presidential Election of 1916*, 137–47.

Living costs, especially for food, increased considerably in the fall of 1916, and Mann seized on the issue. In commenting to the press he criticized Wilson for ignoring the problem in his annual message. His own partial solution he embodied in an amendment to an agricultural appropriations bill. It would provide the Bureau of Marketing with $50,000 to investigate food marketing. The bureau could do more than the Justice Department, which was already investigating for criminality. "There's a great lack of economy in the handling and passage of food products from the farm to the home consumption," Mann argued. "The very purpose of this is to be a practical and not a theoretical investigation." Fitzgerald tried to block the amendment with a point of order, but failed; Asbury Lever, chairman of Agriculture, supported it; and it passed. The amendment was vintage Mann. In a field in which he had a special interest and expertise—food—he would use empirical inquiry by governmental experts to improve an industry for its own good and that of the public. Here was a modern form of promotionalism.[34]

As in previous Congresses, Mann supported an amendment by progressive Republican James Good and the Appropriations Committee to increase funding for the Children's Bureau. The $72,120 that bureau chief Julia Lathrop had requested would chiefly facilitate an investigation of infant mortality. This was a popular project that continued to find its chief opposition among southern Democrats, as Mann knew.[35]

Democrats stood sponsor to the vocational education bill, whose consideration had begun in July. As before, Mann gave the bill hearty support. He likened the program to the agricultural education that the federal government supported at land-grant colleges, which he highly praised. It was the kind of education that puts together "thinking and doing," he said, "the summit of education." Mann lavished praise on the bill's House sponsor, Dudley Hughes of Georgia, who had not been renominated. The landmark Smith-Hughes Act, mainly the work of Senator Hoke Smith of Georgia, became law in February.[36]

Mann was less kindly to the Democrats after the erratic speculator-muckraker Thomas W. Lawson created a sensation. He charged that high administration officials had leaked information about a presidential peace note to Wall Street friends. Compounding Democratic difficulties and the party's vulnerability, Chairman Robert Henry of Rules had presumed to interview Lawson single-handedly and decide whether an investigation was warranted. In the House in January, Mann did the parliamentary work in

[34] *New York Times*, 6 December 1916; *CR* 64:2, pp. 1015–19, 1024 (8 January 1917).

[35] *CR* 64:2, pp. 449–51 (16 December 1916).

[36] *Ibid.*, pp. 764 (2 January 1917), 1081 (9 January 1917); Link, *Wilson: Campaigns for Progressivism and Peace*, 326.

forcing an investigation by the full Rules Committee, and he successfully opposed an effort to limit funds for the investigation to $15,000. After the committee cleared the administration, Mann expressed pleasure at the outcome while gently chastising the many Democrats who had opposed the investigation.[37]

While Mann took progressive positions on the cost of food, the Children's Bureau and vocational education, he was pronouncedly conservative when yet another revenue bill came up. Mann's health caused him to limit his participation in debate, but he did claim for his party credit for first seeing the need to sell bonds in time of emergency, as the bill called for, and he evoked applause from his side in saying that the bonds could be paid for over time with a proper tariff. The most innovative feature of the bill was an excess-profits tax on corporations and partnerships. Mann did not bother to orate against it, but instead pressed Kitchin for assurances that it would not apply unfairly to partnerships. When he got the responses he wanted, he recorded his hope that the Treasury would take guidance from Kitchin's words in construing the law. Fordney's recommittal motion was directed against the new tax and lost with only a few Republican defections, 187–219. When the bill then passed, 211–196, Republicans stood solidly in opposition.[38]

Mann's competent and balanced performance on domestic questions during the short session did not quell the intra-party conflict occasioned by the possibility of organizing the next Congress. In large part, directly and indirectly, the contest was about Mann. He in turn played an important part in it, with the goals of retaining power, keeping the party unified, and steering it to what he considered to be sound and politically effective policies.

The possibility that the Republicans would organize the new House suggested that they might need a floor leader, not just a Speaker. If the Republicans followed the example set by the Democrats since 1911, the floor leader would be more powerful than the Speaker. Soon after the election in November, opponents of Mann talked of making Lenroot the floor leader and reducing Mann to a ceremonial role as Speaker. Mann, some argued, was unsatisfactory due to his past as a Cannon man, "dry" opposition to him, and his reluctance to share power. Lenroot suffered from none of these deficiencies, had become more of a party man than a radical factionalist since his arrival in the House in 1909, had shown high competence and an even temperament, and stood well with Roosevelt. A leading proponent of the floor-leader gambit was Medill McCormick of the *Chicago Tribune* publishing family,

---

[37] Link, *Wilson: Campaigns for Progressivism and Peace*, 251; *Searchlight on Congress*, 2:1 (31 January 1917): 7; *CR* 64:2, pp. 801, 807 (3 January 1917), 1552–54 (17 January 1917), 4950 (3 March 1917).

[38] *CR* 64:2, pp. 2414, 2433, 2440–42 (1 February 1917); Greenlee, "Republican Party," 214.

who had returned from the Progressives to the GOP in 1915 as an advance agent for Roosevelt and in 1916 won election to the House as an Illinois congressman-at-large. McCormick would further redistribute power in a progressive direction by shifting authority over committee assignments from the party leader to a committee.[39]

After the lame-duck session convened, these matters simmered for a time, until on 18 December President Wilson, responding to a peace note from Germany, asked all the belligerents to state their terms for peace. This pressure from the president for a negotiated settlement, published in American papers on 21 December, infuriated Anglophiles, and in the Senate Republicans blocked a resolution to endorse the note.[40] In the House, unexpectedly, Mann interrupted consideration of an appropriations bill to praise Wilson for his peace initiative. "England Stirred as by Hard Blow," headlined the *New York Times*. The response of Augustus P. Gardner was to issue a formal statement opposing Mann for Speaker and backing Lenroot in his place. "This is the fourth or fifth time that Leader Mann has given encouragement to the Kaiser's wicked cause," he said. "I will tolerate such leadership no longer." Gardner quickly supplemented his attack on Mann with a call for a party conference to fix a course of positive policy, instead of merely opposing. Lenroot endorsed that idea, as did many rank-and-file Republicans who wanted to bind prospective committee chairman to progressive principles or displace them.[41]

Mann responded mildly to Gardner's statement. At first he withheld comment altogether, while inspiring an editorial in the *Washington Herald* to the effect that he was not immediately ambitious for the Speakership but preferred to let the Democrats organize, since a House organized by Republicans would be stymied by the Democratic Senate and the president. Furthermore, the editorial said, Mann held Lenroot in high regard. Two days later Mann briefly denied that he was pro-German and said, "I am for America first, last, and all the time."[42] Even so, Gardner's statement caused acceleration in the overall movement for change.

[39] *Superior Telegram*, 10 November 1916, 16 November 1916; *Chicago Tribune*, 14 November 1916; *Chicago News*, 14 November 1916; *Chicago Post*, 22 November 1916, vol. 23, Mann Papers.

[40] Livermore, *Politics Is Adjourned*, 11; Link, *Revolution, War and Peace*, 57.

[41] CR 64:2, p. 713 (22 December 1916); *New York Times*, 23 December 1916, 24 December 1916, 25 December, 1916.

[42] *New York Times*, 26 December 1916; *Washington Herald*, 26 December 1916, vol. 23, Mann Papers; *New York Times*, 28 December 1916.

While Charles Evans Hughes withdrew from politics in favor of his law practice,[43] Theodore Roosevelt, a 1920 presidential prospect, took a strong hand in House Republican affairs, especially through the very active Medill McCormick. Gardner had consulted Roosevelt before issuing his declaration against Mann, and afterwards Roosevelt approved it.[44] But mainly he concerned himself with integration of Moosers into the Republican party and thus lent his weight to the movement for structural and policy reforms rather than the overthrow of Mann. With McCormick, he wanted to achieve his goal without disrupting the party, either in Congress or the Republican National Committee.[45]

In the House Gardner's statement triggered a new wave of anti-Mann expression. A Michigan progressive Republican, Louis Cramton, backed Lenroot over Mann for Speaker on policy grounds, but he stressed other reasons as well. "Mr. Mann is not a party leader," Cramton said. "He is a czar. He arrogates to himself all authority, apparently without ever considering, and certainly without consulting his party colleagues." The party could never be completely unified, he acknowledged, but conference and debate would iron out some difficulties. Another member said "In the last months I have occupied the floor for ten minutes. In consequence I have been complimented by one of my colleagues for being very active." Others complained that Mann publicly humiliated new members.[46] In his impatience, he sometimes did.

In mid-January Gardner petitioned for a party conference, for unstated purposes. Then Madden and Moore, Mann allies, energetically lobbied for a compromise program. They would advance progressive economic policies, but based on the protective tariff principle. They advocated creation of a steering committee to serve as voice of the party and liaison with a similar Senate committee. Finally, they proposed frequent conferences. On 24 January the party convened, but with respect to policy Republicans agreed only in

---

[43]Ralph M. Goldman, *The National Party Chairmen and Committees: Factionalism at the Top* (Armonk, N.Y.: M. E. Sharpe, 1990), 285.

[44]*New York Times*, 25 December 1916; Theodore Roosevelt to Medill McCormick, 5 January 1917, Elting E. Morison et al., editors, *The Letters of Theodore Roosevelt* (Cambridge, Mass.: Harvard University Press, 1951–1954), 8:1140.

[45]McCormick to Roosevelt, 14 December 1916, series 1, box 315; Roosevelt to McCormick, 20 December 1916, series 3, vol. 39; McCormick to Roosevelt, 2 January 1917, series 1, box 317; Roosevelt to McCormick, 5 January 1917, series 3, vol. 100, McCormick to Roosevelt, 12 January 1917, 15 January 1917, series 1, box 318, Theodore Roosevelt Papers, Library of Congress. The ex-Moosers suffered several setbacks in mid-January in a power struggle within the Republican National Committee. Greenlee, "Republican Party," 211–12.

[46]*Marquette Michigan Journal*, 29 December 1916, and *Washington Post*, 15 January 1917, vol. 23, Mann Papers.

opposition to the new Democratic revenue bill and in favor of the protective tariff, while not getting to Gardner's proposals for old-age insurance, minimum-wage legislation for women and children, universal military training, and more. Gardner did get a promise of another conference in two weeks.[47]

Meanwhile, despite the illness that caused him to miss the 24 January conference and limit himself on the revenue bill, Mann joined in a series of meetings with Lenroot, Sydney Anderson, William B. McKinley, and McCormick with an eye towards agreement on reforms that would unify the party and also make it attractive to the third party men and independent who would decide which party would organize in the Sixty-fifth Congress. These leaders came to no full agreement, however. Finally, on 5 February, amidst a new international crisis, the party held its follow-up conference. Mann appealed for harmony and broad statesmanship in the face of the crisis. Anderson offered a motion for creation of a legislative program, but Mann won out with a substitute. Under Mann's motion William Greene of Massachusetts, conference chairman and a regular, would name a twenty-seven-member committee that would make recommendations respecting organizational changes when the new Congress convened. Greene soon appointed Madden to head the committee and named some progressive Republicans but mainly regulars to it.[48]

For the moment Mann and his friends had effected only a small strategic retreat as the price for a continuing intraparty truce. But in February and March jockeying continued in the context of the international crisis to which Mann had referred. On 31 January Germany announced that starting the next day her submarines would sink without warning all ships, neutral as well as belligerent, in a broad zone of the Atlantic and Mediterranean. Neutral ships currently in the zone would have a short grace period. On 3 February, appearing before Congress, Wilson announced that the United States had broken diplomatic relations with Germany, but he professed disbelief that Germany would destroy American ships and take American lives. He proposed no further action until it did. Most congressmen and their countrymen approved, and so did Mann, who said, "I do not see how the President could do any less, and I am very glad that he did not propose at this time to do any more."[49]

---

[47]*Washington Post*, 15 January 1917, and *Chicago Tribune*, 17 January 1917, vol. 23, Mann Papers; *New York Times*, 25 January 1917.

[48]*Superior Telegram*, 30 January 1917; *Washington Post*, 6 February 1917, vol. 23, Mann Papers; Frank Greene to John Esch, 28 February 1917, box 41, John J. Esch Papers, State Historical Society of Wisconsin, Madison; Thomas D. Schall to Theodore Roosevelt, 5 March 1917, series 1, box 323, Roosevelt Papers.

[49]Link, *Wilson: Campaigns for Progressivism and Peace*, 285, 300; *New York Times*, 4 February 1917.

In the following weeks submarine incidents occurred, but none of them met Wilson's vague definition of an "overt act." Wilson had not been explicit as to Americans killed while on belligerent ships. Congress, reflecting the country, divided sharply, and Mann took the popular side as a leader for caution and peace. At the same time, he continued to support preparedness. Despite his efforts to steer a middle course, he aroused the venom of Republicans less opposed to war than he. The unity that he sought was impossible of achievement in the last month of the Congress. The Democrats, however, showed signs of becoming more internally divided than the Republicans. Therein Mann saw patriotic and political possibilities.

In connection with a naval appropriations bill, Mann supported a generous antiaircraft item with these words: "Mr. Chairman, I am not excited. I have not lost my head. and I am as cool as a cucumber, determined to do everything I can to keep the country out of war; but after all, there is some danger of conflict." He went on to urge appropriations for submarines and planes. With Republican support he clashed with Kitchin on a parliamentary point relating to a Republican amendment to raise the number of submarines from three to eighteen. At the same time, he successfully offered an amendment affirming American policy to "settle its international disputes through mediation or arbitration, to the end that war may be honorably avoided." The *New York Tribune*, a major Republican organ, protested that a state of war already existed, and Germany would continue it during arbitration. Henry Cabot Lodge, disgusted with Mann for previous foreign relations offenses, killed his amendment in conference.[50]

On 16 February Mann delivered a short but important speech for peace with Germany and, as the *New York Times* described it, "was greeted by an unusual demonstration." He began with a recollection of his start in Congress, preceding the war with Spain, and commented especially on how unforeseen was the acquisition of the Philippines resulting from that war. Then he read the words of the peace speech he had made on 18 August 1914, soon after war broke out in Europe. Introducing his main point, Mann was careful to say that if the country were drawn into the war, "whatever opinion we may have had in reference to the propriety of being drawn into the struggle will be merged in a universal opinion to stand for the country in what it determines to do." But the country should avoid being drawn in, he said, because of the long-range consequences of belligerency. "If we are a party to the war, we have got to sit in at the final councils. We will have to determine the terms of peace, and at once, at one sweep, we will have abandoned the tradition and long continued policy of the United States to remain supreme

---

[50] *CR* 64:2, pp. 2714 (6 February 1917), 3024, 3037–39 (10 February 1917), 3226 (13 February 1917); *New York Tribune*, 16 February 1917, vol. 23, Mann Papers; Lodge to Theodore Roosevelt, 22 February 1917, series 1, box 322, Roosevelt Papers.

on the American continent and to keep out of the complications of the European Continent." He argued that by participating in the drawing of new boundaries and establishing new nations, the United States would commit itself to continuing enforcement obligations. "And when we undertake to enter a policy which requires us to interfere in European affairs," he went on, "we can no longer ask or insist upon the traditional policy of the United States that European countries shall keep their hands out of American affairs." Martin Dies, Texas Democrat, asked Mann if the United States should relinquish its rights of commerce; Mann dismissed the question as hypothetical and declined to prejudge the issue. "But I will say this for myself: I am determined to do everything within my power to keep our country out of the present European war." Then, without referring specifically to the Monroe Doctrine, he restated his devotion to it, with special reference to the as yet unfulfilled obligation "to help protect and take care of the Republics of Central and South America."[51]

The following day the *New York Times* editorialized in criticism of Mann for stressing avoidance of war rather than defense of American rights. Of greater importance, that day Lenroot delivered a much-noted speech stating his position. Without mentioning Mann or directing all his arguments against Mann's, in two major respects he differed with the floor leader. Lenroot addressed himself to the issue that Mann wanted to postpone, the question of American rights and the appropriate American response to the possible destruction of American ships and lives by Germany. Under those circumstances, Lenroot said, he would fight. But again differing with Mann, he argued that the conflict would be on the seas, not in Europe; "It does not mean that we are to sit in and determine the terms of settlement of European questions." Taken as a whole, Lenroot's speech responded mainly to such strong peace advocates as Warren Worth Bailey, Democrat of Pennsylvania, J. Hampton Moore, and Senator La Follette, who had called for a referendum preceding any war declaration. But because of Mann's prominence as minority leader, newspapers that favored forceful action singled him out as the just object of Lenroot's criticism. Theodore Roosevelt did the same in congratulating Lenroot. Separately, Roosevelt wrote Lodge that "Mann ought to be put out of the position of leader of the minority. He is rather worse than Wilson."[52]

---

[51] *New York Times*, 17 February 1917; *CR* 64:2, pp. 3435–36 (16 February 1917).

[52] *New York Times*, 17 February 1917; *CR* 64:2, p. 3529 (17 February 1917); Herbert F. Margulies, *Senator Lenroot of Wisconsin: A Political Biography, 1900–1929* (Columbia: University of Missouri Press, 1977), 211–13; *Washington Post*, 18 February 1917, 19 February 1917; *New York Tribune*, 19 February 1917; *Milwaukee Sentinel*, 20 February 1917; Roosevelt to Lenroot, 20 February 1917, Roosevelt to Lodge, 20 February 1917, series 3, vol. 104, Roosevelt Papers.

Though Mann could never hope to please the Roosevelts, Lodges, and Gardners, he continued to steer a middle course. The occasion for his speech and Lenroot's was an army appropriations bill, and as the bill moved along, Mann criticized "a large share of this House [who] believe we ought to make no provision for the possibility of war." Near the end of the session, when a bill to permit borrowing for naval construction was reported, Mann restated his position. "I am one of those who believe we ought to keep out of the war, but that we ought to be prepared if war should be forced upon us."[53]

The position that he took in connection with the armed ship bill was consistent with these views. On 26 February Wilson asked Congress for authority to arm American merchant vessels, an approach that had been launched and supported by people seeking an alternative to war. As he spoke, word spread in the chamber of the sinking of a British liner, the *Laconia*, with Americans on board. After the president left the Capitol, Mann and Lenroot conferred with Democrats Clark, Kitchin, Fitzgerald, and Henry Flood of Virginia, chairman of Foreign Affairs, and Senator Furnifold Simmons of North Carolina. Pressured further by the president over the *Laconia*, Flood's committee soon reported a bill authorizing the action Wilson wanted, but submitting a blank-check reference to "other instrumentalities and methods."[54]

Patriotic ardor and outrage surged in the House when it considered the bill on 1 March. That morning the press carried word, released by the administration, of an intercepted telegram from German foreign secretary Arthur Zimmermann to the German minister in Mexico. If the United States entered the war, he should propose to Mexico an alliance by which Mexico, and if possible Japan, would make war on the United States. Mexico would regain territory in the Southwest lost in the nineteenth century. With war fever in the air over the Zimmermann telegram, many among the peace forces took alarm and prepared to support a recommittal motion by Henry A. Cooper of Wisconsin, ranking Republican on Foreign Affairs, that would block the arming of merchant ships carrying munitions to belligerents.[55]

Early on, Mann declared his position in a brief but important speech. Though he made no specific reference to the Cooper proposal, he made it clear that he opposed it, while backing the committee's bill. "I am not willing to cavil over the terms of the power we confer upon the President," Mann said. "When the time comes that our ships shall be assaulted and the limit is passed for patient bearing of the insults or destruction which may be heaped

---

[53] *CR* 64:2, pp. 3834 (21 February 1917), 4960 (3 March 1917).

[54] Link, *Woodrow Wilson: Revolution, War, and Peace*, 67; Link, *Wilson: Campaigns for Progressivism and Peace*, 347; *Milwaukee Sentinel*, 27 February 1917; Link, *Wilson: Campaigns for Progressivism and Peace*, 351–53.

[55] Link, *Wilson: Campaigns for Progressivism and Peace*, 342–43, 353–54.

upon us, it becomes the duty of a free people and a great nation, aye of a small nation, to defend its rights upon the sea and upon the land." He expressed confidence that in conferring the new power on the president "we are more apt . . . to keep out of the war than we are to have a declaration of war. I hope we will not have to declare war. I do not want to become involved in the European war, but I am willing to protect the rights of America," he concluded to prolonged applause.[56]

Later that day, differing with 72 Republicans and 53 peace Democrats, Mann voted against Cooper's motion, which lost, 125–293. Several other conservative Republican peace men, notably Mondell and Cannon, voted as Mann did. But among the conservative leadership Moore and Philip Campbell, ranking Republican on Rules, voted for the motion. Many of those who supported it, especially in the Midwest, had large German-American constituencies. Progressivism, however, seems to have exerted the larger influence, and even Lenroot voted with Cooper.[57]

That more Republicans than Democrats supported the Cooper motion reflected something else—party loyalty on each side. That being so, the substantial Democratic vote for the motion, taken together with the success of agrarian Democrats in committee in weakening the bill,[58] suggested that as the dangerous international situation further evolved, the Republicans might yet establish themselves as the administration's senior partner in Congress in defense of the nation, in accordance with Mann's approach.

The bill passed the House by a vote of 403–14, but fell victim in the Senate to an end-of-session filibuster led by progressive Republicans La Follette, Norris, Cummins, and Asle Gronna of North Dakota. Wilson, however, acting on the basis of an 1819 antipiracy law, on 9 March ordered the navy to put arms and gun crews on liners and merchantmen. Very soon, however, the president judged the plan a failure. Ruefully, he decided on war.[59]

Between 16 and 18 March Germany sank three American merchantmen, two without warning and one with heavy loss of life. The German Admiralty said that it would treat captured crewmen as pirates. Vigorous submarine action against the ships of other neutrals and of belligerents attested to Germany's seriousness of purpose. Under these circumstances, as Wilson later

---

[56] *CR* 64:2, p. 4640 (1 March 1917).

[57] *Ibid.*, p. 4691 (1 March 1917); Greenlee, "Republican Party," 215; John Milton Cooper, Jr., *The Vanity of Power: American Isolationism and the First World War, 1914–1917* (Westport, Conn.: Greenwood Publishing Corp., 1969), 232–34.

[58] Timothy Gregory McDonald, "Southern Democratic Congressmen and the First World War, August 1914–April 1917: The Public Record of Their Support for or Opposition to Wilson's Policies" (Ph.D. diss., University of Washington, 1962), 223.

[59] Link, *Wilson: Campaigns for Progressivism and Peace*, 373–76, 396–402, 411–15.

put it to Congress, armed neutrality was "practically certain to drag us into the war without either the rights or the effectiveness of belligerents."[60]

Wilson was moved by other considerations as well. Public war sentiment, though not truly reflective of majority opinion, was high and loudly expressed. It was fueled by the Zimmermann note, the March sinkings, and news that month of revolution in czarist Russia, which seemed to redefine the war as a conflict of democracies against a brutal autocracy. In addition, Wilson thought that the war was in its last stages, and American entry could hasten its end. Finally, as a belligerent America would earn a place at the peace table, where Wilson hoped to lay the basis for a just and lasting peace settlement.[61] Thus on 21 March he called a special session for 2 April "to receive a communication concerning grave matters of national policy."[62]

When Congress convened, before it could hear the president, each house had to organize itself. In advance of the session, with many questions as to leadership and internal structure undecided, and amidst uncertainty as to which party would organize, the House Republicans continued their earlier intraparty jockeying, while also wooing independents. Their pace accelerated when on 9 March Wilson called a special session for 16 April, and quickened again after the president moved the date to 2 April.

On 10 March Mann came out for bipartisan organization of the new House. Two days later, about to leave for Haiti and "a good rest," he elaborated. "In view of the international complications and the fact that neither party will have a majority in the House, there necessarily will have to be some bipartisan understanding in the House after organization is effected, if not before it is effected. It would be ridiculous to suppose," he argued, "that such a body of men in matters of important legislation would permit themselves to be controlled by the mere whim or caprice of a few men who call themselves independents." Reporters and politicians, speculating on Mann's unstated motives, noted that through a bipartisan organization Henry A. Cooper could be deprived of the chairmanship of Foreign Affairs, and other chairmanships could also be disposed of in accordance with the national interest. Less charitably, anti-Mann Republicans said that he wanted to avoid running for Speaker, fearing that defections among Republicans would show him to be weaker than his party.[63]

Lenroot organized and spoke for progressive Republicans in opposition to Mann's plan, and his activity, combined with Democratic coolness, killed

---

[60] Link, *Woodrow Wilson: Revolution, War, and Peace*, 68–69.
[61] *Ibid.*, 70–71.
[62] Link, *Wilson: Campaigns for Progressivism and Peace*, 408.
[63] *Chicago Examiner*, 10 March 1917, vol. 23, Mann Papers; *New York Times*, 13 March 1917, 10 March 1917; *Chicago Post*, 13 March 1917; and *New York Herald*, 29 March 1917, vol. 23, Mann Papers.

it.[64] The progressive Republicans, plus some Rooseveltian nationalists like Nicholas Longworth, put forth the alternative of temporarily continuing the old organization of the House until emergency legislation was adopted, then organizing on a regular basis. This was part of a larger program that the progressive Republicans hoped the Committee of 27 would recommend to the Republican caucus. They urged that in addition to a candidate for Speaker, the party should choose a floor leader—presumably Lenroot—who would hold that office even if the Speaker nominee lost in the House. They called for creation of a positive program through a Steering Committee and establishment of a Committee on Committees to replace Mann in making committee assignments. As a matter of strategy, some talked of running Lenroot against Mann as Speaker nominee so that if Clark won in the House, Lenroot might become party leader. But only a few would jeopardize their party's effectiveness by an all-out battle, and Republicans quietly negotiated in advance of the 30 March meeting of the Committee of 27.[65]

That committee conceded a little to the dissidents, but decided mainly in favor of the conservative majority and Mann. It recommended creation of an elective Advisory Committee of five on policy and a Committee on Committees of seventeen, both to be chaired by the candidate for Speaker— presumably Mann. In recommending membership for the Committee on Committees, Madden's group ignored two of the six names submitted by progressive Republicans. As to creating a floor-leader position separate from the Speaker nominee, the Committee of 27 recommended that should the party candidate for Speaker (Mann) lose to Clark, as by then seemed certain, then the new Advisory Committee would decide about creating a new floor-leader position—for Lenroot. Conservatives would surely control the Advisory Committee and not recommend displacing Mann in that way. (As it turned out, in June, on the recommendation of the Committee on Committees, the caucus elected Mann, Mondell, Moore, the conservative nationalist Frederick Gillett, and Lenroot, so Mann controlled.) The progressive Republicans, perhaps impressed by the unity of the Democrats, acquiesced in this program and among themselves gave up the idea of nominating Lenroot

---

[64]*New York Sun*, 1 April 1917, box 15, Irvine L. Lenroot Papers, Library of Congress; *New York Times*, 27 March 1917.

[65]*Chicago Post*, 27 March 1917, and *Chicago Tribune*, 29 March 1917, 31 March 1917, and *Washington Post*, 30 March 1917, vol. 23, Mann Papers; Clara Longworth de Chambrun, *The Making of Nicholas Longworth: Annals of an American Family* (New York: Ray Long and Richard R. Smith, 1933), 241; *Chicago Tribune*, 22 March 1917; *Washington Post*, 30 March 1917, vol. 23, Mann Papers.

against Mann for Speaker candidate. They congratulated themselves on creation of the new committees.[66]

At the caucus on 31 March Gardner introduced a discordant note when
he announced that in the House he would vote for Lenroot for Speaker and
moved that the caucus decision not be binding. Despite reassurances as to
that, when his motion was tabled, 127–47, he walked out, with two other
easterners. After that, however, harmony prevailed. Mann was unopposed for
Speaker, and the caucus nominated him. Lenroot and several others escorted
him forward, and he spoke for party harmony. The caucus also approved the
recommendations of Madden's committee. Gardner's defection was no neg-
ligible thing, but on balance the party had successfully handled its factional
conflicts and was ready to work with and against the Democrats in the new
Congress.[67]

The election of Clark as Speaker was made certain days before the House
met because of several deaths and illnesses, the decisions of the independents, and five prospective Republican defections from Mann. What was not
anticipated was that Thomas D. Schall of Minnesota, a blind Bull Mooser,
who had unsuccessfully sought a place on the Republican Committee of 27,
would make an emotional nominating speech for Clark and argue that a
Democratic president should have a Democratic House and Senate. Lenroot,
taking the unusual step of giving a seconding speech for a Speaker nominee,
Mann, aroused strong enthusiasm among Republicans when he responded
that at least one house should be Republican, so the president, who had ignored the Republicans on the great and immediate issue of war and peace,
would be obliged to consult them and thus give the whole country a share in
the government's momentous decisions. He also promised that if the Democrats organized, there would be "no partisanship on the Republican side in
dealing with the situation."[68]

In effect, Lenroot took a dual approach respecting partisanship in the
new Congress—Republicans would help, but not rubber-stamp. Mann agreed
and quickly put that approach into play. In a well-received show of collegiality, after Clark defeated him, 217–205, Mann presented Clark as "the Speaker
you have chosen, the genial, able, impartial, patriotic statesman of Missouri
and the nation." He cooperated with Fitzgerald in permitting suspension of
the rules to pass appropriations bills left over from the last Congress. But he

---

[66] *Superior Telegram*, 31 March 1917; *Washington Post*, 1 April 1917; *Washington
Star*, 1 April 1917; *Chicago Tribune*, 2 June 1917; *Chicago American*, 31 March 1917,
vol. 23, Mann Papers.

[67] *Washington Star*, 1 April 1917; Washington Post, 1 April 1917, vol. 23, Mann
Papers; Maureen R. Romans, "Party Leadership Fights in the House of Representatives: The Cause of Conflict, 1895–1955" (Ph.D. diss., University of Massachusetts,
1976), 43.

[68] *New York Times*, 3 April 1917; CR 65:1, p. 107 (2 April 1917).

delayed the appearance of the president through the afternoon and into the evening in contesting Democratic control notwithstanding Clark's election. First, he demanded roll-call votes on four of the House officers, and he did come within four, five, and six votes of winning three of these contests. Then, when Kitchin nominated Democratic members and chairmen of all the committees, in effect organizing as the majority, Mann demanded a roll-call vote on consideration of the resolution at that time. Although members rarely voted against a party's committee nominations, on this vote Mann lost by a respectable margin, 211–197. By these votes Mann not only contested to the fullest the power of the Democrats to organize, but also showed that Republicans were stronger and better united than Clark's winning margin might have suggested.[69]

Finally Congress was ready to hear the president. At 8:30 Wilson appeared in the House chamber amidst long cheers from senators, representatives, and spectators that were repeated during and after his speech. He began matter-of-factly, reciting German offenses and the reasons armed neutrality would not work. Then he said that Germany was warring on the United States. His country should accept the status of belligerent; it could not back down. The war, though, would be for much more than the defense of American rights and honor. Rather, it would be for a just and lasting peace, secured by a concert of free peoples; it would be a war to make the world "safe for democracy."[70]

The following day Mann named incumbents to their old committees and said that the Committee on Committees would later complete assignments. The key committee at the moment, Foreign Affairs, reported the Senate's war resolution on 4 April. That night the Senate, by a vote of 82–6, opted for war. The House began its debate the next morning.[71]

No one doubted that the House would approve the war resolution, but members showed more seriousness than enthusiasm, and cloakroom comment revealed that many privately opposed the war, but were reluctant to back off in the wake of the president's call. The only consolation for these was the widespread understanding, reinforced by Julius Kahn of Military Affairs, that America's fighting would be confined to the seas.[72]

---

[69] *New York Times*, 3 April 1917; CR 65:1, pp. 107–16 (2 April 1917).

[70] Link, *Wilson: Campaigns for Progressivism and Peace*, 423–26.

[71] CR 65:1, pp. 156–57 (3 April 1917); Link, *Wilson: Campaigns for Progressivism and Peace*, 430.

[72] *Washington Times*, 5 April 1917; Marvin Jones, *Memoirs* (El Paso: Texas Western Press, 1973), 33; Mrs. J. Borden Harriman, *From Pinafores to Politics* (New York: Henry Holt and Company, 1923), 205–7; Edward Keating, *The Gentleman from Colorado: a Memoir* (Denver: Sage Books, 1964), 422; Fiorello H. La Guardia, *The Making of an Insurgent: An Autobiography, 1882–1919* (Philadelphia: J. B. Lippincott, 1948), 140.

More interesting than the early speeches, most of them for the *Record*, was news that Kitchin would both vote and speak against the resolution. When he did speak, in midafternoon, after much soul-searching and discussion, it was the sensation of the day, for his action raised the possibility that, contrary to earlier expectations, many members would vote "nay." The majority leader talked of administration favoritism, British high-handedness, American trade entanglements, and Germany's military necessities. For Kitchin, the speech was the fulfillment of a heart-wrenching duty. When he finished Mann rose in his honor, and the others followed, and applauded him for his courage as he left the chamber.[73]

Six hours later, at about nine in the evening, Mann closed the formal part of the debate with a ten-minute speech. He began by paying tribute to the courage of those who had spoken against the resolution and singled out Kitchin for special praise. "I do not agree with them," he quickly added, "but this is a time when the Members of this body, aye, all the citizens of the country, have the right to express their opposition to the war, for tomorrow, when the war is declared, it will become the duty of all citizens to hold up the honor and the power of the Republic." Mann then reminded members of his prolonged efforts for peace. Finally, he explained his current stand. The president, who represented the country in foreign relations, had asked for war. A resolution was before the House on which members had to vote, declaring themselves to foreign nations whichever way they voted. "What position will we be in both as to our own self-respect and the respect of the world if we should vote down the recommendation of the President and declare to the world that we are afraid to go to war? . . . We can not say to the world that our only goal is gold, that our only desire is wealth. We must, it seems to me, when the question is presented to us declare that we will maintain the rights of Americans abroad as well as at home." He then distinguished between "a deliberate affront" and "an incidental injury." Britain and Germany had both been guilty of the latter. Now Germany was also guilty of the former. Under those circumstances, the only open course was to follow the recommendation of the president "and maintain our rights, our honor, our dignity, our civilization." Members accorded him loud applause.[74]

After Mann finished, he insisted on adherence to an earlier agreement that all who wanted to speak should, under the five-minute rule. The president would receive the resolution at the same time the next day whether the House voted immediately or at six in the morning. Speeches resumed until

---

[73]*Washington Times*, 5 April 1917; *New York Tribune*, 6 April 1917; Richard Kenneth Horner, "The House at War: The House of Representatives During World War I, 1917–1919" (Ph.D. diss., Louisiana State University, 1977), 107; *Washington Times*, 6 April 1917; James F. Byrnes, *Speaking Frankly* (New York: Harper and Brothers, 1947), 34.

[74]*CR* 65:1, pp. 376–77 (5 April 1917).

over a hundred had been made. Finally, at 3:12 A.M., the House voted. By a margin of 373 to 50 it approved the war resolution.[75]

Thirty-two of the opponents were Republicans, 28 of these from the Midwest. Nine of Wisconsin's 11 congressmen voted against the war, in line with La Follette's vote and his private urgings. Lenroot voted for the resolution. In each party progressivism strongly influenced the opponents, perhaps more than the ethnicity of constituents. Among the Republicans, most peace-oriented conservatives, including Moore, Mondell, and Campbell, like Mann, did not go so far as to vote against the resolution.[76]

Republicans felt freer than Democrats to oppose the president on the war vote. But among the latter, Bryanites, led by Kitchin, remained numerous and would surely be heard from in the days ahead. As had been the case with preparedness, so now in war, Republicans could credibly take a preponderant role in support of war measures proposed by the administration. That done, their bona fides established, they could also separate themselves from the administration on some issues respecting the conduct of the war. Mann had helped put them in this politically favorable position. His prowar speech, delivered despite heavy propeace mail from constituents, won press attention and praise, to the advantage of his party.[77] His calculatedly conciliatory words in the first part of his speech invited Republican dissenters on the war vote to reunite with the rest afterwards and receive fair treatment.

Mann had continued to serve his party well. Yet he emerged from the events of November to April somewhat weakened as party leader. Creation of two new party committees did little damage, but reflected the fact of greater and more vocal opposition to him than before. Thus his ability to lead his party and speak for it in the new Congress, while not dramatically reduced, was nevertheless impaired.

The party's consistent recovery since 1912, to the point where after the 1916 election it stood a good chance to organize the House, made conflict between progressive and conservative Republicans again seem worthwhile, since real governmental power might be at stake. There was little Mann could have done about that. Similarly, the criticism of his crusty and autocratic ways that surfaced after the 1916 election reflected not so much any new failing in Mann, but more the impact of time on members' patience combined with the inducement to speak up when the Lenroot supporters challenged

---

[75]*Ibid.*, pp. 390 (5 April 1917), 412–13 (6 April 1917); Link, *Wilson: Campaigns for Progressivism and Peace*, 430.

[76]Horner, "House at War," 113–14; James A. Frear, *Forty Years of Progressive Public Service* (Washington, D.C.: Associated Writers, 1937), 167–68; Cooper, *Vanity of Power*, 235–37; Robert E. Drayer, "J. Hampton Moore: An Old Fashioned Republican" (Ph.D. diss., University of Pennsylvania, 1961), 75.

[77]*Chicago Herald*, 30 March 1917, vol. 23, Mann Papers; *Washington Post*, 6 April 1917; *New York Tribune*, 6 April 1917; *New York Times*, 7 April 1917.

Mann. The minority leader's occasional intemperate remarks did contribute to the dissatisfaction of Gardner and other nationalists and Anglophiles. Yet Mann's basic positions on war issues were politically sound; he suffered mainly from sharp division among Republicans (not unique to them) that he could sometimes paper over, but never eradicate.

The short session revealed another sign of trouble for Mann. He showed intimations of the health problems that soon would interrupt his career. Before that happened, however, and despite his weakened condition politically and physically, he would lead his flock in an effective way through four months of important war legislation. An intense struggle over military conscription was first and foremost.

7

Victory and Defeat:
April 1917–March 1919

Mann was consistently active during the first four months of the war Congress; then illness largely removed him from the scene. The early period was critical, however, and Mann contributed substantially, to the advantage of the country and of his party. Later, in the election of 1918, the Republicans made much of their war record, and it helped them to capture both houses of Congress. Paradoxically, when in early 1919 House Republicans, at last restored to power, chose a Speaker, they rejected Mann in part because of the issue of support for the war that he had himself helped to generate. His vulnerability sprang from votes and statements antecedent to America's declaration of war, as on the McLenore resolution.

The first and most important of the war issues was that of the draft. Wilson alluded to the draft in his 2 April war message to Congress. Four days later Secretary of War Newton Baker submitted a bill to expand the regular army to 298,000 men and the federalized National Guard to 440,000, both through voluntary enlistment. But more men, 500,000 aged nineteen through twenty-five, would be recruited through a selective national draft, with the possibility of another 500,000 later. The bill specified various exemption categories.[1]

Wilson and Baker were latecomers to the idea of a draft, having earlier preferred a volunteer system. They changed their minds for various reasons—to avoid disruption of industry and decimation of the leadership class, as happened in England; to eliminate the need for a divisive emotional appeal for enlistments; to raise a mass army at a predictable rate; and to prevent

---

[1]John Whiteclay Chambers II, *To Raise an Army: The Draft Comes to Modern America* (New York: Free Press, 1987), 153.

Roosevelt from heading a volunteer unit and interfering with the conduct of the war.[2]

Although they had been used before, notably during the Civil War, in the main America had relied on volunteers to fight its wars. Many Democrats, led by Champ Clark, denounced conscription and fought it. The novelty of the plan, the spectacle of conflict over it in Congress, much of it among Democrats, and the importance of the issue combined to make the first great war measure also the most prominent and politically important. Republicans emerged as the saviors of Wilson's plan and benefited accordingly. Their own division and the Roosevelt matter complicated things and ultimately somewhat tarnished their success, but did not destroy it.

For a time Mann kept his own counsel, either because of honest doubt or in deference to the antidraft opinion of constituents and midwestern Republican congressmen. But before the outcome was determined, he threw his support to the draft and thereby strengthened his party's hold on the issue and the general theme of patriotic support for the war effort.

Early on, southern and western Democrats expressed opposition. On 11 April, just days after Congress declared war and Baker submitted his bill, the new chairman of the Rules Committee, Edward W. Pou of North Carolina, wrote Wilson's secretary, Joseph Tumulty, that "the sentiment is overwhelmingly in favor of giving the boys a chance to volunteer first." Tumulty reported to Wilson the next day on his own findings: "There is almost panic in our ranks and our friends assert that the bill cannot pass with this feature in it." Yet both Pou and Tumulty thought that if Wilson insisted on a fight, at cost to his party, he could win.[3]

Members heard protests from their districts. Farm people feared that the draft would fall heavily on their boys, since industrial workers were to be exempt. Boys of nineteen and twenty, not yet legally adults, seemed too young. Southerners had an additional concern—fear of armed Negro soldiers in their communities. Immigrants associated the draft with European militarism and tyranny, while other Americans saw the draft as a blow to individualism and a slur on the people's patriotism.[4]

S. Hubert Dent. Jr., of Alabama, chairman of Military Affairs, backed by other critics of the draft on his committee, launched two weeks of hearings. Dent was not intent on killing the draft altogether. Rather, he wanted to make it politically acceptable by association with a volunteer system. He

---

[2]David M. Kennedy, *Over Here: The First World War and American Society* (New York: Oxford University Press, 1980), 146–48; Chambers, *To Raise an Army*, 136–38, 141–44.

[3]Pou to Tumulty, 11 April 1917, series 2, box 159, Woodrow Wilson Papers, Library of Congress; Tumulty to Wilson, 12 April 1917, box 5, Special Correspondence, Joseph P. Tumulty Papers, Library of Congress.

[4]Chambers, *To Raise an Army*, 154–56.

proposed to authorize the president to establish a Selective Service System to conduct draft registration. But his bill required that before using the system, the president must first try to raise a volunteer army. Wilson would have none of it. A day in advance of the critical 18 April vote in committee, he summoned Dent to a White House interview, set for 5 P.M. He must have expected unsatisfactory results, for he scheduled Mann and Lenroot for 5:30.[5] Lenroot was invited because he might yet become floorleader; the matter had not yet been settled.

Wilson told the Republicans that, as Lenroot later reported it, "it was absolutely essential to the successful prosecution of the war that the views of the gentlemen (Chairman of Military Affairs Committee, Democratic leader of House and Speaker of House) be defeated." Mann and Lenroot promised only that Republicans would consider the draft in a nonpartisan spirit.[6]

By a vote of 13 to 8 the committee rebuffed Wilson, Baker, and the General Staff and approved Dent's plan. Southerners and westerners joined across party lines to make the majority. But Republicans provided five of the eight opposition votes. More important, the ranking Republican, Julius Kahn, stood ready to sponsor the administration's bill and to lead the fight for the draft in the House. In preparation, after the committee's vote, he conferred with Baker. The political implications of the situation were not lost on such Republicans as Senator Henry Cabot Lodge. Although Senate action was not yet completed, in Lodge's judgment the draft had already been saved there by Republicans, he wrote Roosevelt on 23 April, "and can only be saved in the same way in the House. The majority of Democrats seem to be against it. . . . A Republican is going to be in charge of the conscription bill in the House."[7] Mann could claim some of the credit, for over the years he had made the Republican appointments to Military Affairs, including Kahn's, and in advance of the preparedness fight he had persuaded Frank Greene, propreparedness and now prodraft, to stay on the committee.

Dent and Kahn opened debate on 23 April, on predictable lines. Mann remained noncommittal, but the Republican tilt towards the draft became more marked and noted the next day. A subheadline to the *New York Times*'s first-page story said "Lenroot and Anderson Lead the Day's Fight in

[5]From the diary of Thomas W. Braheny, Arthur S. Link, ed., *The Papers of Woodrow Wilson* (Princeton, N.J.: Princeton University Press, 42:9; Ray Stannard Baker, *Woodrow Wilson, Life and Letters* 7:23.

[6]Lenroot to S. D. Slade, 16 December 1918, box 5, Irvine L. Lenroot Papers, Library of Congress; *Milwaukee Sentinel*, 18 April 1917, parentheses Lenroot's in Lenroot to Slade.

[7]Seward W. Livermore, *Politics Is Adjourned: Woodrow Wilson and the War Congress*, 18; *New York Times*, 19 April 1917, 20 April 1917; *Superior Telegram*, 19 April 1917; Lodge to Roosevelt, 23 April 1917, series 1, box 329, Theodore Roosevelt Papers, Library of Congress.

Support of Administration Plan." These, after all, were midwesterners and progressives, hence least likely to back the draft. The episode was the more significant in that Lenroot's prodraft position reflected a change from his earlier, privately expressed view.[8]

Champ Clark provided the highlight of the draft debate on 25 April with a two-hour speech extolling the volunteer system and condemning the draft. House colleagues gave him a good reception, but the press seized on a re-mark that he spoke facetiously to discredit him. "In the estimation of Mis-sourians," he said, "there is precious little difference between a conscript and a convict."[9]

Once Dent's bill reached the amendment stage, Roosevelt's desperate ambition to head a volunteer division or corps complicated matters. Rebuffed by Secretary Baker, Roosevelt enlisted Republican allies in the Senate and House to continue the fight. To minimize the personal connection, Roose-veltians like Medill McCormick stood aside and left sponsorship of an amendment to a Tennessee regular, Richard W. Austin. The amendment would authorize a volunteer corps under Major General Leonard Wood, in which Roosevelt would head one of the three divisions. Only those too old for the draft could join.[10] While adoption of the amendment had some politi-cal attractions for most Republicans, it also would play into the hands of the antidraft forces. In that sense it represented a threat to the party's interest as champion of the administration's measure. Under those circumstances, as debate both heated up and wound down, Mann showed his hand.

"Mr. Chairman," he began, "I had expected to express briefly at a later hour my views on the pending bill, but the amendment now presented causes me to say a word." For days, he went on, the House had been debating be-tween reliance on volunteers or conscripts. "Those who are in favor of letting Col. Roosevelt raise a division can easily give him the opportunity by voting in favor of the volunteer method of raising an army. Those who are in favor of universal liability to service . . . . are utterly inconsistent to maintain that position if they give special preference to a few adventurers, as described by the gentleman from Massachusetts (Mr. Gardner)." Gardner, ardent for both Roosevelt and the draft, tried to respond, but Mann would not yield. Instead he declared, "If the volunteer system should be adopted, men hereafter and the children of men who go into the war will refer to the fact that they them-selves or their ancestors volunteered . . . . and when the volunteer system has not raised sufficient men and men are drafted, for all time in the family his-

[8]*New York Times*, 24 April 1917, 25 April 1917; Herbert F. Margulies, *Senator Lenroot of Wisconsin: a Political Biography, 1900–1929* (Columbia: University of Mis-souri Press, 1977), 223.

[9]*Chicago Examiner*, 26 April 1917, vol. 23, James R. Mann Papers, Library of Congress; Chambers, *To Raise an Army*, 165.

[10]Livermore, *Politics Is Adjourned*, 24–26; *CR* 65:1, p. 1380 (27 April 1917).

tory there will be a blot upon those who have been drafted in. But if you adopt the system now that all men subject equally to liability for service shall be taken according to law, there can be no offense in the term 'drafted in.'" Gardner addressed the chair in an effort to break in, but Mann stoutly and successfully resisted and then finished his comments. "Mr. Chairman, I have reached the conclusion that with the demands that may be made upon us in the war we are now engaged in, where for the safety and honor and dignity of the Republic we must smite our enemy, we ought to start right and make no exceptions, and that we ought to adopt the system that all men are equally liable to service. There then can be no disgrace hereafter in having been drafted."[11]

Minutes later, still in Committee of the Whole, members walked past tellers to be counted. By 170 to 106, they rejected the Roosevelt amendment. Enough Republicans joined Mann and a heavy preponderance of Democrats to form the majority. Pique against Roosevelt may have played a part among some Republican peace men whom he had excoriated, Mann among them, as one historian asserted. But there was more to the Republican antiamendment vote than that, for Lenroot enjoyed Roosevelt's favor, yet said two weeks later: "Mr. Speaker, as the House knows, I supported the conscription policy. I voted against the Roosevelt amendment."[12]

The Roosevelt amendment disposed of, Kahn immediately moved an amendment to strike from the Dent bill the volunteer provisions, thus restoring the bill to the form in which it had come from the War Department. Before debating that, the two sides agreed to vote on it at the start of the next day's session. Amidst high tension, on 28 April members again paraded past tellers and approved the Kahn amendment by an unexpected margin, 279–98. Later, on a roll-call vote in the House, they formalized the decision, 313–109. Seventy-nine percent of the Republicans supported it. A surprisingly high percentage of Democrats also voted for it, 70, but their deathbed conversion did not erase from memory earlier opposition, especially Clark's speech. That night the House passed the bill as further amended, and the Senate adopted its own version. During the late stages Mann explained and defended specific provisions of the bill and also continued, as on the previous day, to speed action on it, in further support of the administration and the war effort.[13] Patriotism came first for Mann in this time of crisis. But by his actions on the bill, he also fulfilled his responsibilities to his party.

---

[11]*CR* 65:1, p. 1385 (27 April 1917).

[12]*Ibid.*, p. 1387 (27 April 1917); *Chicago Tribune*, 28 April 1917, vol. 23, Mann Papers; Livermore, *Politics Is Adjourned*, 26; *CR* 65:1, p. 2205 (12 May 1917).

[13]*CR* 65:1, pp. 1388–90 (27 April 1917), 1503, 1555 (28 April 1917); Richard Kenneth Horner, "The House at War: The House of Representatives during World War I, 1917–1919" (Ph.D. diss., Louisiana State University, 1977), 133; *CR* 65:1, pp. 1524–25, 1547, 1503–05 (28 April 1917), 1368 (27 April 1917).

Many observers expressed astonishment at the turnaround in the House on the issue of selective service within a three-week period. A combination of factors caused it. Preparedness organizations, such as the National Security League, and most of the urban press helped to generate vast prodraft mail, some of it echoing an argument voiced in debate, that "slackers" should not get off. The administration effectively assured southern agrarians that the draft would not adversely affect the farm-labor supply nor race relations. Amendments made the bill more acceptable than before, especially a change in the minimum age from nineteen to twenty-one.[14]

Some difficulties remained. The Senate bill provided for the Roosevelt unit that the House had rejected, and the two houses differed on other things, including the maximum age for draftees. The Roosevelt matter and the Rough Rider's own strenuous efforts seemed the principal cause of deadlock and provoked widespread criticism of him and his supporters. After a time three Republican conferees abandoned Roosevelt and let the bill be reported. In a surprise maneuver the Rooseveltians rallied in the House as Daniel R. Anthony of Kansas moved to recommit with instructions to accept the Senate's Roosevelt amendment. With the draft no longer in danger, other Republicans rallied to the cause and carried the day for the motion, 215–178. Mann, however, with 29 other Republicans, voted "nay." Again the conferees deadlocked, and pressure from the public and the administration mounted. Finally, on 17 May they agreed to permit the president to commission Roosevelt without requiring it. On that basis the two houses adopted the Selective Service Act of 1917.[15] Wilson declined to give Roosevelt a command.

The 12 May Roosevelt gambit in the House conduced to Republican unity. Yet the long deadlock in conference brought on the party some criticism. Even so, on balance it emerged at the end as by far the stronger of the parties in support of the administration's proposal. As for Mann, though quietly at odds with most Republicans on the 12 May Roosevelt vote, he shared with Kahn and a few others the credit for the magnitude of House Republican support for conscription.

A year later Frank Greene reviewed for a friend the history of the draft bill in his Military Affairs Committee. After that legislative experience, he said, the administration had come to rely on the Senate committee to initiate legislation. The House committee, he went on, "is well nigh shot to pieces, and the administration has almost literally to depend upon us Republicans on it for its support in many things it needs." But Greene was not disposed to act as a rubber stamp. Voicing an opinion that had become widespread among Republicans, he wrote that Wilson "had gathered around him a mess of dreamers, theorists, magazine writers, doctrinaires and what not. . . . He

---

[14]Chambers, *To Raise an Army*, 166, 162–64, 157, 148.
[15]Livermore, *Politics Is Adjourned*, 27–30; *CR* 65:1, pp. 2215–16 (12 May 1917).

ignores Congress, and even expresses what is tantamount to contempt for it, in a sense. He is making it a one-man war," Greene concluded, "let his champions say what they will."[16]

Greene's letter reflected a situation that was already developing in the spring and summer of 1917. Republicans stood on firm political ground in support of war measures. But they resented Wilson and had little good to say for many of his associates, including the secretaries of war and the Navy, Baker and Josephus Daniels. Thus in some instances they felt obliged to save the administration from itself and felt secure enough to criticize administration proposals. The major bills that their Democratic colleagues offered did indeed emanate from the executive branch.[17]

During and after consideration of the draft and the Roosevelt amendment, Congress dealt with, among other things, appropriations in several forms, an espionage bill with a contentious censorship section, a major revenue bill, the very important Lever food control bill, and with it the Weeks amendment to establish a congressional oversight committee on expenditures. Mann, with most of his Republican colleagues, was free with criticism and amendments. Though aware that war necessitated extraordinary measures and methods, Mann and other Republicans shied from putting seemingly dictatorial powers in the hands of the administration, and they were loath to still the voice of Congress generally and themselves in particular. They endured some press criticism for causing delay and balking the president, but they did not forfeit their credentials as supportive of the war effort. Politically, the criticism they endured was more than offset by the issues they generated.

More than in previous years, Mann shared the burden of debate with others. The war, the heightened Republican presence, the attacks on Mann after the 1916 election, and perhaps his precarious health stimulated the activity of others. Yet Mann participated vigorously and did credit to his party. Internal division was unavoidable on the revenue bill, and in that instance Mann willingly headed the conservative faction. In the main, however, he at the very least shared the views of his major colleagues, while still providing the cues for the rank and file.

To hasten military appropriations, in early April the Appropriations Committee submitted administration bills, bypassing the military and naval committees. When on 9 April the House considered a one-hundred-million-dollar secret fund, actually for the Secret Service, Mann objected to the absence of specificity and pointed to other instances that week when the House's traditional and treasured role in appropriations had been cavalierly

---

[16]Greene to Howard Hindley, 5 May 1918, box 3, Frank L. Greene Papers, Library of Congress.

[17]Livermore, *Politics Is Adjourned*, 37–39; Horner, "House at War," 25.

treated. There had been, for example, a two-billion-dollar appropriation to the War Department with no terminal date, as the Constitution required, and a Treasury Department request for almost three billion dollars spelled out in just six lines. "Now, is it the expectation that Congress is simply to be dissolved?" he asked. "Will we say that we will turn over all the money that can be raised . . . . to be expended by the direction of the President, who personally can not know what it is to be expended for or the need for the expenditure, and practically end the theory that Congress is in control of the appropriations for the government?" Mann was willing to make all necessary appropriations. "But I hope that we will not be asked, in the endeavor to spread democracy throughout the world, to abolish it at home." To put billions in the hands of the president "without any control whatever on our part" abolished real democracy, he said. Though Mann lost out respecting the Secret Service appropriation, he had put Democratic leaders on the defensive, and John Fitzgerald, John Nance Garner, and Swagar Sherley promised more specificity.[18]

"We ought not to get into a panic. We ought to retain some coolness," Mann said, in criticizing the short-circuiting of Congress on huge appropriations. He brought the same attitude to bear in connection with what he considered an overly broad antisabotage bill.[19] Then he opposed a press censorship provision of the espionage bill.

Suspicious and antagonistic towards the press, Wilson was insistent on press censorship. The foreign-language press, fearing charges of disloyalty, did not object, but the English-language press raised a hue and cry and likened the proposal to the odious Sedition Act of 1798. In the House Mann voiced early opposition, then gave strong support to George S. Graham of Pennsylvania, a member of the Judiciary Committee and a distinguished constitutionalist, who led the opposition to the provision and others in the bill.[20]

The bill, Mann said on 3 May, allowed criticism of the government, but not use of facts. So what good would the criticism do? "The best way for us to conduct the war is to let the people know what is going on." He opposed allowing "a clerk in the War Department" to decide what could be published, including lists of dead and captured. The following day, by a vote of 221–167, the House approved Graham's motion to strike the section, as 86 percent of the Republicans voted with Graham. After some Republicans left the chamber and Democrats entered, Democrat Warren Gard of Ohio offered what he described as compromise language. Vainly, Mann protested that few knew anything of the amendment and suggested recommittal. The Demo-

---

[18]Horner, "House at War," 135–36; *CR* 65:1, pp. 496–98 (9 April 1917).
[19]*CR* 65:1, pp. 497 (9 April 1917), 819–21 (18 April 1917).
[20]Livermore, *Politics Is Adjourned*, 32–34; Kennedy, *Over Here*, 25–26.

crats controlled, however, and by 191–185 adopted the amendment. As the House moved on with the bill, Mann successfully supported lesser Graham amendments, but he was not able to do anything about a provision that would later prove important, allowing the postmaster general to ban publications from the mails. "There seems to be a great idea just now abroad in the land that nobody shall be permitted to express an opinion unless it agrees with your own," he said. "Freedom is to be attained by having liberty, not by curtailing it." On that basis, Mann joined the minority in a 260–107 vote against the bill. Only 10 Democrats voted with Mann, while 96 Republicans did.[21]

The Senate rejected the censorship provision, but when the bill went to conference the president publicly insisted on it and obtained a compromise provision. Wilson's intervention reinvigorated Republican opponents in the House. They held a nonbinding caucus, perhaps at Mann's initiative, certainly with his complicity, and resolved against the compromise. Wilson again insisted on it at a meeting with House Democratic leaders, and a nonbinding party caucus so resolved. The Republicans proved the better unified. By a vote of 184–144 the House recommitted the conference report with instructions to remove the censorship section, effectively killing it given the Senate's stance on the issue. Just 10 House Republicans opposed recommittal, while 37 Democrats approved it.[22]

The surviving Espionage Act retained stringent provisions against interference with the armed forces, including recruitment, and for control of the mails. Politically, though, Congress's rejection of censorship benefited the Republicans in several ways. They aligned themselves with the press on the issue; and their victory kept the press open as an avenue of criticism of the administration.[23]

Mann took a libertarian stance again in mid-July in connection with the Trading with the Enemies Act. The House was marking time, and fewer than fifty members participated in Committee of the Whole deliberations. Mann, however, abetted by Lenroot and Fiorello La Guardia of New York, won attention with a successful attack on various repressive features of the bill. Most important, he brought about the withdrawal of sections for drastic mail censorship and to prohibit sending of any letter or other form of communication to an enemy country or its ally, topics covered in the Espionage Act. In debate Mann suggested that the State Department use the good offices of neutrals to help families at least discover whether relatives in Germany or other enemy countries were alive. The *New York Times* featured Mann's role

---

[21]*CR* 65:1, pp. 1765–66 (3 May 1917), 1816, 1818–19, 1837–39, 1821–22, 1841 (4 May 1917); Horner, "House at War," 128.

[22]Livermore, *Politics Is Adjourned*, 34–36; Horner, "House at War," 429–30.

[23]Kennedy, *Over Here*, 25–26.

and said that he "enlivened debate" with the statement that "the departments have gone crazy on these matters. They see a German spy on every house top and every street corner, and they are afraid of the spies. They are scared stiff and there is no occasion for it."[24] German Americans, including citizens by naturalization, were the principal beneficiaries of Mann's efforts, and by extension those of his party.

Earlier, Mann showed himself equally free to attack a Democratic revenue bill, even though the Ways and Means Committee treated it as a war measure and reported it unanimously. From a different perspective, progressive Republicans led by Lenroot also attacked it, and Mann found himself at odds with them. In this two-front conflict Mann upheld economic conservatism, both within his party and against the Democrats. Mann realized that the wartime need for revenue had provided occasion for the further advance of progressive revenue principles with respect both to high tax rates and to heavy reliance on taxes as against bond sales. This he resisted. His approach was not wholly ideological, however, for he also found in the bill some bias towards the South, and he embraced the potent sectional issue for partisan advantage. Given the commitment to the bill of the GOP members of Ways and Means, headed by Joseph Fordney, Nicholas Longworth, and Ebenezer Hill, Mann did double duty as leader for Republicans against Democrats and for Republican conservatives against the party's progressives. J. Hampton Moore and Martin Madden lent him strong support, the latter on postal provisions.

The committee bill undertook to raise $1.8 billion from tax increases, half from income and profits taxes, half from consumer excises. In addition, it proposed a new zone rate system for second-class mail to raise an additional $1.5 billion. In combination, these increases would approximately match the amount to be raised from the initial sale of bonds, as earlier authorized with bipartisan support. As reported on 9 May, the bill proposed to double the normal and corporation tax rate to 4 percent, boost the surtax to a maximum of 33 percent, double the excess profits tax to 16 percent, and substantially increase excises. Its provisions reflected in part the inclinations of Claude Kitchin, chairman of Ways and Means and majority leader still, who favored progressive taxation under any circumstances, and most especially in the context of causing those who promoted the war and profited from it to bear much of the cost. In this outlook, carried over from the preparedness and revenue debates of 1916, Kitchin mirrored the views of many progressives of both parties.[25]

---

[24]*New York Times*, 10 July 1917; Horner, "House at War," 173–74; *CR* 65:1, pp. 4912–15, 4920, 4924 (10 July 1917), 1970–73, 4978–79 (11 July 1917).

[25]Homer Larry Ingle, "Pilgrimage to Reform: A Life of Claude Kitchin" (Ph.D. diss., University of Wisconsin, 1967), 143–44; Richard L. Watson, Jr., *The Development of National Power: The United States, 1900–1919* (Boston: Houghton Mifflin,

Since the bill was unanimously reported, congressmen anticipated no substantial amendments.[26] Very soon they discovered otherwise. A Democratic leader, Swagar Sherley, and Irvine Lenroot led a drive to boost surtaxes on upper-income people yet more. Initially, Kitchin suspected that Lenroot's real purpose was to make possible cuts in certain proposed excises, and so, after defeating Sherley's amendments, he also opposed the first of Lenroot's, to raise the surtax on incomes of from forty to sixty thousand dollars. Nevertheless, the Committee of the Whole adopted the amendment, 98–87. Suddenly, Secretary McAdoo revised the government's revenue needs upwards, and Kitchin the next day agreed to Lenroot's full program of amendments, which raised the surtaxes on incomes over forty thousand dollars by 25 and put a 45 percent surtax on incomes over a million dollars. The Committee of the Whole approved the composite amendment on 17 May, 147–107.[27]

Preliminary adoption of the Lenroot amendments increased what was already strong opposition to the bill from publishers, business leaders, and such conservative Republicans as Nicholas Murray Butler and Senator John W. Weeks of Massachusetts.[28] Mann spoke and acted for these interests and for himself. First, however, on 21 May he set out to exploit the sectional issue for party advantage. At odds with progressive Republicans on some things, he had their support in this effort.

Moore offered an amendment to add to the excises a war tax on cotton at $2.50 a bale. Charles R. Crisp of Georgia immediately made a point of order against the motion. At this point Mann took over for the Republicans. Criticizing the rules the Democrats had made as "more restrictive than any body in the history of the world has ever made," he acknowledged that there were precedents in favor of the point of order, but asked the chair to overrule these and go to the merits. Under the rules, new items could not be added by amendment. Yet, Mann argued, the House "has the right to originate revenue legislation itself and not be confined to the sweet will of 23 members who happen to be elected to the Ways and Means committee."

1976), 231; Charles Gilbert, *American Financing of World War I* (Westport, Conn.: Greenwood Publishing Corp., 1970), 75–91.

[26]John J. Esch to Odin J. Oyen, 12 May 1917; and to Robert M. La Follette, 14 May 1917, box 42, John J. Esch Papers, State Historical Society of Wisconsin, Madison.

[27]John Wylie Hillje, "The Progressive Movement and the Graduated Income Tax, 1913–1919" (Ph.D. diss., University of Texas, 1966), 235; Ingle, "Pilgrimage to Reform," 145; *Washington Times*, 18 May 1917; *CR* 65:1, pp. 2419 (16 May 1917), 2462, 2474 (17 May 1917).

[28]Ingle, "Pilgrimage to Reform," 144; Livermore, *Politics Is Adjourned*, 58–61; Butler to James R. Mann, 11 May 1917, 25 May 1917, James R. Mann file, Nicholas Murray Butler Papers, Butler Library, Columbia University; *Washington Post*, 18 May 1917.

Fitzgerald and Lenroot supported Mann with the argument that items recommended for taxation by McAdoo could not be added under the rules, and
Mann named some of these. They included tobacco, alcohol, and sugar, a
short list with both sectional and moral overtones. Champ Clark then ruled
against the amendment, and Mann duly appealed the ruling. Thomas Heflin,
with whom Mann had often clashed, then moved to table the appeal. "You
can not lay the appeal on the table," Mann snapped at Heflin. "If you knew
anything about it, you would not undertake to do that." When Mann then
reiterated that the chair was right respecting the precedents, but the House
should make a new precedent, tempers heated. Mann was trying to change
the rules in an irregular way, several members charged, while others yelled
for the vote. Quickly it came, and the House sustained the Chair, 137–117.
Amidst a general assault on the excises, this vote had the closest margin, sug-
gestive of Republican unity on a major partisan issue.[29]

The party was less united on other amendments in part because of the
committee Republicans' commitment to the bill, and also because of division
along progressive/conservative lines. Mann debated several excise amendments and showed himself in mild disagreement with his Ways and Means
colleagues.[30] He became more fully and actively engaged in supporting
Moore's amendment to strike the section raising second-class mail rates.
Mann argued in terms of the education of youth from magazines and newspapers. He argued also that there was a close correlation between the second-
class-mail rate and business growth.[31]

As on 23 May the Committee of the Whole neared the end of its work,
Mann took the floor to say, "I regret very much that I will not be able to
vote for the bill on its final passage." In light of his earlier criticisms, the announcement warranted no surprise; still, the bill was an important war measure and had the backing of Fordney and his committee colleagues. Mann
spelled out his reasons. The government had to raise large sums, he acknowledged. But the diversion of resources would drive up prices of food and
clothing for ordinary Americans. "I think it is a mistake to add to that the
effort to raise one-half of the money necessary to carry on the war by additional burdensome taxation," Mann said. "It is far better . . . to levy a small
tax upon the people now, and to continue that tax during a series of years
after the war is closed." If new taxes were later needed to maintain the nation's credit, they could be incorporated in new bond legislation. The bill, he
concluded, went far in the direction of killing the goose that lays the golden
egg.[32] That he referred to the bill's impact on business and investment be-

---

[29]*CR* 65:1, pp. 2661–65 (21 May 1917); Ingle, "Pilgrimage to Reform," 146.
[30]*CR* 65:1, pp. 2275, 2284 (14 May 1917), 2603, 2619 (19 May 1917), 2685, 2689
(21 May 1917).
[31]*Ibid.*, p. 2765 (22 May 1917).
[32]*Ibid.*, p. 2806 (23 May 1917).

came clear in the votes that followed as the bill went to the House for final action.

In the roll-call votes Mann showed himself staunchly conservative. Overall, the Republican members proved divided along both sectional and ideological lines.[33] Yet, given the fact of these divisions, and the further fact that this was unanimously reported war legislation, the conservative vote was noteworthy.

Mann took charge for his side and got a roll-call vote on the Lenroot income tax amendment. By a margin of 344–66 it passed. Mann was one of 50 Republicans in the minority. The House then rejected an amendment by Frank Doremus, Michigan Democrat, to ease certain business taxes, 173–235. Mann, with 71 percent of the Republicans, supported the amendment. Then committee postal rate-amendments won approval, 257–150, over the opposition of Mann and 65 percent of Republicans. The amendments disposed of, Mann moved recommittal. The House rejected the motion, 161–247. On this vote 77 percent of the Republicans voted with Mann, and under other circumstances the 10 on Ways and Means would have. Mann then asked for a roll-call vote on the bill, and it passed, 329–76. All the opponents were Republicans, Mann among them.[34]

Mann's involvement, especially because it came early in the bill's course, was politically significant. He encouraged and led a partisan opposition even though the bill was an early major war measure, unanimously reported. He helped to reinvigorate the sectional issue in connection with the cotton tax amendment, and that issue, nourished by other events, would be very important in the 1918 elections. In the vital and rapidly changing field of taxation, Mann had shown the flag for conservatism against the Democrats and within his own party.

Early on, Mann took the German threat very seriously. Urging authorization for more vice-admirals, he said, "The sooner we get over the idea in this country and in this House that we are conducting a woman's sewing circle, or a pink tea affair, the better it will be for us all. We are at war with the greatest war power that the world has ever seen." The Allies alone could not defeat it.[35] At the same time, he saw a need for economy and found in administration practice disturbing instances of wasteful favoritism and incompetence.[36] Accordingly, in July Mann strongly supported creation of a bipartisan Joint Committee on the War to serve as a watchdog on expenditures. Such a committee, of course, would enhance Republican influence.

---

[33]Horner, "House at War," 151, 155.

[34]CR 65:1, pp. 2815–19 (23 May 1917); Horner, "House at War," 143–51.

[35]CR 65:1 p. 1966 (8 May 1917).

[36]Ibid., pp. 3203, 3187 (1 June 1917), 3294 (7 June 1917), 2893 (25 May 1917).

Bills for the committee had been introduced on 9 April by Weeks in the Senate and Madden in the House. The president, however, hastened to the Capitol and succeeded in burying the bills.[37] In connection with the important Lever food-control bill, Weeks, abetted especially by the spectacular failure of the Shipping Board, revived the plan and won its adoption in the Senate as an amendment. Wilson, who thought that Abraham Lincoln had been seriously hamstrung in conduct of the Civil War by just such a committee, wrote Asbury Lever, in charge of the bill in the House, urging rejection of the amendment and spelling out his reasons. Accordingly, Lever offered a resolution opposing all Senate amendments, including Weeks's, and calling for a conference. Against that, Mann argued for a separate vote on the Weeks amendment. The House managers would kill it in conference, he said, so this was the only chance for a vote. Lever would not yield, and Mann thereupon blocked action for the day, despite the importance of the legislation and the fact of public impatience over earlier delay. Again the next day, 25 July, Lever refused a separate vote and Mann withheld unanimous consent. At that point Acting Rules Chairman Finis J. Garrett submitted a rule, earlier adopted in committee on a straight party vote, to the effect that the House should disagree to all Senate amendments, ask for a conference, and the Speaker "shall immediately appoint the conferees." There would be no separate vote on the Weeks amendment. The country and patriotism demanded immediate action, Garrett explained, and he then moved the previous question. By a vote of 163–101 the House approved the rule. Thirty-one Republicans voted with Garrett, and the rest supported Mann. The press criticized him and his colleagues, along with Senate proponents of the amendment, both on the merits and for delay. But Weeks persisted in the months ahead, and his proposal served as a rallying point for Republicans.[38]

Mann took no part in debate on the food-control bill. The bill addressed the problem of food shortages and skyrocketing prices by giving the president unprecedented powers to stimulate production with price guarantees, while also protecting the public against extortion. In connection with an earlier companion bill that Mann helped shape, for a food survey and seed distribution program, Mann endorsed the large wartime extension of controls embodied in the Lever Food and Fuel Control Act.[39] But his silence on that law probably resulted less from approval than from deteriorating health.

In August, while the Senate wrestled with the revenue bill, the House took a series of three-day adjournments. Mann took the opportunity to try

---

[37]*Ibid.*, p. 497 (9 April 1917); Livermore, *Politics Is Adjourned*, 15–17.

[38]*CR* 65:1, pp. 5435–36 (24 July 1917), 5473 (25 July 1917); *New York Times*, 26 July 1917.

[39]*CR* 65:1, p. 2938 (26 May 1917).

to repair his health. As it turned out, however, except for a few appearances, he was unable to resume his duties for sixteen months.

Mann suffered from severe "needle pains" in his legs that deprived him of sleep. His friends and eventually doctors blamed persistent overwork for his troubles; but in August 1917 one physician prescribed extraction of all his teeth, which when done only worsened matters. Intermittently he was confined at Johns Hopkins Hospital in Baltimore, where he was treated by diet and surgery. In the main, however, he worked in his Chicago truck garden, under orders to ignore public affairs.[40] On 19 September 1918 his only child, twenty-eight and for years the victim of tuberculosis, killed himself with a revolver. "I am pretty nearly all in, and I do not want to wait for the end by tuberculosis," he wrote his mother.[41] Even so, Mann's recovery progressed, and in December 1918, with the start of the third session of the Sixty-fifth Congress, he resumed full activity. He deluded himself with the belief that his recovery was complete.

One of Mann's infrequent appearances in Washington during the hiatus came in late November 1917, in advance of the second session. He told colleagues that he would not remain long, but nevertheless he proposed not to relinquish his leadership, but to delegate it, principally to Frederick Gillett, ranking Republican on Appropriations and on the GOP steering committee. Augustus P. Gardner, Mann's outspoken critic, had enlisted in the army and so was not present to challenge the arrangement. Mann and his allies Mondell and Moore controlled the five-member steering committee. Furthermore, no one could then have definitely predicted that the session would last for almost a year nor that Mann would be unable to resume his duties in that time. During his absence, Martin Madden took care of Illinois matters.[42]

Mann did not entirely forsake public affairs during his illness and recuperation. Some of his activity was collegial. From his hospital bed he sent a letter to be read by Gillett in tribute to John Fitzgerald on the occasion of his last appropriations bill before retiring from the House. After Ebenezer Hill died, Mann came to the Capitol to deliver a short eulogy. When the death of Senator William Stone of Missouri opened the Senate seat for Champ Clark, Mann conferred with Republican leaders and told Clark that he could take the appointment without fear that the GOP would challenge for the speakership. Clark chose not to.[43]

---

[40]*Calumet Index*, 21 June 1918, vol. 23, Mann Papers, *CR* 67:4, pp. 1717, 1720 (14 January 1923); *New York Times*, 28 November 1917; *CR* 65:3, p. 2405 (30 January 1919); *Washington Post*, 29 December 1917; *Calumet Index*, 21 June 1918, vol. 23, Mann Papers, Library of Congress.

[41]*Chicago Tribune*, 21 September 1918.

[42]*New York Times*, 26 November 1917.

[43]*CR* 65:2, pp. 316 (14 December 1917), 2952 (3 March 1918); *Chicago Tribune*, 26 April 1918.

In January, his health at its worst, Mann took his life in his hands to come from the hospital to cast a critical vote for the woman suffrage amendment, to give it the bare two-thirds margin that was required. He was cheered whenever he appeared during the months of his illness; on this occasion members on both sides of the aisle rose and applauded for several minutes when he entered the chamber and took his seat. Although Wilson had belatedly come out for the amendment, the Republicans, following a caucus, gave it the larger share of its vote. Later it narrowly failed in the Senate.[44] Mann's risky action in coming for the vote reflected his partisanship, but more than that his attachment to the suffrage cause and the personal values of courage and bravery that he considered rare among politicians and statesmen.[45]

A month later Mann was well enough to attend a joint session to hear a presidential address. Wilson had laid down his Fourteen Points for a generous and liberal peace in an 8 January speech. Austria responded more favorably than did Germany. Now, on 11 February, Wilson called Congress's attention to the divergence and restated in general terms a liberal peace program, based on the welfare and national aspirations of the people involved. Afterwards, Mann commended the address for in several ways opening the door to peace, as by widening the breach between Germany and Austria.[46]

Perhaps sympathy for Wilson's peace efforts and for his plans for future peace through a League of Nations had something to do with a later statement by Mann that was favorable to the administration. On 8 May he announced in the House that though he felt well, instead of resuming his legislative duties, he would leave Washington to tend his garden through the spring and summer. He left with his colleagues some advice. Some Republicans, including Gillett, had strongly criticized the administration's conduct of the war for extravagance, delay, incompetence, and partisanship. Earlier, Mann had himself made such criticism. Now, however, he said that "we must have patience. We are appropriating here unbelievable sums of money. . . . Mistakes will occur here, mistakes will occur there. . . . Let us help to correct them, but never forget that they are natural and cannot be avoided," Mann concluded. "We must not be too hurried in our judgment. . . . I know the feeling, I think, on both sides of this House: In the war there is no partisanship." The press noted Mann's comments, and so did Colonel Edward House, Wilson's friend and adviser. In a letter to the president, House expressed hope of dividing "such Republicans as Taft, Root and Hughes on the

---

[44]*CR* 66:1, p. 88 (21 May 1919); *CR* 67:4, p. 1723 (14 January 1923); *CR* 65:2, p. 810 (10 January 1918); Clara Lenroot Diary, entry for 10 January 1918, Lenroot Papers Addition; *Chicago Tribune*, 11 January 1918.

[45]*CR* 65:2, p. 316 (14 December 1917).

[46]Arthur S. Link, *Woodrow Wilson: Revolution, War, and Peace* (Arlington Heights, Ill.: Harlen Davidson, 1979), 84–85; *New York Times*, 12 February 1918.

one hand and such Republicans as Sherman, Brandegee, Penrose and their ilk on the other." He thought that might be done and noted in evidence Mann's speech and one by Root. In the event, no breach occurred that was so severe as to hurt the Republicans in their political recovery. But internal divisions were developing that would affect both the future direction of the party and public policy, most importantly the postwar decision about joining the League of Nations.[47]

Mann's illness presented no obstacle to his renomination and reelection. Early on, Edwin W. Sims took charge and assured Mann that he need not campaign. As promised, Mann won renomination without opposition and in the general election defeated the Democrat with 59.5 percent of the vote. His victory came despite charges that he had not supported Wilson, as on the McLemore resolution.[48]

Reelection in 1918 carried special significance for Mann, in that his party won majorities in both houses. With a plurality of 1,200,000, the largest since 1906, the Republicans gained 7 Senate seats and 30 in the House. In the Senate their margin was a precarious 49–47, but enough to organize the body. In the House the party majority was 239–193, plus three minor-party candidates.[49] There, too, Republicans would organize. If all went well, they would elect Mann speaker. Whether they did or not, the election marked the party's reunion and revival after the years of division and defeat that had set in in 1910 and 1912.

In some respects the Republican victory sprang from transitory factors, especially resentment of northern farmers and ranchers over the fact of price controls on their wheat and wool but not on southerners' cotton.[50] In addition, though, in 1918 Republicans and Moosers cemented their reunion, partly through the efforts of Roosevelt. When the National Committee elevated the young GOP chairman of the Indiana Republicans, Will Hays, to the national chairmanship, the event marked a further triumph for conciliation and put in authority a man who practiced and preached party reunion.

---

[47]*Chicago Tribune*, 19 April 1918; CR 65:2, p. 6218 (8 May 1918); *New York Times*, 9 May 1918; House to Wilson, 9 May 1918, Arthur S. Link, ed., *The Papers of Woodrow Wilson*, (Princeton, N.J.: Princeton University Press, 1984), 47:584.

[48]Sims to Mann, 18 February 1918, vol. 23, Mann Papers; *Chicago Tribune*, 16 May 1918; *New York Times*, 12 September 1918; John L. Moore, ed., *Congressional Quarterly's Guide to U.S. Elections* 2nd ed. (Washington, D.C.: Congressional Quarterly, 1985), 736; *Chicago Tribune*, October 24, 1918; Thomas Robert Bullard, "From Businessman to Congressman: The Careers of Martin B. Madden" (Ph.D. diss., University of Illinois at Chicago Circle, 1973), 17.

[49]William H. Harbaugh, "The Republican Party, 1893–1932," in *History of U.S. Political Parties*, vol. 3, *1910–1945: From Square Deal to New Deal*, ed. Arthur M. Schlesinger, Jr. (New York: Chelsea House Publishers in association with R. R. Bowker Co., 1973), 2103; Livermore, *Politics Is Adjourned*, 224.

[50]Harbaugh, "Republican Party," 2104; Livermore, *Politics Is Adjourned*, 224, 243.

Though in January 1919 death would take Roosevelt, there was every reason
to believe that the Moosers' return was permanent. The disillusionment with
Wilson and his administration that in 1920 would convert a tendency into an
electoral avalanche had not yet set in, but even so the 1918 returns suggested
that the Republicans had regained their status as the majority party and that
the unstable Wilsonian coalition had been broken. If after the returns were
in, Mann looked backward over the previous decade, he surely took satisfaction in his own very considerable incremental contributions to the outcome.[51]

When the lame-duck session of the Sixty-fifth Congress convened on 2
December 1918, Mann was in his place and ready to resume his duties. By
then the war was over, and the president was about to embark for Europe as
head of the American delegation to the Paris peace conference. Above all, he
would press for a League of Nations and would preside over its creation. In
advance of his departure he addressed an unfriendly Congress. The day before the speech, Democratic Senator Henry Ashurst of Arizona wrote of the
president's precipitous loss of popularity. He attributed it to Wilson's failure
to demand unconditional surrender, his many notes to Germany, his 25
October appeal for a Democratic Congress, his refusal to appoint a senator
to the peace delegation, and his appointment of himself. Ashurst might have
added to his list skepticism among many Republicans about the League of
Nations and bipartisan resentment over being ignored during the war.[52]

Wilson was coolly received, especially by Republicans, most of whom
withheld applause. The president did not improve matters when he failed to
confide the details of his plans. The chilly atmosphere was not lost on Wilson, and later that day he referred to it in conversation and said that he was
interested in remarks made to him by the reception committee. "Mann is a
bitter partisan but he is a sport," Wilson remarked. "He wished me a good
voyage and success." Lodge, who had succeeded to party leadership on the

---

[51]Harold Ickes to Gifford Pinchot, 21 January 1918, box 210, Gifford Pinchot
Papers, Library of Congress; Walter Brown to James R. Garfield, 18 February 1918,
box 162, and Ickes to Garfield, 18 February 1918, box 115, James R. Garfield Papers,
Library of Congress; Livermore, *Politics Is Adjourned*, 106–10; Will H. Hays, *The
Memoirs of Will H. Hays* (Garden City, N.J.: Doubleday, 1955), 168; Lewis L. Gould,
Reform and Regulation: American Politics from Roosevelt to Wilson 2nd ed. (New
York: Alfred A. Knopf, 1986), 206; Jerome Clubb, William Flanagan and Nancy Zin-
gale, *Partisan Realignment: Voters, Parties, and Government in American History*
(Beverly Hills, Calif.: Sage Publications, 1980), 113.

[52]George F. Sparks, ed., *A Many-colored Toga: The Diary of Henry Fountain
Ashurst* (Tucson: University of Arizona Press, 1962), 1 December 1918, 90–91; David
Lawrence, *The True Story of Woodrow Wilson* (New York: George H. Doran Com-
pany, 1924), 269.

death of Jacob Gallinger, pointedly wished him only a good voyage, he noted.[53]

Less severely than others, Mann criticized Wilson's vagueness. But when Senator Lawrence Sherman offered a resolution to declare the presidency vacant and to install Vice President Thomas Marshall in the office because of Wilson's absence from the country, and Senator Philander Knox of Pennsylvania offered a resolution to separate the League of Nations from the rest of the treaty and make peace first, Mann strongly dissented. He announced that "there will be no concerted effort on the part of the Republicans of the House to embarrass the president in any way while he is abroad." The people would not approve, he said, and he did not himself favor the Sherman or Knox resolutions. William Howard Taft, president of the League to Enforce Peace, which favored a world organization, quickly echoed and endorsed Mann's statement, and Wilson, just before leaving, gratefully acknowledged it.[54]

In February and at the session's end in March, Mann defended the league against criticism from Senate Republicans, and his remarks attracted some attention. In opposing a large naval increase, he expressed hope that "the President will be successful in his aspirations for a league of nations which will, through orderly and peaceful methods, prevent the settlement of disputes in the future by war."[55] Thus Mann continued what had begun during the period of his illness, to take a hand in the battle to determine his party's approach to international affairs in the postwar world.

Congress achieved little in the short session. The administration had no coordinated plan for postwar reconstruction, and neither did the Republicans. Politics loomed large as both parties, fresh from their 1918 clash, looked ahead to 1920, a presidential year. Simultaneously, Republicans fought an intraparty battle looking towards an end-of-session caucus, when Mann would be challenged for the speakership in the next Congress. In these several contexts Mann tried to show himself again equal to his varied leadership duties.

Mann exhibited his usual strong institutional concern and capacity. He had complimentary words for Democrats Carter Glass and Swagar Sherley, the former appointed Secretary of the Treasury and the latter ending his

[53]Ellen M. Slayden, *Washington Wife: Journal of Ellen Maury Slayden from 1897–1919* (New York, Harper and Row, 1962), 350–51; "From the Diary of Josephus Daniels," 2 December 1918, Arthur S. Link, ed., *The Papers of Woodrow Wilson*, (Princeton, N.J.: Princeton University Press, 1986), 53:301.

[54]*New York Times*, 4 December 1918; Link, *The Papers of Woodrow Wilson*, 53:323, n. l; Wilson to Mann, 3 December 1918, Link, *The Papers of Woodrow Wilson*, 53:308.

[55]*CR* 65:3, p. 3151 (11 February 1919); *New York Times*, 4 March 1919.

House career after defeat in the election.[56] Occasionally he clarified arcane rules in a nonpartisan way, and criticized "crude methods . . . in enacting important legislation."[57] Though favorable to a much-needed and publicized reform in the budgeting process, on several occasions, as he had two years earlier, he warned against any sacrifice of congressional power to the executive branch.[58]

Mann, with most of his party colleagues, took familiar proconservation ground in opposition to the most recent version of the coal, oil, and gas leasing bill. After a conference report died in the Senate, Gifford Pinchot complimented Mann on his work and correctly predicted better things ahead.[59]

Mann gave his usual close attention to appropriations, pushed for economy, and won some.[60] In that connection he picked up on a wartime theme that remained popular—vast waste and extravagance by such executive agencies as the Shipping Board—and warned of an investigation in the next Congress.[61] Late in the war Mann had urged his colleagues to curb that kind of criticism, but with war's end the Democratic administration became fair game. Nor, apparently, did Mann feel that such criticism undermined Wilson's position at the peace conference.

Mann reserved his fullest energy, attention, and emotion for current outrages against American soldiers by the American government. In that connection he solicited letters of grievance and asked his colleagues to channel their letters of complaint to him. He pressed individual cases with Secretary of War Baker and others, but when no satisfactory outcome resulted, he criticized the army, the War Department, and the War Risk Insurance Bureau. Using appropriations bills as the setting for his remarks, Mann told of slowness in paying dependents from allotments made by the soldiers out of their pay; he complained of slowness to discharge soldiers, even when they had jobs that would remain open only temporarily; he recited complaints of ill-treatment of wounded soldiers and indifferent efforts to get mail to them or to help families locate them; and he talked of inadequately marked graves

---

[56]*CR* 65:3, pp. 518 (16 December 1918), 2241 (28 January 1919).

[57]*Ibid.*, pp. 1119 (17 January 1919), 2455 (31 January 1919), 3370–71 (14 February 1919), 3469 (15 February 1919).

[58]*CR* 64:2, p. 4035 (25 February 1917).

[59]*CR* 65:3, pp. 3171 (11 February 1919), 3708–10 (18 February 1919); Margulies, *Senator Lenroot*, 255–56; Pinchot to Mann, 19 March 1919, vol. 24, Mann Papers.

[60]*CR* 65:3, pp. 2251 (28 January 1919), 2837 (6 February 1919).

[61]*Ibid.*, pp. 1455 (15 January 1919), 2241–42 (28 January 1919), 4180 (24 February 1919), 4910–14, 4917–19 (3 March 1919).

in France.[62] To hasten mobilization, Mann, in concert with Julius Kahn and with the backing of 154 Republicans, opposed a bill to restore the National Defense Act of 1916 and its system of enlistment for three years in service and four years in reserve. An insufficient number of men would enlist, he argued, and the president, under color of an "emergency," would keep the draftees in Europe. Without prejudice to a separate army bill, Mann, Kahn, and his committee favored a temporary program for one-year enlistments as the practical way to speed demobilization.[63]

While serving his party and his country during the short session, Mann also served his own strong ambition for the speakership in successfully performing his duties as before his prolonged absence. Through the session he felt intense enemy fire and knew that it would be difficult to win out for speaker at the caucus on 27 February.

After the 1916 elections, when Republicans thought that they might organize the House in the next Congress, Augustus P. Gardner had stepped forth to champion the candidacy of Irvine Lenroot against Mann. In January 1918 Gardner died in an army camp, and in April Lenroot won a special election to the Senate. But their attack on Mann, and his illness, encouraged others to oppose him in 1919, despite all the precedents in favor of the elevation of former minority leaders.[64]

The first and most formidable challenger was Frederick Gillett of Massachusetts. A congressman since 1893, Gillett was a fair and genial, unaggressive man without enemies. Satisfactory to eastern conservatives, as compared to Mann his backers called him a liberal.[65]

Two Ohioans, Nicholas Longworth, Roosevelt's able son-in-law, and Simeon Fess, head of the Congressional Campaign Committee, stirred up opposition to Mann among midwesterners, and in January Fess announced his candidacy. Eventually most of his supporters switched to Gillett. Towards the end Philip Campbell, who had supported Mann, offered himself, possibly in order to divert votes from Gillett on the first ballot.[66]

---

[62]*Ibid.*, pp. 955–56, 964 (2 January 1919), 1217 (10 January 1919), 1405–18 (14 January 1919), 1560, 1574 (16 January 1919), 2043 (25 January 1919), 2550 (1 February 1919), 2916, 2923, 2929 (7 February 1919), 3500 (15 February 1919).

[63]*Ibid.*, pp. 3715–19, 3724–28 (18 February 1919); *New York Times*, 19 February 1919.

[64]George B. Galloway, *History of the House of Representatives* (New York: Thomas Y. Crowell Co., 1961), 109.

[65]Chang-Wei Chiu, *The Speaker of the House of Representatives since 1896* (1928; reprint, New York, AMS Press, 1968), 304–5; Cyrenus Cole, *I Remember, I Remember* (Iowa City: State Historical Society of Iowa, 1936), 383; *New York Times*, 20 January 1919.

[66]*New York Times*, 28 February 1919.

The anti-Mann campaign drew powerful support from outside. Senators Henry Cabot Lodge, Boise Penrose of Pennsylvania, and Reed Smoot of Utah brought influence to bear, as did National Chairman Will Hays. At the February caucus Joseph Cannon singled out Penrose and Hays especially for vilification.[67] Many newspapers applied their own special pressure against Mann.[68]

The motives of the anti-Mann campaigners were not fully mirrored in the campaign against him. Lodge, hostile to Mann on other grounds, was further angered by Mann's refusal to embarrass Wilson while he was at the peace conference.[69] Gillett, Fess, and Longworth did not raise that divisive issue, however. For Hays, Lodge, Penrose, and Smoot, the overriding concern was party victory in 1920. After consultation with others, including members of the National Committee, Hays joined the senators in concluding that Mann's election would pose unnecessary risks and embarrassments.[70]

Mann's "war record" was one of his main liabilities, as the Gillett campaign letter hinted.[71] After Wilson, late in the 1918 campaign, called for a Democratic Congress to support his administration, Republicans responded with fury at what they took to be an unjust aspersion on their support of war measures. Making the case that their party had been more reliable than the Democrats, Lodge, Smoot, Gillett, and Fess issued a statement attacking Democrats Dent, Kitchin, and Clark for their opposition to conscription and, in the case of Kitchin, the war declaration.[72] Hoping to continue the counterattack into 1920, anti-Mann Republicans ignored the minority leader's votes in favor of the war and conscription and found in his prewar record a source of embarrassment. In particular, as others had done before, his detractors quoted him against himself from the McLemore resolution debate of 1916, when, as they saw it, he derided the victims of the *Lusitania* sinking in saying "I hope that our citizens may be so advised that we shall

[67]*Ibid.*, 27 January 1919; William Stafford in *CR* 67:4, p. 1720 (14 January 1923); Charles Hilles to Nicholas Murray Butler, 27 February 1919, Hilles folder, Butler Papers; *Milwaukee Sentinel*, 27 February 1919; *New York Times*, 28 February 1919.

[68]Frank Greene to Fred A. Howland, 2 February 1919, box 3, Greene Papers.

[69]Maureen R. Romans, "Party Leadership Fights in the House of Representatives: The Cause of Conflict. 1895–1955." (Ph.D. diss., University of Massachusetts, 1976), 158.

[70]*New York Sun*, 13 January 1919, and *St. Joseph Missouri News Press*, 1 February 1919, vol. 23, Mann Papers; Richard B. Cheney and Lynne V. Cheney, *Kings of the Hill: Power and Personality in the House of Representatives* (New York: Continuum, 1983), 145; Nicholas Murray Butler to Charles Hilles, 28 February 1919, Hilles folder, Butler Papers.

[71]Gillett to Frank Greene, 30 December 1918, box 16, Greene Papers.

[72]*Milwaukee Sentinel*, 26 October 1918.

never be put to the test whether we have to fight because some fool had entered upon a joy ride or voyage."[73]

Anti-Mann forces also feared that Mann's elevation would hurt the party in 1920 because of his close association with Cannon, and they raised the argument against him. The party should learn its lesson and not again choose a leader with reactionary tendencies, the argument went. The Gillett people warned also that Mann would turn the clock back and rule with an iron hand, as Cannon had. Mann's long record as minority leader, and his often stated comments on rules questions lent weight to the argument as to strong leadership.[74]

Longworth and Fess most aggressively, and then Gillett, to broaden his appeal, raised an issue that was important to many House members personally. They proposed that seniority be disregarded in the choice of committee chairmen. The proposal, appealing to the self-interest of newer members, was clothed as conducive to more progressive policies and to reduction in the power of party leaders.[75] Longworth hoped to displace, and possibly himself replace, the ranking Republican on Ways and Means, Joseph Fordney, an archprotectionist.

The anti-Mann appeal was the more potent because Mann had made many enemies over the years. Ellen Maury Slayden, wife of the Texas Democrat, hoped that Mann would win, but was rueful. "One always feels that Mann is *straight* though his Scotch bluntness antagonizes many people," she wrote. Vermont Republican Frank Greene at the time, and James Frear of Wisconsin and Alben Barkley of Kentucky afterwards, felt that personal animosities weighed heavily against Mann's candidacy.[76]

For members disinclined to support Mann, charges against him of impropriety offered a convenient excuse. The perennially unpopular meat packers

---

[73]"Mr. Mann and the Lusitania Test," *Outlook* (12 February 1919): 260; *New York Times*, 15 January 1919, 20 January 1919; Martin Madden in *CR* 67:4, p. 1715 (14 January 1923); John Andrew Russell, *Joseph Warren Fordney, an American Legislator* (Boston: Stratford Company, 1928), 177.

[74]*New York Times*, 28 February 1919, 20 January 1919; Rena Mitchell, "The Congressional Career of James R. Mann" (M.A. thesis, University of Chicago, 1938), 66; L. Ethan Ellis, "James Robert Mann," in *Dictionary of American Biography*, vol. 6, pt. 2, ed. Allen Johnson and Dumas Malone (New York: Charles Scribner's Sons, 1933), 244; Mann in *CR* 65:3, p . 4639 (28 February 1919).

[75]*New York Times*, 19 January 1919, 20 January 1919; Gillett to Frank Greene, 30 December 1918, box 16, Greene Papers; *Review of Reviews* 59 (March 1919): 244.

[76]Slayden, *Washington Wife*, 349; Greene to Fred A. Howland, 2 February 1919, box 3, Greene Papers; James A. Frear, *Forty Years of Progressive Public Service* (Washington, D.C.: Associated Writers, 1937), 225; Alben W. Barkley, *That Reminds Me* (Garden City, N.Y.: Doubleday, 1954), 98. A journalist and a historian concurred, in retrospect. George Rothwell Brown, *The Leadership of Congress* (1922; reprint, New York: Arno Press, 1974), 248; Ellis, "James Robert Mann," *DAB* , 6:244.

came under investigation by the Federal Trade Commission and the Senate Agriculture Committee. Among the lesser findings was that in 1907 Mann accepted from Swift and Company an aged horse worth $150 for use in his truck garden, and a $3.50 beef steak. Immediately, Mann's opponents adopted a campaign hymn, "Can, can, the Packers' Mann."[77]

Against all this the Mann campaign, led by Martin Madden, proved woefully insufficient. Thus, at the 27 February caucus of members-elect to the Sixty-sixth Congress, Gillett defeated Mann by a vote of 138–69, with 18 other votes scattered. The East was solid for the Massachusetts man, and the Longworth-Fess forces brought votes from some midwesterners. After the roll call was done, in a show of sportsmanship, Mann moved to make Gillett's nomination unanimous.[78]

Soon after that, Mann perpetrated a coup against his tormentors. Gillett's manager, Samuel Winslow of Massachusetts, offered a resolution for the election of a seventeen-member Committee on Committees, consisting of some Mann allies but chiefly Gillett people. Mann was ready with a substitute. Each of the thirty-six Republican state delegations should elect a member of the Committee on Committees, presumably the head of the delegation. Each of these members would cast a number of votes equal to his state's Republican representation in the House. On the surface the proposal seemed to the Gillett coalition to be inoffensive, since the motion would provide additional places on the committee, and quick calculation indicated that Gillett men would be in the majority. Thus the caucus gave noisy approval to Mann's motion without a record vote. Only later did the Gillett men realize that mainly because of the seventy-five votes that would be cast by the members from New York, Pennsylvania, and Illinois, Thomas Dunn, J. Hampton Moore, and Mann, the Mann forces would easily control. The committee would virtually choose committee chairmen and members, a Steering Committee, and a floor leader. The outcome was a triumph for those who had climbed the ladder of seniority on committees, and for Mann, who would surely lead the committee and largely control assignments, as before.[79]

When Mann appeared in the House the next day, he received a great ovation. It came, in the opinion of the *Washington Post*, because he had showed himself a game loser, and also in tribute to his sagacity at the caucus. No doubt, also, some members felt a combination of sympathy, guilt, and outrage over the denial of the speakership to Mann. In the "love feast" that

[77]*New York Times*, 16 January 1919, 17 January 1919.

[78]Chiu, *Speaker of the House of Representatives*, 304–5; Cole, *I Remember, I Remember*, 383; *New York Times*, 28 February 1919; *Chicago Tribune*, 28 February 1919.

[79]*Washington Post*, 1 March 1919, 2 March 1919, vol. 24, Mann Papers, *New York Times*, 28 February 1919; Paul DeWitt Hasbrouck, *Party Government in the House of Representatives* (New York: Macmillan Company, 1927), 43–44.

marked the end of the Congress on 3 March, Champ Clark referred to Mann's earlier reception and said, "It was genuine. It came from the hearts of the Members. It was not a partisan performance. I never tried to stop it, the truth is, I joined in it. It is the only time since I have been Speaker that I have clapped my hands and applauded anybody about anything."[80]

Responding to Clark, Mann said in part that he had long been prepared for defeats and would not sulk. "I love the House of Representatives," he said, "and had worked until there was danger that I might be overcome physically." After an absence of a year and a half, he again felt well. Thus, though he implied that he would not take the floor leadership, neither would he end his active service.[81] Most of his intimates and colleagues agreed that Mann was deeply disappointed over his rejection as Speaker, but that he tried not to show it. Nor would he use the power he retained in a petty way.[82]

Whatever the justice or injustice of Mann's defeat for the speakership, the overall outcome was probably in the best interests of the Republican party. Minority leader Mann had made a major contribution in a period of adversity. Now that the party had fully recovered, and the administration was the object of a myriad of complaints related to the war and reconstruction, prudence dictated a strategy of caution. In the event, no damage Mann might have done as speaker could have derailed the Republican express, but at the time, his occasional impulsiveness, his penchant for strong leadership, and his vulnerabilities from past associations and statements combined to pose a risk that the party had every reason to avoid.

Furthermore, the GOP was able to have it both ways, for less conspicuously than as Speaker, Mann would continue to provide leadership through the Committee on Committees and simply as a vigilant member on the floor. Indeed, freed of obligations as party spokesman, he could more easily offer honest and seasoned judgment. The new role better suited the condition of his health and energies than would the daily obligations of the speakership. As it turned out, despite his disappointment, Mann adjusted to his changed situation with grace and even some relish.

---

[80]*Washington Post*, 1 March 1919, vol. 24, Mann Papers, *CR* 65:3, p. 4953 (3 March 1919).

[81]*Chicago Tribune*, 4 March 1919, vol. 24, Mann Papers.

[82]Barkley, *That Reminds Me*, 98; Cole, *I Remember, I Remember*, 384; Frear, *Forty Years*, 144; Harold Knutson, William Stafford, and Edward Little in *CR* 67:4, pp. 1716, 1720, 1723 (14 January 1923).

8

Aftermath: March 1919–November 1922, and Retrospect

Swiftly in early March Mann and his allies on the Committee on Committees fulfilled their promises and put in place in the House committees, the Steering Committee, the floor leadership, and as whip a preponderance of political friends. Nicholas Longworth led a spirited opposition, but Mann responded with equal spirit and greater success.

Over Longworth's strong objections, Mann adhered to seniority respecting committee chairmanships. Most of those who benefited had earlier aligned themselves with Mann, so his friends controlled nine of the eleven most important posts and twenty of twenty-five overall. Almost complete adherence to seniority, while occasioned in part by factional strife, met institutional needs and persisted in subsequent Congresses. Mann had more leeway, especially in dealing with new members, as a committee of one on remaining committee assignments.[1]

The Committee on Committees elected a Steering Committee of five, three of them allies of Mann's—J. Hampton Moore, Martin Madden, and Thomas B. Dunn. Longworth, though a member of the committee, yet protested its makeup and urged that it be enlarged. He personalized the matter, charging that the composition of the Steering Committee, taken together with decisions as to the floor leadership and the whip, made Mann "the dominating figure in the next House" and "is the most complete triumph of

---

[1]*New York Times*, 6 March 1919, 31 March 1919; Nelson Polsby, *Congress and the Presidency*, 4th ed. (Englewood Cliffs, N.J.: Prentice-Hall, 1986), 77; *New York Times*, 12 March l919.

reactionism."[2] Mann took umbrage and rejoined in a long statement. He detailed his progressive accomplishments dating to the Roosevelt administrations, while Longworth, famous as a high-society bon vivant, "was attending pleasant social functions." Mann called Longworth a poor loser and appealed for party harmony against disruption. Will Hays, Frederick Gillett, and others backed Longworth, but when Congress convened in May, the caucus declined to enlarge the Steering Committee.[3]

The post of floor leader figured to be important since the incoming Speaker, Gillett, had been chosen with the understanding that in contrast to his opponent Mann, he would be unassertive. Later a reporter said of Gillett that he did not drink coffee in the morning "for fear it would keep him awake all day."[4]

Of his two principal lieutenants, J. Hampton Moore and Frank Mondell, Mann preferred Moore as floor leader. Mondell forcefully pressed his claims, which included seniority, and Moore gracefully opted for the second-ranking position on Ways and Means, where he could look after his district's tariff needs.[5]

At the 11 March meeting of the Committee on Committees, as a courtesy Moore nominated Mann in an eloquent speech and Mann permitted himself to be elected, with 154 of 161 votes cast, before declining. He said that by reason of his service he had expected the speakership as a reward. He would do his full part on the floor, but to conserve his health he preferred to avoid the daily drudgery of the floor leadership. At that point Longworth urged delay, but instead the committee immediately chose Mondell. Then it elected Harold Knutson of Minnesota, just a one-termer but among Mann's strongest supporters, as whip.[6]

After his resounding victory over Longworth—a sort of vindication—Mann indulged himself in a public comment: he felt like the cat that had swallowed the canary, he said. That same day he further consolidated his

---

[2]*Washington Post*, 14 March 1919, vol. 24, James R. Mann Papers, Library of Congress.

[3]*New York Times*, 16 March 1919, 17 March 1919; *Washington Times*, 1 April 1919, and *Washington Post*, 2 April 1919, vol. 24, Mann Papers; Randall B. Ripley, *Party Leaders in the House of Representatives* (Washington, D.C.: Brookings Institution, 1967), 48.

[4]Randall B. Ripley, *Congress: Process and Policy* (New York: W. W. Norton and Company, 1975), 53; George Rothwell Brown, *The Leadership of Congress* (1922; reprint New York: Arno Press, 1974), 245; Richard B. Cheney and Lynne V. Cheney, *Kings of the Hill: Power and Personality in the House of Representatives* (New York: Continuum, 1983), 167.

[5]Frank Mondell, "My Story," *Wyoming State Tribune*, 13 December 1935; *Washington Star*, 7 March 1919, vol. 24, Mann Papers.

[6]*New York Times*, 12 March 1919.

power with the announcement that he would take but one committee assignment, as head of a special committee on woman suffrage. That committee's work would be quickly done, and Mann would be free to exert full vigilance on the floor.[7]

A number of Mann's colleagues and outside observers regarded Mann as the leader of the House until his death in November 1922. His power sprang from his control of committee assignments and from his role on the floor, where from a front seat reserved for leaders he brought to bear his knowledge of legislation, precedent and parliamentary law. Thus a new member in 1919, Robert Moore of Virginia, was astonished by "the range, the power and the influence of his activities" and considered him the "outstanding figure here." Harry Slattery, in August 1919, advised Gifford Pinchot to develop a personal relationship with Mann, for though Mann was not in good health, he still held the House "in the hollow of his hands." After Mann's death, the *New York Times* observed that "Mr. Mann, so far as his health permitted, never lost the prime position won by his knowledge, experience and acumen."[8]

But ill-health limited his activity. Thus, for instance, he did not attend the May meeting of the Committee on Committees that preceded the special session of the new Congress, sending Madden to act for him, and he missed the caucus as well.[9] Present for the start of the session, to lead for woman suffrage, he soon absented himself for two months.[10] So it went for the remainder of his career. When he was present, the stoop of his shoulders and his slow, shuffling gait betrayed the effects of time and overwork and illness, and when he spoke, though always to the point, he was even briefer than before.[11]

---

[7]*Philadelphia North American*, 14 March 1919, in Robert Edward Drayer, "J. Hampton Moore: An Old Fashioned Republican" (Ph.D. diss., University of Pennsylvania, 1961), 82; *Washington Post*, 14 March 1919, vol. 24, Mann Papers.

[8]*New York World*, 4 December 1919, vol. 24, Mann Papers; *CR* 67:4, p. 1718 (14 January 1923); Slattery to Pinchot, 21 August 1919, box 1842, Gifford Pinchot Papers, Library of Congress; *New York Times*, 2 December 1922. For similar testimony see also L. Ethan Ellis, "James R. Mann, Legislator Extraordinary," *Journal of the Illinois State Historical* Society 46 (Spring 1953): 44; Brown, *Leadership of Congress*, 205–10; Cyrenus Cole, *I Remember, I Remember* (Iowa City: State Historical Society of Iowa, 1936), 304–5; Ronald M. Peters, Jr., *The American Speakership: The Office in Historical Perspective* (Baltimore: Johns Hopkins University Press, 1990), 100; and Edward Little in *CR* 67:4, p. 1722 (14 January 1923).

[9]Mann to J. Hampton Moore, 9 May 1919, J. Hampton Moore Papers, Historical Society of Pennsylvania, Philadelphia.

[10]*Washington Post*, 22 July 1919, vol. 24, Mann Papers.

[11]Cole, *I Remember, I Remember*, 304; Carl Chindblom in *CR* 67:4, p. 1721 (14 January 1923).

Besides that, Mann was not disposed to undermine the authority of Mondell, Rules chairman Philip Campbell, and other leaders. He had too much respect for them and for the welfare of the party for that. Rather, to a considerable degree he worked with them. Mondell, whose party feared the issue of Cannonism, presided over a system of formally diffused authority in which, for example, no chairman of a major committee could be on the Steering Committee, and Mondell himself, unlike floor leader Sereno Payne in Cannon's day, or even Underwood and Kitchin among the Democrats, did not preside over Ways and Means. Leadership inhered in an unofficial group, of which Mann was a part.[12] In addition, exploiting his freedom from formal responsibility, to an extent Mann free-lanced on the floor, a sort of "emeritus . . . peppery oracle," acting on his own and sometimes in conflict with the majority of Republicans, but always in what he saw as his party's best interests.[13]

The political setting for Mann's activity in the Sixty-sixth and Sixty-seventh Congresses was one of relative harmony among House Republicans. The leadership system was transitional to a stronger speakership, but effective. Mondell proved able and conciliatory, and Longworth assumed a share in leadership, while Gillett was treated with respect.[14]

Republican margins were comfortable after the elections of 1918 and especially 1920. In that year, benefiting from many discontents, the GOP completed its revival and restoration. Warren G. Harding was easily elected president and Republicans took the House by a margin of 300–132 and the Senate by 59–37.[15] The restoration was no passing thing, for the Republicans held the presidency and Congress through the decade.

In the interests of harmony, after the victories of 1918 and 1920 the dominant regulars deferred to progressives where they could without sacrifice to their goals respecting tariffs, internal taxes, and economy. Most progressives reciprocated. Mann could work comfortably in this context, which reflected his own earlier approach and perhaps also his continuing leadership.

At the start of the Sixty-sixth Congress, which met in special session on 19 May 1919, Mondell indulged Mann in his desire to lead for the woman suffrage amendment as chairman of a Woman Suffrage Committee. Success

---

[12]Brown, *Leadership of Congress*, 189–90, 196–97, 203–12; Robert Luce, *Congress: An Explanation* (Cambridge, Mass.: Harvard University Press, 1926), 117; Peters, *American Speakership*, 101–2.

[13]L. Ethan Ellis, "James Robert Mann," *Dictionary of American Biography* vol. 6, pt. 2, ed. Allen Johnson and Dumas Malone (New York: Charles Scribner's Sons, 1933), 6:244.

[14]Brown, *Leadership of Congress*, 218, 222; Cheney and Cheney, *Kings of the Hill*, 148–49.

[15]Paul DeWitt Hasbrouck, *Party Government in the House of Representatives* (New York: Macmillan Company, 1927), 239.

was a foregone conclusion, but Mann made it his business to bring House action before Wilson, from Paris, could take the lead and the credit.[16]

After that, occasionally Mann capitalized on his formal independence from party leadership by going his own way on significant questions in the Sixty-sixth Congress. Thus he was part of a minority in a 330–6 vote when the House, for the second time, refused to seat Victor Berger of Milwaukee, who had been convicted of violating the Espionage Act by attacks on the war. Before the vote Mann denounced the action from an institutional standpoint.[17]

Later, he vainly opposed centralizing appropriations in a single committee.[18] Against Mondell and most of his party, he opposed a soldiers' bonus bill, arguing for economy. The bill failed in the Senate but came up again in the next Congress.[19]

In that Congress Mann continued to occasionally free-lance. Again he opposed the soldiers' bonus, which passed both houses but was vetoed.[20] He went his own way also in favoring continued appropriations for a dam at Muscle Shoals in order to produce cheap nitrates for farmers.[21] That initiative failed for a time, but Mann was temporarily successful on another matter, delaying restriction of immigration.[22] He failed in opposing "American valuation" in a tariff bill, a complicated device to raise tariffs more than Mann thought prudent. The provision was dropped in conference.[23] He also chastised Mondell for prolonging a "dog days" session.[24]

---

[16]Eileen L. McDonagh, "Issues and Constituencies in the Progressive Era: House Roll Call Voting on the Nineteenth Amendment, 1913–1919" *Journal of Politics* 51 (February 1989): 130; Rena Mitchell, "The Congressional Career of James R. Mann" (M.A. thesis, University of Chicago, 1938), 58; *CR* 66:1, pp. 24 (19 May 1919), 66–70 (20 May 1919), 78–94 (21 May 1919); *New York Times*, 22 May 1919; John Milton Cooper, Jr., *Pivotal Decades: The United States, 1900–1920* (New York: W. W. Norton and Company, 1990), 308.

[17]*New York Times*, 6 January 1920; *CR* 66:2, pp. 1339–40, 1343 (10 January 1920); David M. Kennedy, *Over Here: The First World War and American Society* (New York: Oxford University Press, 1980), 289–90.

[18]*CR* 66:2, pp. 8106–8, 8120–21 (1 June 1920).

[19]*CR* 66:2, pp. 6647–48 (6 May 1920), 7924, 7927, 7929–30 (29 May 1920); *New York Times*, 30 May 1920.

[20]*CR* 67:2, pp. 4398, 4447 (23 March 1922); John D. Hicks, *Republican Ascendancy, 1921–1933* (New York: Harper and Row, 1960), 52.

[21]*CR* 66:3, pp. 356 (4 January 1921), 3857–79 (25 February 1921), 4505 (3 March 1921).

[22]*Ibid.*, pp. 288 (13 December 1920), 520, 523 (18 December 1920), 640 (22 December 1920), 1109–10 (7 January 1921), 2127 (27 January 1921), 3010 (11 February 1921), 3073 (12 February 1921), 4075 (28 February 1921).

[23]*CR* 67:1, pp. 3703 (13 July 1921), 4143, 4190, 4192 (20 July 1921).

[24]*New York Times*, 26 July 1921; *CR* 67:1, pp. 4264–65 (25 July 1921).

When he was not required to sacrifice his own views, Mann gave full and important support to the party leaders. After the power of the Appropriations Committee was expanded, the able chairman, James Good, announced that soon he would retire. Mondell felt that the second-ranking committee Republican, seventy-one-year-old Charles Davis of Minnesota, was not equal to the job and proposed Martin Madden instead. Mann agreed and set to work. The job was formidable, for seniority was holy, and to many Madden seemed crude. Nevertheless, Mann accomplished the task, and as chairman Madden vindicated his judgment.[25]

Mann agreed fully with the president and congressional leaders on the importance of a ship subsidy bill to subsidize the transfer into private hands of mothballed ships built by the government for the war.[26] Harding called a special session to meet on 20 November 1922 to act on the issue. Mann was in his seat when the session began. Then, however, he came down with painful pleurisy and was confined to his bed. Nevertheless, Mann sent word to Mondell that if needed for a close vote, he would come. In the event, he could not, for suddenly his condition turned into pneumonia, and on 30 November he died.[27]

In death Mann received high honors. Funeral services in the House were attended by the president, the cabinet, justices of the Supreme Court, and scores of representatives and senators. His body was taken to Chicago, where notables again attended services. On a Sunday in January 1923, the House held a memorial service and twenty-one colleagues, new and old, Republican and Democrat, extolled Mann, none more extravagantly than did Joseph Cannon. In the main they dwelt on his greatness as a legislator and on the goodness of a character that had been concealed from some because of his no-nonsense manner. The encomiums, while fulsome, were nevertheless incomplete, for this was not the occasion to dwell on Mann's services to his party in its times of trouble, especially as chairman of Interstate and Foreign Commerce in the Sixty-first Congress and then for eight years as minority

---

[25]Thomas Robert Bullard, "From Businessman to Congressman: The Careers of Martin B. Madden" (Ph.D. diss., University of Illinois at Chicago Circle, 1973), 254–55; George B. Galloway, *History of the House of Representatives* (New York: Thomas Y. Crowell Co., 1961), 69; Brown, *Leadership of Congress*, 209–10, 241; Charles H. Stewart III, *Budget Reform Politics: The Design of the Appropriations Process in the House of Representatives, 1865–1921* (New York: Cambridge University Press, 1989), 200; CR 66:2, pp. 8109, 8120–21 (1 June 1920); Mondell, "My Story," *Wyoming State Tribune*, 6 January 1936; Cole, *I Remember, I Remember*, 387–88.

[26]CR 67:2, p. 9110 (21 June 1922); Hicks, *Republican Ascendancy*, 52.

[27]CR 67:3, p. 4 (20 November 1922); *Chicago Tribune*, 1 December 1922; CR 67:3, p. 439 (1 December 1922).

leader. Yet these contributions had been considerable and constitute part of the story of Republican reconciliation and revival.[28]

In 1909 Mann brought to the Interstate and Foreign Commerce post and to floor responsibilities a number of assets that would allow him to help his party at a time when it was already beginning to divide and decline. Among his assets was extraordinary legislative competence. He brought to bear a good education and seventeen years of legislative experience in Chicago and Washington. His knowledge, which included parliamentary law and precedent, combined with copious industry, ingenuity, acuity, and orderliness, made him the master of whatever legislation was coming up.

Already he enjoyed among his colleagues admiration and respect, if not always great fondness. He had successfully led in the preparation and adoption of important legislation, especially the Pure Food and Drug Act and Panama Canal bills, had played a large part in the development of the Hepburn Act of 1906 expanding railroad regulation, and impressed the House with the evenhandedness and thoroughness of his print-paper investigation. Enjoying the confidence of Joseph Cannon, he had shown himself astute in advising on committee assignments and had effectively guarded the Treasury on appropriations bills and as the "Great Objector" on private bills. Often he offended with sharp remarks to members who seemed uninformed or ignoble. Yet these bursts of temper sprang in part from a devotion to the House as an institution that his colleagues could appreciate. One among many manifestations of that institutional feeling was his path-breaking fairness in treatment of disputed elections.

Mann's ideas and general outlook suited the needs of the time, too. He was a moderate conservative. Progressivism was on the rise, yet the Republican base, and its ultimate future, lay with economic conservatism, especially since the Democrats were in the process of transforming themselves into a progressive party. The Republicans, however, could hardly afford to abandon progressivism altogether, partly because within their ranks were progressives from traditionally Republican states who in 1909 called themselves insurgents. In the short run, because of the revival of the Democratic party and the growing division in the GOP, the most that a leader like Mann could contribute was damage control. In the long run he could facilitate party reconciliation and revival. For both of these purposes, his moderate conservatism was suitable.

Neither his conservatism nor his moderateness is wholly separable from his relationship to the Republican party. A strong partisan, he upheld party positions, but he was no party hack. In Chicago politics he was a luminary whose relationship with machine politicians such as Thomas "Doc" Jamieson was not as a subordinate but as a wary ally, possessed of his own

---

[28]*New York Times*, 3, 5 December 1922; *CR* 67:4, pp. 1712–25 (14 January 1923).

sources of power and his own convictions. In Congress, though strongly loyal to Speaker Cannon and the party, he also exercised a measure of independence that accorded with the political culture of the time. A vote against a Dingley tariff provision in 1897 gave early indication of his flair for independence.

Mann's conservatism was rooted in his faith in America's prospects for economic growth, and in the key role of the producer, especially but not exclusively the businessman. He had seen the wonders of material progress in his younger days, and in his nurseryman father he had a model of a man who, despite some adversity, yet contributed to society through the use of American economic traits, ingenuity, intelligence, perseverance, and optimism. Mann's father also demonstrated to his son the possibilities of science as an engine of progress.

The Republican party of Mann's early years was only selectively devoted to laissez-faire economics and belief in small government. On the contrary, in contrast to the Democrats before their transformation, it was the party of governmental activism. Mann, with his party, married that approach to his faith in the producer and emerged an ardent advocate of promotionalism. For example, in his Chicago days and after he consistently urged tariff protection. To promote trade, in Congress he gave sustained attention to the Panama Canal and to the origin and development of the Department of Commerce and Labor.

Enterprisers required something even more basic than promotionalism from the national government, in a view that Mann shared with most in his party. That was a sound currency, based on unshakable credit. In the 1896 campaign Mann mastered the arguments against Bryan's free-silver vagaries. In Congress his unceasing attention to economy related less to the modern conservative idea of keeping taxes low and government small than it did to concern for the condition of the Treasury, whose gold supply stood behind the currency.

As a staunch Cannon man, too, Mann was a strong conservative. In part, he was moved by admiration for and devotion to the Speaker, and also by self-interest. In addition, however, Mann believed in party government, party responsibility, and party leadership. He never agreed with those who called Cannon a tyrant, but saw him as an effective leader of the majority.

By 1909, though, "Cannonism" connoted to many citizens and to congressional insurgents not only tyranny, but reaction. The times called for moderate policies and conciliatory behavior by House Republican leaders. Mann was equipped to accommodate. On the Chicago City Council he had been a reformer of the "good-government" sort, and in the face of the depression of the 1890s he took moderate positions on the tariff and treatment of labor. While always concerned to avoid measures that were punitive towards businessmen, yet he took a leading role in adoption of progressive regulatory measures. He wanted to cooperate with the ever more progressive President Theodore Roosevelt to meet rising public demand, to parry the thrusts of progressive Democrats, and to serve the national interest. Besides, reasonable regulation of some businessmen, such as railroaders, served the interests of other businessmen, such as merchants. In addition, Mann lusted for achievement, and as he got into a subject that came before him on Interstate and Foreign Commerce, his zeal for thoroughness took him to more advanced positions than initially he had contemplated. Certainly this was true of the Pure Food and Drug Act, and the enactment of that act, more than any other, marked Mann as at least moderate in his conservatism.

Foreign relations were of no great national concern in 1909, but later they would be. Mann repudiated early jingoism in connection with Cuba, but his support for the annexation of Hawaii, for the questionable methods of Roosevelt in facilitating the Panamanian revolution, and for a strong Philippines policy all reflected a concern for trade that implied a willingness to fight. But conflicts over trade he projected into the distant future. In the present, year after year Mann voted as a small-navy man, and he spoke as a devotee of the peace movement. He wanted no distractions and diversions from the American mission of economic growth, which for Mann also promised the improvement of all aspects of American civilization.

Though as president William Howard Taft did not initiate Republican division and decline, he contributed to both. Committed to a continuation of progressivism, by associating himself with Cannon, the Payne-Aldrich tariff, and Richard Ballinger he came to be seen as a "standpatter." Attacks by progressives in and out of Congress then made him one, and in 1910 he tried to purge insurgents. The effort failed, and in the election that faction gained in relative weight within the party, while the Democrats, as the anti-Cannon progressive party, captured the House.

Mann, especially in his role as chairman of Interstate and Foreign Commerce, did much to limit the damage. Though far from insurgency himself, he yet saw room in the party for insurgents, and he also saw the need to preserve for the GOP some semblance of progressivism against the Democrats. What the insurgents needed, and Mann helped to supply, was a basis to defend themselves against the Democrats in the 1910 election and later, in 1912, an excuse to remain in the Republican party rather than join Roosevelt and the Bull Moosers. In the Sixty-first Congress Mann assisted chiefly through the Mann Act against "white slavery" and still more through the Mann-Elkins Act that further regulated railroads.

With regard to "white slavery," Mann's contribution was to use fully the constitutional power to regulate interstate and foreign commerce to attack an evil that was not traditionally subject to federal control. As to the Mann-Elkins Act, Mann first seized control in committee, at the expense of a more conservative administration bill; then, although bested on the floor over certain amendments, he secured in the House a measure that pleased both insurgents and the administration; and finally, he pushed through the conference committee a bill that was more progressive than either the House or Senate versions.

Even at the height of the Progressive movement, conservatism remained preponderant in the GOP in Congress and latent in the electorate, and after the progressive wave receded, conservatism would again be rewarding to the party. Mann blended with his concessions to progressivism strong expressions of conservatism. On some of the issues, he took the lead for conservative Republicanism and performed creditably.

As always, Mann closely guarded the Treasury. On the railroad bill he vainly promoted provisions that, had they been enacted, would have helped the companies and probably the national economy. In particular, he wanted to facilitate mergers and rate agreements. As to Cannon and the rules, he organized for Cannon's reelection as Speaker and for a conservative victory on the rules in 1909. The following year Mann strongly led in defense of both the Speaker and the rules in the face of a successful rules rebellion.

After the 1910 election, when Cannon said that he would not serve as minority leader in the new Congress, no one challenged Mann for the post. The attributes and attainments already mentioned commended him to his colleagues. In addition to these, insurgents liked his vote against the Payne-Aldrich bill, while regulars realized that this show of independence betrayed no unreliability on protectionism, but pique over the pulp and print-paper rates. Furthermore, Mann had demonstrated a genius for harassing the Democrats that would be highly useful in the days ahead.

During Mann's first term as minority leader, chiefly in 1911 and 1912, he could do little to arrest the further division of his party or the rise of the Democrats. Roosevelt joined and then led the progressive Republican revolt against Taft, and the former friends contested for the nomination with a bitterness that pervaded the party. Failing to win the nomination, Roosevelt, whose popularity with voters far exceeded Taft's, launched a new party that threatened the very survival of the GOP. The Democrats, meanwhile, acted effectively in the House under the leadership of Oscar Underwood. Then, in 1912, in Woodrow Wilson they nominated a reformer who commanded more widespread respect than had William Jennings Bryan in earlier campaigns.

If damage control had been the order of the day for Mann in the Sixty-first Congress, that was even more the task in the Sixty-second. As before, part of the job was to placate the insurgents to keep them in the party, and also to help them establish records on which they could successfully run in 1912. Along the way, Mann set out to get from them some measure of cooperation. In these tasks he was notably successful. He showed himself fair, even generous, on committee assignments. He abandoned the binding caucus, to which insurgents objected, while joining them in condemnation of caucus rule and "gag rules" by the Democrats. Mann joined them also in anti-Southernism in debate and voting on some Democratic tariff proposals, as on rice. In connection with the tariff, he stressed a Tariff Board, which appealed to insurgents. Finally, he backed some progressive legislation.

The progressive legislation that Mann helped to win gave to beleaguered Republicans some talking points in the 1912 elections. In particular, Mann put his party to the left of the Democrats on parcel post, outlawry of phosphorus matches, and various conservation issues. He also helped his party by his work on appropriations. In addition, Mann scored points against the Democrats on the traditional issue of incompetence and by demonstrating the weaknesses in the Democrats' Discharge Calendar rules reform.

Though the insurgents believed otherwise, the Republicans could compete with the modernized Democrats only at the margins for the label "progressive." In many districts, especially in the East and portions of the Midwest, the party relied on conservatism. Despite the shifts in balance in 1910, regulars remained preponderant among congressional Republicans. Notwithstanding his attentions to the insurgents, Mann gave leadership for Republican conservatism in the Sixty-second Congress. Especially was this so on tariff bills, which the Democrats offered in two sessions of the Congress. Also, while not belligerent about it, Mann came out for Taft against Roosevelt for the presidential nomination. When an insurgent member of the Rules Committee from Kansas died, Mann successfully battled to replace him with a Kansas regular, Philip Campbell.

Mann's performance in the Sixty-second Congress was less than perfect and foreshadowed similar difficulties in future Congresses. He overplayed his hand as to the scope of the "money trust" investigation and contributed to the unification of the Democrats for a broad and politically damaging investigation. He made an offhand and injudicious comment on the occasion of a woman's suffrage parade that caused trouble. Often he spoke caustically to errant members regardless of party. He offended Republican colleagues by limiting their floor time and dominating proceedings for his party. In making enemies, in some measure he lessened his own unifying capacities.

But even some of Mann's seeming flaws had redeeming features. Thus, for example, in crowding out others for floor time as party spokesman, he ensured for the GOP a consistently high level of competence. His penchant for speaking his mind eased matters when issues cut across party lines, for on such occasions Republicans who differed with Mann could plausibly say and feel that he spoke only for himself on the issue in question. Such was the case during the lame-duck session of the Sixty-second Congress when Mann opposed a literacy test for immigration and also opposed the Webb-Kenyon temperance bill.

Mann and the Republicans were strongly challenged after the election of 1912. The Democrats, ably led by Woodrow Wilson and in the House by Underwood, made good on campaign promises. The Bull Moosers were energized by the strong election showing of Roosevelt. Yet in 1912 and 1914 the Republicans, aided by a slump in the economy, regained their confidence and much of their popularity. In the 1914 elections they reclaimed sixty-six House seats and but for the outbreak of war in Europe in the summer of 1914 would have done still better. The Moosers' House delegation, meanwhile, was reduced from eighteen to eight, and the party, which also lost Senate and governorship races, seemed no longer a serious threat to the GOP.

Mann served as principal spokesman for Republicans in 1913 and 1914, as well as the one who molded and implemented their tactics in the House. To the extent that Republican gains sprang from the actions of people and not just from impersonal forces, he more than any other person engineered Republican recovery in this period. One is tempted to say, therefore, that in the Sixty-third Congress Mann was at his very best. That generalization must be qualified, however, for in 1913 and 1914 the course of action required of Mann was much more easily perceived and executed than would be the case after the war issues became acute. Certainly, though, in the Sixty-third Congress Mann did what needed to be done with high levels of spirit, energy, and competence.

The voters endorsed progressivism in the election of 1912. But Mann retained his faith in the long-run attractiveness of economic conservatism, and he scored points against the administration from that standpoint. After the economy began to worsen late in 1913, Republicans could plausibly blame the Democrats and boast of their own record.

The Democrats had strongly capitalized on the tariff issue since 1909 and in 1913 they made downward revision their first order of business. Mann embraced the challenge, called the tariff the key issue, secured party unity in the House against the Underwood bill, and periodically revived the issue as the economy weakened. The Federal Reserve Act offered fewer political opportunities, but Mann directed attention to its most vulnerable aspect, the danger of political control of the Federal Reserve Board. On the related issues of antitrust and a Federal Trade Commission, Mann allied himself with business, and in his public appeal he stressed the needs of business. He opposed punitive, intimidating antitrust restrictions in the Clayton bill. But he embraced the Federal Trade Commission Act as facilitating government-business cooperation and claimed for his party some of the credit. When war came in Europe, Mann spoke of new American industrial and commercial opportunities, and as the 1914 election approached, he helped his party develop a useful issue as he attacked a war revenue bill. Mann urged economy instead and chastised the Democrats for extravagance.

Notwithstanding his heavy reliance on economic conservatism, as before he kept the insurgents content and also fortified them in their districts. He again treated them well in committee assignments, starting with the nomination of Sydney Anderson to Ways and Means. He held no binding caucuses and even opened the caucus, while again joining in attacks on Democrats for their reliance on the caucus and "gag rules." To this, he and the insurgents now added the charge of presidential dictation. In handling the tariff issue, Mann again stressed the alternative of a Tariff Commission, which still appealed to insurgents, and he urged schedules based on Tariff Board reports. He also supported progressive legislation that did not conflict with his economic conservatism, especially conservation bills for an Alaska railroad and leasing federal mineral lands and dam sites.

Now that the Democrats controlled the presidency as well as Congress, they presented for Mann a larger target than in the previous Congress. Adroitly and aggressively he exploited openings, while occasionally also pointing up the legendary competence of his side. Thus he attacked on the Diggs-Caminetti "white slave" case, suggesting high-level intrusion; he used his own expertise in again arguing against repeal of the Panama Canal Tolls exemption; he took advantage of lingering troubles and irresolute administration policies in Mexico; and on the Tariff Commission, conservation, and the appropriation for the Children's Bureau he outflanked the Democrats on the left.

Helpful on nonpartisan legislation and attentive to institutional matters, Mann enhanced his own reputation and, indirectly, his party's. Antiopium bills and the Hetch Hetchy Valley bill for San Francisco's water supply were but two of many laws of the Sixty-third Congress that he helped to perfect and pass.

Occasionally Mann spoke not for his party but for himself, as in opposition to the Mexican intervention after the Tampico affair. He thus earned among colleagues admiration for saying what they privately believed, and he also again legitimized and made less troublesome the instances when others in his party, especially insurgents, went their own way.

Mann could not deny Wilson the national support that came with the war in Europe, but he did limit the damage. Quite as strongly as Wilson, Mann called for American neutrality.

The year 1916 was a presidential election year; well in advance, both major parties prepared for this test of Republican rejuvenation and Democratic staying power. By the time the campaign began, and as it ensued, the Democrats seemed to have the best of it. Through their own actions and a liberal dose of luck, they could present themselves as the party of peace, progressivism, and prosperity. German submarine warfare had brought on the danger of war. Its suspension in May 1916, temporary as it turned out, but sustained through the campaign, lent credibility to the claim for Wilson that "He kept

us out of war." A new rash of progressive laws in 1916 shored up the Democrats' appeal to key segments of the electorate, especially about 20 percent of
the Moosers. At the time, their party was breaking up and they were choos-
ing between the party of origin, the GOP, and the Democrats. With war orders came prosperity, an obvious advantage to the party in power. In addition, in Woodrow Wilson the Democrats had a far more attractive candidate
than the cold and lackluster Charles Evans Hughes, and the Democratic
campaign organization was the stronger one as well.

Despite it all, Wilson won by only a very small margin. The two parties
tied in the House elections, and which would organize was not known for
some months and turned on five minor-party congressmen. The GOP also
gained two seats in the Senate. Although the Republicans were disappointed
at the outcome, viewed historically, their showing in 1916 marked a further
major stride back towards power. James R. Mann substantially contributed
to his party's gains.

Issues stemming from the Great War became paramount in the period
1914–1916. Domestic questions relating to the economy were also salient
and intertwined with the foreseeable breakup of the Progressive party and
the battle for Mooser votes. Mann gave close attention to both areas in activity that began in December 1914 with the lame-duck session of the Sixty-
third Congress and concluded with the first session of the Sixty-fourth Congress, which began in December 1915 and continued into the fall campaign
season of 1916.

Mann was at his best in dealing with the treacherous and important issue
of preparedness. German submarine warfare, above all, increased the attractiveness of the new issue politically, especially in the East. But midwestern
Republican peace advocates opposed any military buildup that seemed to
increase the chance of American belligerency. Initially, as the bellicose
Augustus P. Gardner took the lead for preparedness, Mann shied from it. By
September of 1915, however, after Wilson publicly switched to the preparedness side, Mann followed suit. In the Sixty-fourth Congress he set out to
exploit deep Democratic division on the subject and capture the issue for his
own party without either alienating Republican peace forces or suggesting to
the public that his party favored war. Ultimately, Wilson secured compromise army and navy bills from Democrats and thus prevented Mann from
fully accomplishing his purpose. Mann did, however, achieve considerable
success. He helped bring about a large measure of party unity behind army
and navy alternatives that were stronger than the Democratic bills. There
were dissidents, still, in Congress and the electorate, but Mann did much to
ease their fears. Most spectacularly, the minority leader defended the party's
proposal to enlarge the army by 80,000 more troops than the Democrats
proposed with the astonishing statement that he saw more danger of war
with Great Britain than with Germany. That was reassuring to those who

most feared war with Germany, while alarming no one, since the likelihood of war with Great Britain was very slender. In the same vein, periodically Mann defended preparedness as directed towards trouble with Mexico, as well as likely disturbances after the end of the European war. In arguing for defense of neutral rights, he stressed British violations more than German.

Consistently, Mann outdid Wilson as the advocate of peace. Thus, in particular, he argued and voted against tabling the McLemore resolution to warn Americans off belligerent merchant ships. The temporary halt to submarine warfare salvaged the issue for the Democrats. Yet Hughes was also given the chance to appeal to peace forces, and so were the Republican congressional candidates who needed that issue.

Economic conservatism had less appeal with the return of prosperity than before, while progressivism received a new lease on life from the improved economy. Yet, though progressivism was a valuable Democratic tool in 1916 with some voters, the strong reform movement of the Roosevelt-Taft years had run its course, as Americans turned to war-related questions, the assimilation of immigrants, temperance, and more. At the same time, economic conservatism, long established in the electorate as the formula for growth and opportunity, persisted. It behooved Mann to present his party as the champion of economic conservatism while at the same time placating insurgents and Moosers and guarding his party against charges of being reactionary.

In opposing the Democrats' war revenue bill of 1916, which immediately became a campaign issue, Mann strongly denounced heavy reliance on the income tax through higher rates. He also revived themes that he had often expressed earlier. Thus Mann recapitulated the case for the tariff and for economy in government and denounced Democratic extravagance. In another important expression of economic conservatism, Mann helped develop for Hughes and other Republicans the issue of the Adamson Act. He attacked the disguised government-mandated wage increase for railroad workers as of doubtful constitutionality, and he criticized the Democrats for dropping provisions relating to settlement procedures for the future. Earlier, Mann had attacked the administration's shipping bill as being socialistic.

On clearly popular progressive measures Mann went along with the administration. In some cases, such as respecting child-labor legislation or creation of a Tariff Commission, he claimed Republican priority. Mann also sometimes took more progressive ground than the Democrats, especially on issues on which southerners balked at reform. One of these was the woman suffrage amendment. He also stood with insurgents in familiar attacks on the Democrats for their use of the caucus, for restrictive rules, and for engaging in spoils politics.

Mann helped his party, too, on issues foreign and domestic that were neither progressive nor conservative. He persistently exploited an administration weakness respecting outrages against Americans in and by Mexico. He also unified House Republicans on the Philippines issue in accepting a vague compromise as an alternative to independence within four years. In connection with the revenue bill, especially, he supplied campaign fodder for all Republicans in detailing the southern stake in the bill.

Inevitably, Mann antagonized some in his party, as by his stand on the McLemore resolution. He continued to make enemies by his characteristic brusqueness and his domination of proceedings. In the main, however, he more than his party suffered in consequence.

The possibility of organizing the next House sharpened internal conflicts among House Republicans, and such conflict could easily weaken the party nationally. Mann undertook to maintain his own party leadership and keep the party true to conservative principles, while at the same time minimizing internal division. In considerable degree he succeeded.

Within the party, from November 1916 until the new Congress met in April 1917, Mann encountered a strong movement to displace him as party leader and to alter the party's machinery. The rebels were insurgents such as Augustus P. Gardner and former Progressives like Medill McCormick, along with ordinary members unhappy with Mann's dominating ways. Not fully unified themselves, they put forth various proposals. Gardner, in particular, would replace Mann with Lenroot, either by creating a floor-leader post for Lenroot or making him the candidate for Speaker. McCormick, on the other hand, concerned for the successful reintegration of the Moosers into the party, played down opposition to Mann and stressed other aspects of the insurgents' program—structural changes such as creating a Committee on Committees, and also the development of a positive legislative program.

During the short session Mann negotiated with the more tractable dissidents, such as McCormick and Sydney Anderson, and secured agreement on creating a Committee of 27 that would make recommendations when the new Congress convened. While the committee, headed by Martin Madden, had progressive representation, its members were mainly of the dominant conservative wing. Eventually the committee made its predictable recommendations. There would be concessions with the creation of a new Advisory Committee and a new Committee on Committees. But Mann would chair both and, with the help of allies, control both. The matter of creating a new floor-leader post was deferred, but doomed, partly because by 2 April, when Congress met, it was clear that Democrats would organize and Mann would be not the Speaker but again the minority leader.

Meanwhile, and related to Mann's success in quelling rebellion, he dealt effectively with international issues in the sense that he staked out moderate and popular positions and minimized internal discord. Persistently Mann advocated peace. But he also urged heightened preparedness after Germany resumed submarine attacks on neutral merchantmen. In that connection he opposed Henry Cooper's amendment to block the arming of American merchant ships. When finally he had to cast his vote for war or peace, his decision was for war. At the same time, by his compliments for the antiwar stand of Claude Kitchin and in other ways, he tried to minimize divisiveness, not only in the House, but in his own party.

Mann served just four months in the war Congress before illness intervened, but in that time he helped to set a politically wise course for his party. Above all on the draft bill, which he supported and Champ Clark strongly opposed, Mann helped establish his party as more supportive of the war effort than were the Democrats. That record, constantly maintained, stood the party in good stead after Wilson appealed for a Democratic Congress just in advance of the 1918 elections. Protected against charges of disloyalty, Mann encouraged Republican opposition to some administration proposals, and he helped defeat the press censorship provisions of the espionage bill. He also supported creation of a Joint Committee on the War to oversee expenditures, an issue that rallied the GOP and highlighted charges of waste and extravagance.

During the war Mann continued to uphold economic conservatism as against both Democrats and some Republicans. He fought a revenue bill and talked against heavy reliance on taxes rather than bond sales. Spread the cost over several years, he urged; don't hurt consumers or weaken business incentive by excessive rates. Mann also used the bill to partisan advantage by raising a sectional issue. He led in a parliamentary effort to get a vote on an amendment to tax cotton. In the 1918 elections Republicans would benefit heavily from the sectional theme.

Because of prolonged absences due to health problems, Mann contributed less to the 1918 victory than to the party's gains in 1914 and 1916 and to the minimization of losses in 1910 and 1912. His contribution, especially in his handling of war issues and internal discord among House Republicans, was nevertheless significant. In any case, just as Republican recovery was a cumulative process spanning six years, so Mann's contribution to that recovery must be seen in terms of his total record, dating even to the years preceding the breakup of 1912. Taken as a totality, his contribution was unmatched by any other representative or senator and was far greater than that of the defeated presidential candidates, Taft and Hughes. Among other things, it consisted in demonstrating Republican competence, often in contrast to Democratic failings; in generating electoral issues that reflected a blend of basic conservatism with flourishes of progressivism; and in keeping the party both open and helpful to the insurgents and their followers without alienating the dominant conservatives or their supporters back home.

Mann believed in the Republican party and zealously served its interests. but in his public career he had other ambitions and accomplishments as well, which in this book have been treated only as they related to his political role.

As Mann receives further attention from historians, they will more fully explore his role as a legislator, which was astonishingly productive over a long period of years and a wide range of subjects. They will recognize his love for the House as an institution and his many and varied efforts to improve it. While these aspects of his career await their historian, they can already be recognized as significant in the life and service of James R. Mann.

Some things are already evident. Mann, in cooperation with House Republicans, had a greater impact than has generally been recognized on the legislation and politics of the Wilson era. Historical attention has been devoted too much to the presidency, too little to Congress, too much to the Senate and maverick senators, too little to the House, too much to the majority party, too little to the minority. Yet it was Mann and the House Republicans who through pressure or direct involvement helped to shape and adopt the Federal Trade Commission bill, legislation for a Tariff Commission, child-labor bills, conservation measures great and small, preparedness legislation, the draft law and other war measures, the woman suffrage amendment, various appropriations, and more. If history is to present a balanced picture of the Wilson era, it must draw the appropriate lessons from the career of James R. Mann and the House Republicans.

Similarly, the story of James R. Mann has lessons for those who would understand the development of the Republican party from Taft to Harding. Again, Congress, and especially the House, has been unduly slighted in favor of the presidency and presidential candidates. To explain Republican reconciliation and revival, and the party's shift to the right, historians must study the House Republicans.

Their story has many aspects. Insurgent and regular factions developed internally and increasingly accommodated one another. The GOP outdid the Progressives in the House, then reabsorbed them. In battling the Democrats, the House Republicans responded to their opponents' initiatives and took advantage of their vulnerabilities. The GOP adapted to external events such as the business slump of 1913–14 and then the war in Europe. Always, House Republicans influenced elections in various ways. Routinely, they projected a party image and denigrated the Democrats. They also generated specific issues for campaigners, as with the Adamson Act and tax and tariff laws. On the issues that were more local than national, such as temperance and immigration, they created a conveniently ambiguous record. James R. Mann was deeply involved with all these matters. The facts of his career point to avenues for further exploration.

Selected Bibliography

MANUSCRIPT COLLECTIONS

Butler, Nicholas Murray. Papers, Butler Library, Columbia University, New York City.

Culbertson, William S. Papers, Library of Congress.

Depew, Chauncey M. Papers, Sterling Library, Yale University, New Haven, Connecticut.

Esch, John J. Papers, State Historical Society of Wisconsin, Madison.

Fisher, Walter L. Papers, Library of Congress.

Garfield, James R. Papers, Library of Congress.

Greene, Frank L. Papers, Library of Congress.

Hill, Ebenezer J. Papers, Sterling Library, Yale University, New Haven, Connecticut.

Hilles, Charles D. Papers, Sterling Library, Yale University, New Haven, Connecticut.

Kent, William. Papers, Sterling Library, Yale University, New Haven, Connecticut.

Kitchin, Claude. Papers, University of North Carolina Library, Chapel Hill.

Lehman, Frederick William. Papers, Washington University, St. Louis, Missouri.

Lenroot, Irvine L. Papers, Library of Congress.

McCormick, Joseph Medill. Papers, Hanna-McCormick Family Papers, Library of Congress.

Mann, James R. Papers, Library of Congress.

Merriam, Charles E. Papers, University of Chicago Library.

Moore, J Hampton. Papers, Historical Society of Pennsylvania, Philadelphia.

Murdock, Victor. Papers, Library of Congress.

Needham, James C. Papers, Bancroft Library, University of California, Berkeley.
Nelson, John M. Papers, Library of Congress.
Norris, George W. Papers, Library of Congress.
O'Laughlin, John C. Papers, Library of Congress.
Parsons, Herbert. Papers, Butler Library, Columbia University, New York City.
Perkins, George W. Papers, Butler Library, Columbia University, New York City.
Pinchot, Gifford. Papers, Library of Congress.
Poindexter, Miles. Papers, University of Virginia, Charlottesville.
Roosevelt, Theodore. Papers, Library of Congress.
Sherman, James S . Papers, New York Public Library.
Stimson, Henry L. Papers, Sterling Library, Yale University, New Haven, Connecticut.
Taft, William Howard. Papers, Library of Congress.
Tumulty, Joseph P. Papers, Library of Congress.
Vanderlip, Frank A. Papers, Butler Library, Columbia University, New York City.
Wilson, Woodrow. Papers, Library of Congress.

PUBLISHED DOCUMENTS

Congressional Record. Washington, D.C.: U.S. Government Printing Office, 1909–1923.
United States Census Reports. No. 13 Washington, D.C.: U.S. Government Printing Office, 1913.
U.S. Congress. *Biographical Directory of the American Congress, 1774–1971*. Washington, D.C.: U.S. Government Printing Office, 1971.
U.S. House of Representatives. *Report*, no. 47, "White Slave Traffic," 61st Cong, 2d sess. Washington, D.C.: U.S. Government Printing Office, 1910.

AUTOBIOGRAPHIES, MEMOIRS, AND PUBLISHED LETTERS

Abbot, Willis J. *Watching the World Go By*. Boston: Little, Brown, 1933.
Ashurst, Henry Fountain, *Diary of Henry Fountain Ashurst*. Tucson: University of Arizona Press, 1962.
Barkley, Alben W. *That Reminds Me*. Garden City, N.J.: Doubleday, 1954.
Bartholdt, Richard. *From Steerage to Congress: Reminiscences and Reflections*. Philadelphia: Dorrance and Company, 1930.
Butt, Archibald. *Taft and Roosevelt: The Intimate Letters of Archie Butt, Military Aide* 2 vols. Garden City, N.Y.: Doubleday, Doran, and Company, 1930.
Byrnes, James F. *All in One Lifetime*. New York: Harper and Brothers, 1958.

————. *Speaking Frankly*. New York: Harper and Brothers, 1947.

Clark, Champ. *My Quarter Century of American Politics*, 2 vols. New York: Harper and Brothers, 1920.

Cole, Cyrenus. *I Remember, I Remember*. Iowa City: State Historical Society of Iowa, 1936.

Cox, James M. *Journey through My Years*. New York: Simon and Schuster, 1946.

Cullom, Shelby M. *Fifty Years of Public Service: Personal Recollections*. Chicago: A. C. McClurg and Company, 1911.

Darling, Arthur B., ed. *The Public Papers of Francis G. Newlands*. 2 vols. Boston: Houghton Mifflin, 1932.

Ford, Worthington Chauncey, ed. *Letters of Henry Adams, 1892–1918*. Boston: Houghton Mifflin, 1938.

Frear, James A. *Forty Years of Progressive Public Service*. Washington, D.C.: The Associated Writers, 1937.

Gardner, Constance, ed. *Some Letters of Augustus Peabody Gardner*. Boston: Houghton Mifflin, 1920.

Gompers, Samuel. *Seventy Years of Life and Labor*. 2 vols. New York: E. P. Dutton and Company, 1925.

Harriman, Mrs. J. Borden. *From Pinafores to Politics*. New York: Henry Holt and Company, 1923.

Hays, Will H. *The Memoirs of Will H. Hays*. Garden City, N.Y.: Doubleday, 1955.

Hull, Cordell. *The Memoirs of Cordell Hull*. 2 vols. New York: Macmillan Company, 1948.

Ickes, Harold L. *The Autobiography of a Curmudgeon*. New York: Reynal and Hitchcock, 1943.

Jones, Marvin. *Memoirs*. El Paso: Texas Western Press, 1973.

Keating, Edward. *The Gentleman from Colorado, a Memoir*. Denver: Sage Books, 1964.

La Guardia, Fiorello H. *The Making of an Insurgent: An Autobiography, 1882–1919*. Philadelphia: J. B. Lippincott, 1948.

Link, Arthur S., ed. *The Papers of Woodrow Wilson*. Vols. 28, 35, 38, 42, 47, 50, 53, Princeton, N.J.: Princeton University Press, 1978–1986.

Longworth, Alice Roosevelt. *Crowded Hours: Reminiscences of Alice Roosevelt Longworth*. New York: Charles Scribner's Sons, 1933.

McAdoo, William G. *Crowded Years: The Reminiscences of William G. McAdoo*. Boston: Houghton Mifflin, 1931.

Mondell, Frank. "My Story". *Wyoming State Tribune*, 1 August 1935–4 February 1936.

Morison, Elting E., ed. *The Letters of Theodore Roosevelt*. 8 vols. Cambridge, Mass.: Harvard University Press, 1951–1954.

Norris, George W. *Fighting Liberal: The Autobiography of George W. Norris*. New York: Macmillan Company, 1945.

Seymour, Charles, ed. *The Intimate Papers of Colonel House*, Vol. 1, Boston: Houghton Mifflin, 1926.
Slayden, Ellen M. *Washington Wife: Journal of Ellen Maury Slayden from 1897–1919*. New York, Harper and Row, 1962.
Watson, James E. *As I Knew Them: Memoirs of James E. Watson*. Indianapolis: Bobbs-Merrill, 1936.
Wiley, Harvey W. *An Autobiography*. Indianapolis: Bobbs-Merrill, 1930.

NEWSPAPERS

Chicago Herald, 1917.
Chicago Tribune, 1894, 1896, 1918.
Clippings, miscellaneous papers, 1894–1922, James R. Mann Papers.
Milwaukee Sentinel, 1917.
New York Times, 1909–1923.
New York Tribune, 1917–1919.
Superior Telegram, 1909–1918.
Washington Post, 1916–1919.
Washington Times, 1917.
Wisconsin State Journal, 1909–1918.

PERIODICALS

American Magazine, April 1916.
Current Opinion, January 1914.
Independent, 4 February 1909.
Literary Digest, 1911–1916.
Nation, 8 June 1916.
Outlook, 13 March 1909, 12 February 1919, 6 June 1923.
Review of Reviews, July 1910, May 1911, July 1913, March 1919, January 1923.
Searchlight on Congress, February 1916–July 1918.

DISSERTATIONS AND THESES

Barfield, Claude Ercell. "The Democratic Party in Congress, 1909–1913." Ph.D. diss., Northwestern University, 1965.
Bullard, Thomas Robert. "From Businessman to Congressman: The Careers of Martin B. Madden." Ph.D. diss., University of Illinois at Chicago Circle, 1973.
Clubb, Jerome Martin. "Congressional Opponents of Reform, 1901–1913." Ph.D. diss., University of Washington, 1963.
Drayer, Robert Edward. "J. Hampton Moore: An Old Fashioned Republican." Ph.D. diss., University of Pennsylvania, 1961.
Ellis, Lewis Ethan. "A History of the Chicago Delegation in Congress, 1843–1925." Ph.D. diss., University of Chicago, 1927.

Greenlee, Howard Scott. "The Republican Party in Division and Reunion, 1913–1920." Ph.D. diss., University of Chicago, 1950.

Havig, Alan Rolf. "The Poverty of Insurgency: The Movement to Progressivize the Republican Party, 1916–1924." Ph.D. diss., University of Missouri, Columbia, 1966.

Hillje, John Wylie. "The Progressive Movement and the Graduated Income Tax, 1913–1919." Ph.D. diss., University of Texas, 1966.

Horner, Richard Kenneth. "The House at War: The House of Representatives during World War I, 1917–1919." Ph.D. diss., Louisiana State University, 1977.

Ingle, Homer Larry. "Pilgrimage to Reform: A Life of Claude Kitchin." Ph.D. diss., University of Wisconsin, 1967.

Kenkel, Joseph Frederick. "The Tariff Commission Movement: The Search for a Nonpartisan Solution of the Tariff Question." Ph.D. diss., University of Maryland, 1962.

McCarthy, Michael Patrick. "Businessmen and Professionals in Municipal Reform: The Chicago Experience, 1887–1920." Ph.D. diss., Northwestern University, 1970.

McCulley, Richard Todd. "The Origins of the Federal Reserve Act: Banks and Politics during the Progressive Era, 1897–1913." Ph.D. diss., University of Texas at Austin, 1980.

McDonald, Timothy Gregory. "Southern Democratic Congressmen and the First World War, August 1914–April 1917: The Public Record of Their Support for or Opposition to Wilson's Policies." Ph.D. diss., University of Washington, 1962

McKnight, Gerald D. "A Party against Itself—The Grand Old Party in the New Freedom Era, 1913–1916." Ph.D. diss., University of Maryland, 1972.

Mayhill, George Roger. "Speaker Cannon under the Roosevelt Administration, 1903–1907." Ph.D. diss., University of Illinois, 1942.

Meyer, Jonah Nathan. "The Presidential Election of 1916 in the Middle West." Ph.D. diss., Princeton University, 1966.

Mitchell, Rena. "The Congressional Career of James R. Mann." M.A. thesis, University of Chicago, 1938.

Morrison, Geoffrey F. "A Political Biography of Champ Clark." Ph.D. diss., St. Louis University, 1972.

Palermo, Patrick Francis. "Republicans in Revolt: The Sources of Insurgency." Ph.D. diss., State University of New York at Stony Brook, 1973.

Pegram, Thomas Ray. "Progressivism and Partisanship: Reformers, Politicians, and Public Policy in Illinois, 1870–1922." Ph.D. diss., Brandeis University, 1987.

Phillips, Virginia. "The Early Congressional Career of James R. Mann: A Conservative in a Progressive Era, 1897–1913." M.A. thesis, American University, 1959.

Rager, Scott William. "The Fall of the House of Cannon: Uncle Joe and His Enemies, 1903–1910." Ph.D. diss., University of Illinois at Urbana-Champaign, 1991.

Roady, Elston E. "Party Regularity in the Sixty-Third Congress." Ph.D. diss., University of Illinois, 1951.

Romans, Maureen R. "Party Leadership Fights in the House of Representatives: The Cause of Conflict, 1895–1955." Ph.D. diss., University of Massachusetts, 1976.

Sayre, Ralph Mills. "Albert Baird Cummins and the Progressive Movement in Iowa." Ph.D. diss., Columbia University, 1958.

Straetz, Ralph Arthur. "The Progressive Movement in Illinois, 1910–1916." Ph.D. diss., University of Illinois, 1951.

Woodbury, Robert Louis. "William Kent: Progressive Gadfly, 1864–1928." Ph.D. diss., Yale University, 1967.

ARTICLES

Baker, John D. "The Character of the Congressional Revolution of 1910." *Journal of American History* 60 (December 1973): 679–91.

Barfield, Claude E. "'Our Share of the Booty' The Democratic Party, Cannonism, and the Payne-Aldrich Tariff." *Journal of American History* 57 (September 1970): 308-23.

Boxerman, Alan. "Kahn of California." *California Historical Quarterly* 55 (Winter 1976): 340-51.

Brady, David W., and Althoff, Philip. "Party Voting in the U.S. House of Representatives, 1890–1910: Elements of a Responsible Party System." *Journal of Politics* 36 (August 1974): 753-75.

Brady, David W.; Cooper, Joseph; and Hurley, Patricia. "The Decline of Party in the U.S. House of Representatives, 1877–1968." *Legislative Studies Quarterly* 4 (August 1979): 381-407.

Broesamle, John J. "The Democrats from Bryan to Wilson." In *The Progressive Era*, edited by Lewis L. Gould, 83-113 (Syracuse: Syracuse University Press, 1974).

Burdick, Frank. "Woodrow Wilson and the Underwood Tariff." *Mid-America* 50 (October 1968): 270-90.

Burner, David. "The Democratic Party, 1910–1932." In *History of U.S. Political Parties*, vol. 3, *1910–1945: From Square Deal to New Deal*, edited by Arthur M. Schlesinger, Jr., 1811–1834 (New York: Chelsea House Publishers in association with R. R. Bowker Co., 1973).

Burnham, Walter Dean. "Critical Realignment, Dead or Alive?" In *The End of Realignment? Interpreting American Electoral Eras*, edited by Byron E. Shafer, 101-140 (Madison: University of Wisconsin Press, 1991).

Cooper, John Milton, Jr. "Progressivism and American Foreign Policy: A Reconsideration." *Mid-America* 51 (1969): 260-277.

Cooper, Joseph, and Brady, David W. "Institutional Context and Leadership Style: The House from Cannon to Rayburn." *American Political Science Review* 75 (June 1981): 411-425.

Dixon, Frank H. "The Mann-Elkins Act." *Quarterly Journal of Economics* 24 (August 1910): 593-633.

Ellis, L. Ethan. "James R. Mann, Legislator Extraordinary." *Journal of the Illinois State Historical Society* 46 (Spring 1953): 28–43.

———. "James Robert Mann." In *Dictionary of American Biography*, vol. 6 pt. 2, edited by Allen Johnson and Dumas Malone, 244 (New York: Charles Scribner's Sons, 1933).

Gould, Lewis L. "The Republican Search for a National Majority." In *The Gilded Age*, edited by H. Wayne Morgan, 171-198 (Syracuse: Syracuse University Press 1970).

———. "The Republicans Under Roosevelt and Taft." In *The Progressive Era*, edited by Lewis L. Gould, 55–82 (Syracuse: Syracuse University Press 1974).

Hahn, Harlan. "President Taft and the Discipline of Patronage." *Journal of Politics* 28 (May 1966): 368–390.

Harbaugh, William H. "The Republican Party, 1893–1932." In *History of U.S. Political Parties*, vol. 3, *1910–1945 From Square Deal to New Deal*, edited by Arthur M. Schlesinger, Jr., 2069–2128 (New York: Chelsea House Publishers in association with R. R. Bowker Co. 1973).

Johnson, Arthur M. "Theodore Roosevelt and the Bureau of Corporations." *Mississippi Valley Historical Review* 45 (March 1959): 571–590.

Jones, Charles O. "Joseph G. Cannon and Howard W. Smith: An Essay on the Limits of Leadership in the House of Representatives." *Journal of Politics* 30 (August 1968): 617–646.

Keller, Morton. "The Pluralist State: American Economic Regulation in Comparative Perspective, 1900–1930." In *Regulation in Perspective: Historical Essays*, edited by Thomas K. McCraw, 56-94, (Cambridge, Mass.: Harvard University Press 1981).

Leake, James M. "Four Years in Congress." *American Political Science Review* 11 (May 1917): 242-283.

Link, Arthur S., and Leary, William M., Jr. "Election of 1916." In *History of American Presidential Elections 1789–1968*, vol. 3, edited by Arthur M. Schlesinger, Jr., 2245–2270 (New York: Chelsea House Publishers in association with McGraw-Hill Book Co. 1971).

McCormick, Richard L. "The Discovery That Business Corrupts Politics: A Reappraisal of the Origins of Progressivism." *American Historical Review* 86 (April 1981): 247–274.

McDonagh, Eileen Lorenzi. "Electoral Bases of Policy Innovation in the Progressive Era: The Impact of Grass Roots Opinion on Roll-Call Voting in the House of Representatives, Sixty-Third Congress, 1913–1915." *Journal of Policy History* 4 (no. 2 1992): 162–187.

————. "Issues and Constituencies in the Progressive Era: House Roll Call Voting on the Nineteenth Amendment, 1913–1919." *Journal of Politics* 51 (February 1989): 119–136.

McKnight, Gerald D. "Republican Leadership and the Mexican Question, 1913–1916: A Failed Bid for Party Resurgence." *Mid-America* 62 (April–July 1980): 105–122.

Morrison, Geoffrey. "Champ Clark and the Rules Revolution of 1910." *Capitol Studies* 2 (Winter 1974): 43–56.

Polsby, Nelson W. "The Institutionalization of the U.S. House of Representatives." *American Political Science Review* 62 (March 1958): 144–168.

Sarasohn, David. "The Insurgent Republicans: Insurgent Image and Republican Reality." *Social Science History* 3 (1979): 245–261.

Silbey, Joel H. "Congressional and State Roll Call Studies by U.S. Historians." *Legislative Studies Quarterly* 6 (November 1981): 597–607.

Sinclair, Barbara Deckard. "Determinants of Aggregate Party Cohesion in the U.S. House of Representatives, 1901–1956." *Legislative Studies Quarterly* 2 (May 1977): 155-175.

Solvick, Stanley D. "William Howard Taft and Cannonism." *Wisconsin Magazine of History* 48 (August 1964): 48–58.

————. "William Howard Taft and the Insurgents." *Papers of the Michigan Academy of Science, Arts, and Letters* 45 (1963): 279–295.

————. "William Howard Taft and the Payne-Aldrich Tariff." *Mississippi Valley Historical Review* 50 (December 1963): 424–442.

Sosna, Morton. "The South in the Saddle: Racial Politics during the Wilson Years." *Wisconsin Magazine of History* 54 (Autumn 1970): 30–49.

Tarr, Joel A. "William Kent to Lincoln Steffens: Origins of Progressive Reform in Chicago." *Mid-America* 47 (January 1965): 48–57.

Vander Meer, Philip R. "Congressional Decision-Making and World War I: A Case Study of Illinois Congressional Opponents." *Congressional Studies* 8 (Autumn 1981): 49–79.

Vietor, Richard H. K. "Businessmen and the Political Economy: The Railroad Rate Controversy of 1905." *Journal of American History* 64 (June 1977): 47–66.

OTHER BOOKS

Alexander, DeAlva S. *History and Procedure of the House of Representatives.* Boston: Houghton Mifflin, 1916.

Allen, Howard W. *Poindexter of Washington: A Study in Progressive Politics.* Carbondale: Southern Illinois University Press, 1981.

Allswang, John M. *The Political Behavior of Chicago's Ethnic Groups, 1918–1932.* 1967 Reprint, New York: Arno Press, 1980.

Anderson, Donald F. *William Howard Taft: A Conservative's Conception of the Presidency.* Ithaca, N.Y.: Cornell University Press, 1973.

Anderson, Judith Icke. *William Howard Taft: An Intimate History*. New York: W. W. Norton, 1981.

Anderson, Oscar E. *The Health of a Nation: Harvey W. Wiley and the Fight for Pure Food*. Chicago: University of Chicago Press, 1958.

Bates, J. Leonard. *The Origins of Teapot Dome: Progressives, Parties and Petroleum, 1909–1921*. Urbana: University of Illinois Press, 1963.

Bensel, Richard F. *Sectionalism and American Political Development, 1880–1980*. Madison: University of Wisconsin Press, 1984.

Block, Jean F. *Hyde Park Houses: an Informal History, 1856–1910*. Chicago: University of Chicago Press, 1978.

Blum, John M. *Joe Tumulty and the Wilson Era*. Boston: Houghton Mifflin, 1951.

Bolles, Blair. *Tyrant from Illinois: Uncle Joe Cannon's Experiment with Personal Power*. New York: W. W. Norton and Company, 1951.

Bolling, Richard. *Power in the House: A History of the Leadership of the House of Representatives*. New York: E. P. Dutton, 1968.

Briggs, John E. *William Peters Hepburn*. Iowa City: State Historical Society of Iowa, 1919.

Broesamle, John J. *William Gibbs McAdoo: A Passion for Change, 1863–1917*. Port Washington, N. Y: Kennikat Press, 1973.

Brown, George Rothwell. *The Leadership of Congress*. 1922. Reprint. New York: Arno Press, 1974.

Buechler, Steven M. *The Transformation of the Woman Suffrage Movement: The Case of Illinois, 1850–1920*. New Brunswick, N.J.: Rutgers University Press, 1986.

Burnham, J. H. *History of Bloomington and Normal in McLean County, Illinois*. Bloomington, Ill.: Burnham Publishing Co., 1879.

Busbey, L. White. *Uncle Joe Cannon: The Story of a Pioneer American*. New York: Henry Holt and Company, 1927.

Chambers, John Whiteclay, II. *To Raise an Army: The Draft Comes to Modern America*. New York: Free Press, 1987.

Cheney, Richard B., and Cheney, Lynne V. *Kings of the Hill: Power and Personality in the House of Representatives*. New York: Continuum, 1983.

Chiu, Chang-Wei. *The Speaker of the House of Representatives since 1896*. 1928. Reprint. New York: AMS Press, 1968.

Clements, Kendrick A. *The Presidency of Woodrow Wilson*. Laurence: University Press of Kansas, 1992.

Clubb, Jerome; Flanigan, William; and Zingale, Nancy. *Partisan Realignment: Voters, Parties and Government in American History*. Beverly Hills, Calif.: Sage Publications, 1980.

Coletta, Paolo E. *The Presidency of William Howard Taft*. Lawrence: University Press of Kansas, 1973.

Cooper, John Milton, Jr. *Pivotal Decades: The United States, 1900–1920*. New York: W. W. Norton and Company, 1990.

————. *The Vanity of Power: American Isolationism and the First World War, 1914–1917*. Westport, Conn.: Greenwood Publishing Co., 1969.

————. *The Warrior and the Priest: Woodrow Wilson and Theodore Roosevelt*. Cambridge, Mass.: Harvard University Press, 1983.

Davis, Allen F. *Spearheads for Reform: The Social Settlements and the Progressive Movement, 1890–1914*. New York: Oxford University Press, 1967.

Davis, Oscar King. *Released for Publication: Some Inside Political History of Theodore Roosevelt and His Times, 1898–1918*. Boston: Houghton Mifflin, 1925.

de Chambrun, Clara Longworth. *The Making of Nicholas Longworth: Annals of an American Family*. New York: Ray Long and Richard R. Smith, 1933.

Ellis, L. Ethan. *A History of the Chicago Delegation in Congress, 1843–1925*. Springfield: Illinois State Historical Society, 1930.

————. *Newsprint: Producers, Publishers, Political Pressures*. New Brunswick, N.J.: Rutgers University Press, 1960.

————. *Print Paper Pendulum: Group Pressures and the Price of Newsprint*. New Brunswick, N.J.: Rutgers University Press, 1948.

————. *Reciprocity, 1911: A Study in Canadian-American Relations*. New Haven, Conn.: Yale University Press, 1939.

Ewing, Cortez A. M. *Congressional Elections, 1896–1944* . Norman: University of Oklahoma Press, 1947.

Fausold, Martin L. *Gifford Pinchot: Bull Moose Progressive*. Syracuse: Syracuse University Press, 1961.

————. *James W. Wadsworth, Jr.: The Gentleman from New York*. Syracuse: Syracuse University Press, 1975.

Finnegan, John Patrick. *Against the Specter of a Dragon: The Campaign for American Military Preparedness, 1914–1917*. Westport, Conn.: Greenwood Press, 1974.

Fuller, Wayne E. *RFD: The Changing Face of Rural America*. Bloomington: Indiana University Press, 1964.

Gable, John A. *The Bull Moose Years: Theodore Roosevelt and the Progressive Party*. Port Washington, N.Y.: Kennikat Press, 1978.

Galloway, George B. *History of the House of Representatives*. New York: Thomas Y. Crowell Co., 1961.

Gardner, Joseph L. *Departing Glory: Theodore Roosevelt as Ex-President*. New York: Charles Scribner's Sons, 1973.

Garraty, John A. *Right-Hand Man: The Life of George W. Perkins*. New York: Harper and Brothers, 1960.

Gilbert, Charles. *American Financing of World War I*. Westport, Conn.: Greenwood Publishing Company, 1970.

Goldman, Ralph M. *The National Party Chairmen and Committees: Factionalism at the Top*. Armonk, N.Y.: M. .E. Sharpe, 1990.

Gould, Lewis L. *The Presidency of Theodore Roosevelt*. Lawrence: University Press of Kansas, 1991.

————. *Reform and Regulation: American Politics from Roosevelt to Wilson.* 2nd ed. New York: Alfred A. Knopf, 1986.

Gwinn, William R. *Uncle Joe Cannon: Archfoe of Insurgency.* New York: Bookman Associates, 1957.

Haines, Lynn. *Law Making in America: The Story of the 1911–12 Session of the Sixty-Second Congress.* Bethesda, Md.: Lynn Haines, 1912.

————. *Your Congress: An Interpretation of the Political and Parliamentary Influences that Dominate Law Making in America.* Washington, D.C.: The National Voters League, 1915.

Harbaugh, William H. *The Life and Times of Theodore Roosevelt.* New York: Oxford University Press, 1975.

Harstad, Peter T., and Lindemann, Bonnie. *Gilbert N. Haugen: Norwegian-American Farm Politician.* Iowa City: State Historical Society of Iowa, 1992.

Hasbrouck, Paul DeWitt. *Party Government in the House of Representatives.* New York: Macmillan Company, 1927.

Hechler, Kenneth W. *Insurgency: Personalities and Politics of the Taft Era.* New York: Russell and Russell, 1964.

Heckscher, August. *Woodrow Wilson.* New York: Charles Scribner's Sons, 1991.

Hicks, John D. *Republican Ascendancy, 1921–1933.* New York: Harper and Row, 1960.

Higgs, Robert. *Crisis and Leviathan: Critical Episodes in the Growth of American Government.* New York: Oxford University Press, 1987.

Hobson, Barbara Meil. *Uneasy Virtue: The Politics of Prostitution and the American Reform Tradition.* New York: Basic Books, 1987.

Holt, James. *Congressional Insurgents and the Party System, 1909–1916.* Cambridge, Mass.: Harvard University Press, 1967.

Hoogenboom, Ari, and Hoogenboom, Olive. *A History of the ICC: From Panacea to Palliative.* New York: W. W. Norton and Company, 1976.

Hull, Denison Bingham. *The Legislative Life of Morton Denison Hull.* Chicago: Privately printed, 1948.

Johnson, Evans C. *Oscar W. Underwood: A Political Biography.* Baton Rouge: Louisiana State University Press, 1980.

Jones, Charles O. *The Minority Party in Congress.* Boston: Little, Brown, 1970.

————. *The Republican Party in American Politics.* New York: Macmillan Company, 1965.

Keller, Morton. *Regulating a New Economy: Public Policy and Economic Change in America, 1900–1933.* Cambridge, Mass.: Harvard University Press, 1990.

Kenkel, Joseph F. *Progressives and Protection: The Search for a Tariff Policy, 1866–1936.* Lanham, Md.: University Press of America, 1983.

Kennedy, David M. *Over Here: The First World War and American Society.* New York: Oxford University Press, 1980.

Kent, Elizabeth T. *William Kent, Independent: A Biography.* n.p.: Privately published, 1951.

Kolko, Gabriel. *Railroads and Regulation, 1877–1916.* Princeton, N.J.: Princeton University Press, 1965.

La Follette, Belle, and La Follette, Fola. *Robert M. La Follette.* 2 vols. New York: Macmillan Company, 1953.

La Forte, Robert Sherman. *Leaders of Reform: Progressive Republicans in Kansas, 1900–1916.* Lawrence: University Press of Kansas, 1974.

Lake, David A. *Power, Protection, and Free Trade: International Sources of U.S. Commercial Strategy, 1887–1939.* Ithaca, N.Y.: Cornell University Press, 1988.

Larson, Bruce L. *Lindbergh of Minnesota: A Political Biography.* New York: Harcourt Brace Jovanovich, 1973.

Link, Arthur S. *Wilson: Campaigns for Progressivism and Peace, 1916–1917.* Princeton, N.J.: Princeton University Press, 1965.

———. *Wilson: Confusions and Crises, 1915–1916.* Princeton, N.J.: Princeton University Press, 1964.

———. *Wilson: The New Freedom.* Princeton, N.J.: Princeton University Press, 1956.

———. *Wilson: The Struggle for Neutrality, 1914–1915.* Princeton, N.J.: Princeton University Press, 1960.

———. *Woodrow Wilson: Revolution, War, and Peace.* Arlington Heights, Ill.: Harlan Davidson, 1979.

Livermore, Seward W. *Politics is Adjourned: Woodrow Wilson and the War Congress, 1916–1918.* Middletown, Conn.: Wesleyan University Press, 1966.

Livingston, James. *Origins of the Federal Reserve System: Money, Class, and Corporate Capitalism, 1890–1913.* Ithaca, N.Y.: Cornell University Press, 1986.

Lovell, Samuel D. *The Presidential Election of 1916.* Carbondale: Southern Illinois University Press, 1980.

Lowitt, Richard. *George W. Norris: The Making of a Progressive, 1861–1912.* Syracuse: Syracuse University Press, 1963.

Luce, Robert. *Congress: An Explanation.* Cambridge, Mass.: Harvard University Press, 1926.

———. *Legislative Procedure: Parliamentary Practices and the Course of Business in the Framing of Statutes.* Boston: Houghton Mifflin, 1922.

McCall, Samuel W. *The Business of Congress.* New York: Columbia University Press, 1911.

McCraw, Thomas K. *Prophets of Regulation: Charles Francis Adams, Louis D. Brandeis, James M. Landis, Alfred E. Kahn.* Cambridge, Mass.: Belknap Press of Harvard University Press, 1984.

McCulley, Richard T. *Banks and Politics during the Progressive Era: The Origins of the Federal Reserve System, 1897–1913*. New York: Garland, 1992.

McGeary, M. Nelson. *Gifford Pinchot: Forester–Politician*. Princeton, N.J.: Princeton University Press, 1960.

McGerr, Michael E. *The Decline of Popular Politics: The American North, 1865–1928*. New York: Oxford University Press, 1986.

Margulies, Herbert F. *The Decline of the Progressive Movement in Wisconsin, 1890–1920*. Madison: State Historical Society of Wisconsin, 1968.

———. *Senator Lenroot of Wisconsin: A Political Biography, 1900–1929*. Columbia: University of Missouri Press, 1977.

Martis, Kenneth C., and Rowles, Ruth A. *The Historical Atlas of United States Congressional Districts, 1789–1983*. New York: Free Press, 1982.

Merrill, Horace S., and Merrill, Marion G. *The Republican Command, 1897–1913*. Lexington: University Press of Kentucky, 1971.

Moore, J. Hampton. *Roosevelt and the Old Guard*. Philadelphia: Macrae Smith Co., 1925.

Moore, John L., ed. *Congressional Quarterly's Guide to U.S. Elections*. 2nd ed. Washington: Congressional Quarterly, 1985.

Mowry, George E. *The Era of Theodore Roosevelt and the Birth of Modern America, 1900–1912*. New York: Harper and Row, 1958.

Myers, William S. *The Republican Party: A History. 1928*. Reprint, New York: Johnson Reprint Corporation, 1968.

Nord, David Paul. *Newspapers and New Politics: Midwestern Municipal Reform, 1890–1900*. Ann Arbor: UMI Research Press, 1981.

Odegard, Peter H. *Pressure Politics: The Story of the Anti-Saloon League*. New York: Columbia University Press, 1928.

Olin, Spencer C., Jr. *California's Prodigal Sons: Hiram Johnson and the Progressives, 1911–1917*. Berkeley: University of California Press, 1968.

Paxson, Frederic L. *American Democracy and the World War: Pre-War Years, 1913–1917*. Boston: Houghton Mifflin, 1936.

Peters, Ronald M., Jr. *The American Speakership: The Office in Historical Perspective*. Baltimore: Johns Hopkins University Press, 1990.

Pinchot, Amos R. E. *History of the Progressive Party, 1912–1916*, Edited by Helene Maxwell Hooker. New York: New York University Press, 1958.

Polsby, Nelson. *Congress and the Presidency*. 4th ed. New York: Prentice Hall, 1986.

Pringle, Henry F. *The Life and Times of William Howard Taft*. 2 vols. New York: Farrar and Rinehart, 1939.

Quirk, Robert E. *An Affair of Honor: Woodrow Wilson and the Occupation of Veracruz*. Lexington: University Press of Kentucky, 1962.

Reckless, Walter C. *Vice in Chicago*. 1933. Reprint, Montclair, N.J.: Patterson Smith, 1969.

Richardson, Elmo R. *The Politics of Conservation: Crusades and Controversies, 1897–1913*. Berkeley: University of California Press, 1962.

Ripley, Randall B. *Congress: Process and Policy*. New York: W. W. Norton and Company, 1975.

———. *Party Leaders in the House of Representatives*. Washington: Brookings Institution, 1967.

Robertson, James Oliver. *No Third Choice: Progressives in Republican Politics, 1916–1921*. New York: Garland, 1983.

Rosen, Ruth. *The Lost Sisterhood: Prostitution in America, 1900–1918*. Baltimore: Johns Hopkins University Press, 1982.

Russell, John Andrew. *Joseph Warren Fordney, an American Legislator*. Boston: Stratford Company, 1928.

Sarasohn, David. *The Party of Reform: Democrats in the Progressive Era*. Jackson: University Press of Mississippi, 1989.

Semonche, John E. *Charting the Future: The Supreme Court Responds to a Changing Society, 1890–1920*. Westport, Conn.: Greenwood Press, 1978.

Shannon, W. Wayne. *Party Constituency and Congressional Voting: A Study of Legislative Behavior in the United States House of Representatives*. Baton Rouge: Louisiana State University Press, 1968.

Sklar, Martin J. *The Corporate Reconstruction of American Capitalism, 1890–1916: The Market, the Law, and Politics*. Cambridge, Eng.: Cambridge University Press, 1988.

———. *The United States as a Developing Country*. Cambridge, Eng.: Cambridge University Press, 1992.

Skowronek, Stephen. *Building a New American State: The Expansion of National Administrative Capacities, 1877–1920*. Cambridge, Eng.: Cambridge University Press, 1982.

Sprout, Harold, and Sprout, Margaret. *The Rise of American Naval Power, 1776–1918*. Princeton, N.J.: Princeton University Press, 1966.

Stewart, Charles H., III. *Budget Reform Politics: The Design of the Appropriations Process in the House of Representatives, 1865–1921*. New York: Cambridge University Press, 1989.

Tarr, Joel Arthur. *A Study in Boss Politics: William Lorimer of Chicago*. Urbana: University of Illinois Press, 1971.

Terrill, Tom E. *The Tariff, Politics, and American Foreign Policy, 1874–1901*. Westport, Conn.: Greenwood Press, 1973.

Timmons, Bascom N. *Garner of Texas: a Personal History*. New York: Harper and Brothers, 1948.

Van Riper, Paul. *History of the United States Civil Service*. Evanston, Ill.: Row, Peterson, 1958.

Waller, Robert Alfred. *Rainey of Illinois: A Political Biography, 1903–1934*. Urbana: University of Illinois Press, 1977.

Watson, Richard L., Jr. *The Development of National Power: The United States, 1900–1919*. Boston: Houghton Mifflin, Company, 1976.

Widenor, William C. *Henry Cabot Lodge and the Search for an American Foreign Policy*. Berkeley: University of California Press, 1980.

Wiebe. Robert H. *Businessmen and Reform: A Study of the Progressive Movement*. Cambridge, Mass.: Harvard University Press, 1962.

Wilensky, Norman M. *Conservatives in the Progressive Era: The Taft Republicans of 1912*. Gainesville: University of Florida Press, 1965.

Wiseman, John B. *The Dilemmas of a Party out of Power: The Democrats, 1904–1912*. New York: Garland, 1988.

Wolman, Paul. *Most Favored Nation: The Republican Revisionists and U.S. Tariff Policy, 1897–1912*. Chapel Hill: University of North Carolina Press, 1992.

Wright, James. *The Progressive Yankees: Republican Reformers in New Hampshire, 1906–1916*. Hanover, N.H.: University Press of New England, 1987.

Young, James Harvey. *Pure Food: Securing the Federal Food and Drugs Act of 1906*. Princeton, N.J.: Princeton University Press, 1989.

Index

About the Author

HERBERT F. MARGULIES is Emeritus Professor of History at the University of Hawaii in Manoa. He is the author of *The Decline of the Progressive Movement in Wisconsin, 1890–1920* (1968), *Senator Lenroot of Wisconsin: A Political Biography, 1900–1929* (1977), and *The Mild Reservationists and the League of Nations Controversy in the Senate* (1989).

Recent Titles in
Contributions in American History

Christian Science in the Age of Mary Baker Eddy
Stuart E. Knee

Northern Labor and Antislavery: A Documentary History
Philip S. Foner and Herbert Shapiro, editors

Loyalists and Community in North America
Robert M. Calhoon, Timothy M. Barnes, and George A. Rawlyk, editors

Abraham Lincoln: Sources and Style of Leadership
Frank J. Williams, William D. Pederson, and Vincent J. Marsala, editors

Zebulon Butler: Hero of the Revolutionary Frontier
James R. Williamson and Linda A. Fossler

Clio Confused: Troubling Aspects of Historical Study from the
Perspective of U.S. History
David J. Russo

Federal Antitrust Policy During the Kennedy-Johnson Years
James R. Williamson

The Home-Front War: World War II and American Society
Kenneth Paul O'Brien and Lynn Hudson Parsons, editors

Portrait of an Abolitionist: A Biography of George Luther Stearns
Charles E. Heller

No King, No Popery: Anti-Catholicism in Revolutionary New England
Francis D. Cogliano

James Glen: From Scottish Provost to Royal Governor of South Carolina
W. Stitt Robinson

The Journalist as Reformer: Henry Demarest Lloyd and *Wealth Against
Commonwealth*
Richard Digby-Junger

ISBN 0-313-29817-3